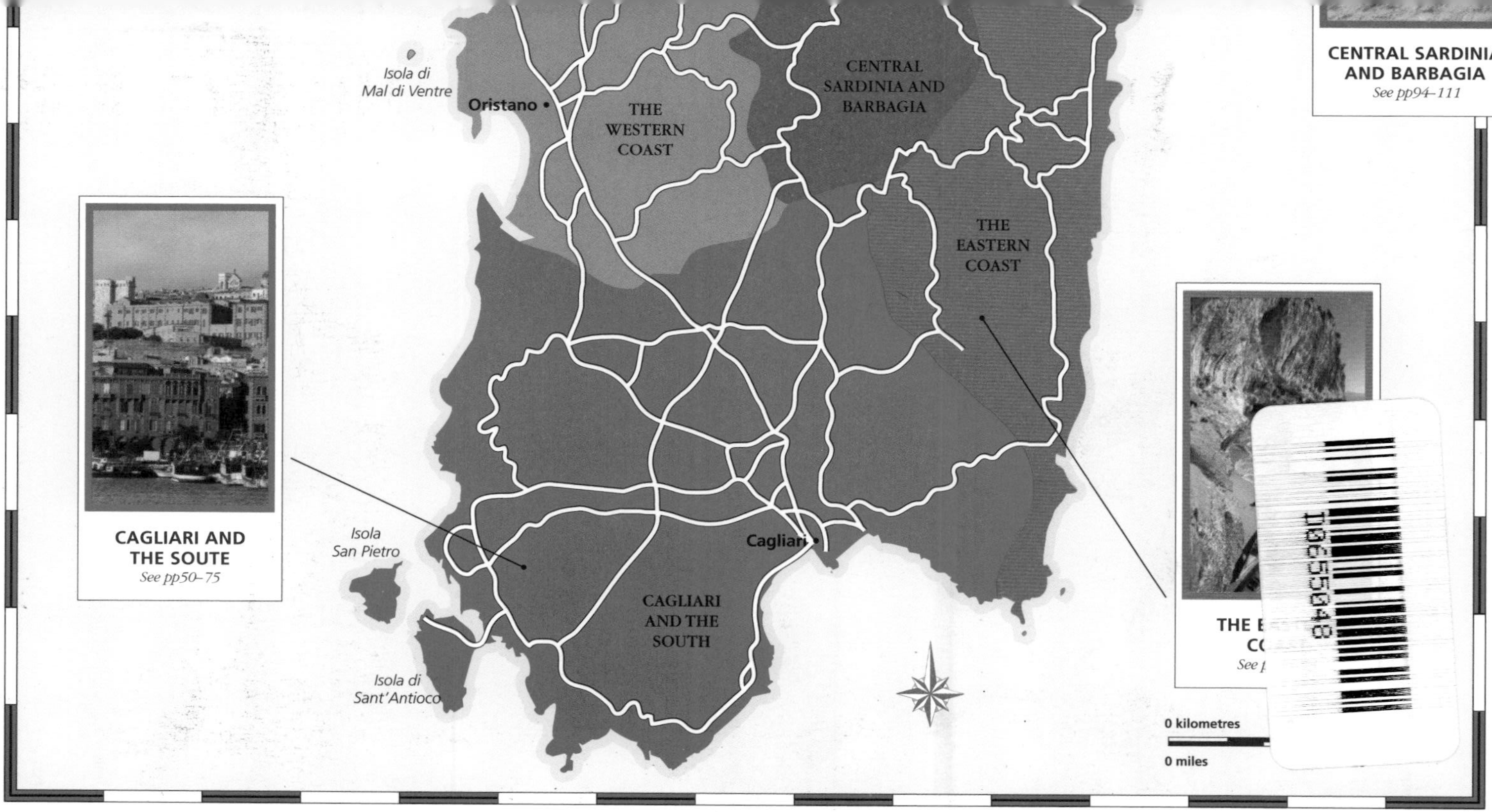

CENTRAL SARDINIA
AND BARBAGIA
See pp94–111

THE E
CO
See p

0 kilometres

0 miles

CENTRAL
SARDINIA AND
BARBAGIA

THE
EASTERN
COAST

Cagliari

THE
WESTERN
COAST

Oristano

CAGLIARI
AND THE
SOUTH

*Isola di
Mal di Ventre*

*Isola
San Pietro*

*Isola di
Sant'Antioco*

CAGLIARI AND
THE SOUTE
See pp50–75

EYEWITNESS TRAVEL

SARDINIA

MAIN CONTRIBUTOR: FABRIZIO ARDITO

LONDON, NEW YORK,
MELBOURNE, MUNICH AND DELHI
www.dk.com

Produced by Fabio Ratti
Editoria Libraria e Multimediale, Milano, Italy

PROJECT EDITOR Diana Georgiacodis
EDITORS Anna Lia Deffenu, Giovanni Francesio,
Renata Perego, Laura Recordati
DESIGNERS Paolo Gonzato, Stefania Testa, Studio Matra
MAPS Paul Stafford
PICTURE RESEARCH Fabio De Angelis, Riccardo Villarosa

Dorling Kindersley Ltd
PROJECT EDITOR Fiona Wild
EDITOR Francesca Machiavelli
DTP Cooling Brown
DTP DESIGNER Ingrid Vienings

MAIN CONTRIBUTOR Fabrizio Ardito
ADDITIONAL CONTRIBUTORS Patrizia Giovannetti, Raffaella Rizzo

ILLUSTRATORS Giorgia Boli, Alberto Ipsilanti,
Daniela Veluti, Nadia Viganò

ENGLISH TRANSLATION Richard Pierce

Reproduced in Singapore by Colourscan
Printed and bound in China by L. Rex Printing Co. Ltd

First published in Great Britain in 1998
by Dorling Kindersley Ltd, 80 Strand, London WC2R 0RL

Reprinted with revisions 2000, 2001, 2002, 2003, 2006, 2008

*Front cover main image: Roccia dell'Elefante,
Cala di Volpe, Costa Smeralda*

**The information in this
DK Eyewitness Travel Guide is checked regularly.**

Every effort has been made to ensure that this book is as up-to-date
as possible at the time of going to press. Some details, however,
such as telephone numbers, opening hours, prices, gallery hanging
arrangements and travel information are liable to change. The
publishers cannot accept responsibility for any consequences
arising from the use of this book, nor for any material on third party
websites, and cannot guarantee that any website address in this
book will be a suitable source of travel information. We value the
views and suggestions of our readers very highly. Please write to:
Publisher, DK Eyewitness Travel Guides,
Dorling Kindersley, 80 Strand, London WC2R 0RL, Great Britain.

CONTENTS

Sheep grazing in pastures filled
with spring flowers

INTRODUCING
SARDINIA

A prehistoric tower of the Santu
Antine nuraghe at Torralba

◁ **The promontory of Castelsardo on the northern coast**

The beach at Stintino on the tip of the northwestern coast

Knight on horseback during the Sa Sartiglia festival at Oristano

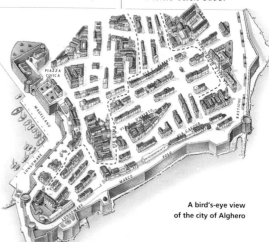

A bird's-eye view of the city of Alghero

HOW TO USE THIS GUIDE

This guide helps you get the most from your visit to Sardinia, providing expert recommendations as well as detailed practical information. *Introducing Sardinia* sets the island in its geographical, historical and cultural context. The five area chapters in *Sardinia Area by Area* describe the main sights and monuments in detail, with maps, pictures and illustrations. *Travellers' Needs* offers recommendations on hotels, restaurants and bars, as well as features on what to eat, drink and where to shop. The *Survival Guide* contains practical information on everything from transport to safety.

SARDINIA AREA BY AREA

Sardinia has been divided into five main sightseeing areas, each coded with a coloured thumb tab for quick reference. A map illustrating how the island has been divided can be found on the inside front cover of this guide. The sights covered within the individual areas have been plotted and numbered on a *Regional Map*.

Each area can be identified quickly by its colour coding.

1 Introduction
The landscape, history and character of each region is described here, showing how the area has developed over the centuries and what it has to offer visitors today.

A locator map shows the region in relation to the other areas of Sardinia.

2 Regional Map
This gives an illustrated overview of the whole area. All the sights covered in the chapter are numbered and there are useful tips on getting around by car and public transport.

Features and story boxes highlight special or unique aspects of an area or sight.

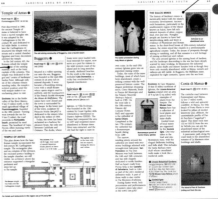

3 Detailed Information
All the important towns and other places of interest are described individually. They are listed in order, following the numbering on the Regional Map. *Within each entry there are details on the important buildings and other major sights.*

4 Major Towns

All the important towns are described individually. Within each entry there is further detailed information on important buildings and other sites. The Town Map *shows the location of the main sights.*

A Visitors' Checklist gives you the practical details to plan your visit, including transport information, the address of the tourist office, market days and festivals.

The Town Map shows all major and minor roads. The key sights are plotted, along with train and bus stations, parking areas, churches and tourist information offices.

5 Street-by-Street Map

Towns or districts of special interest to the visitor are given a bird's-eye view in detailed 3D with photographs and descriptions of the most important sights.

A suggested route for a walk covers the most interesting streets in the area.

Opening hours, telephone number and transport details for the sight are given in the Visitors' Checklist.

6 The Top Sights

These are given two or more pages. Historic buildings are dissected to reveal their interiors, while the photographs highlight the most interesting features.

Stars indicate sights that visitors should not miss.

INTRODUCING SARDINIA

DISCOVERING SARDINIA

Encircled by the dazzling blue waters of the Mediterranean, the Italian island of Sardinia offers incredible contrasts. The beautiful beach resorts clustered along the fashionable northern coastline, provide a striking contrast to the surprisingly rugged mountainous interior and quieter

Traditional Barbagia dress

southern areas. The countryside is dotted with curious monumental nuraghe; these prehistoric tombs and fortresses are fascinating and are worth taking the time to explore. The following pages will help visitors plan their holiday, pinpointing the many highlights this extraordinary island has to offer.

Flamingoes in flight at the salt marshes on the outskirts of Cagliari

CAGLIARI AND THE SOUTH

- Bustling capital, Cagliari
- Marshes for birdwatching
- Sant'Antioco & San Pietro
- Su Nuraxi archaeological site

Cagliari *(see pp54–61)* in the far south of the island has a laid-back atmosphere, good-value restaurants and pleasant sightseeing. A leisurely walk around the Spanish ramparts, the inspiring belvedere and the **Castello district** *(see pp56–7)* reveals delightful craft shops and graceful churches dating back to the time when the Pisans were in charge of the city.

Stretching west and east of the city are extensive **marshes and salt flats** *(see pp60–61)*, a joy for birdwatchers keen to observe migratory species, which stop over in the autumn months.

Off the western coast lies the island of **Sant'Antioco** *(see p72)*, easily visited via a

causeway. Dotted with ancient necropolises, it boasts a lively town and secluded bays. A short ferry trip from the mainland is the attractive island of **San Pietro** *(see p70)*, home to hard-working fishermen who celebrate their patron saint in style.

Arguably Sardinia's largest and most impressive nuraghe, **Su Nuraxi** *(see pp64–5)* contains the evocative ruins of a prehistoric fortified settlement, and a visit to this upland site cannot fail to leave a lasting impression.

The scenic Mandas-Arbatax train on its long journey

THE EASTERN COAST

- Trek in Gennargentu NP
- Cala Luna bay by footpath
- Mandas-Arbatax train ride
- Cannonau wine region

Rugged and windswept, the mountainous **Gennargentu National Park** *(see pp82–3)* is home to a population of hardy wildlife, not to mention memorable treks, such as the one up Punta La Marmora,

Sardinia's highest peak at 1,834 m (6,017 ft). In contrast, the northeastern edge of the park offers a beautiful coastline with divine bays for swimming. The highlight is **Cala Luna** *(see p85)*. Backed by soaring limestone cliffs, it is best reached from the resort village of Cala Gonone by either a pretty footpath or a less strenuous boat trip.

One original way to reach the coast from the inland is to take a seat on the summertime **Mandas-Arbatax train** *(see pp92–3)*, a rattling five-hour journey through a wilderness only punctuated by shepherds' settlements.

Hillsides carpeted with vines in the **Jerzu district** *(see p89)* are a welcome sight for wine lovers, as this is the homeland of Sardinia's top red wine, **Cannonau**.

CENTRAL SARDINIA AND BARBAGIA

- Supramonte scenery
- Trek to Tiscali
- Barbagia traditions

Wilderness and desolate upland landscapes often associated with the early inhabitants of the island characterize the **Supramonte** mountain group. The region is best explored by driving along the winding roads.

Walkers with suitable footwear and plenty of drinking water can spend a satisfying if tough day trekking up **Monte Tiscali** *(see pp104–5)*. Besides the wide-reaching panoramas, the reward is a well-concealed prehistoric

The village of Burgos, with the 12th-century castle ruins atop the hill

settlement hidden inside a vast natural cavity in the mountain top.

Surrounded by swathes of Mediterranean woods, villages in the **Barbagia district** retain much of their traditional feel, with flourishing crafts and age-old festivities. Try to visit the castle at **Burgos** *(see p100)*, a reminder of the ancient rivalries that thrived between the villages; **Orgosolo** *(see p106)*, which is traditional in feel; **Bitti** *(see p100)* for the island's best-known folk ensemble and **Sarule** *(see p102)*, which is famous for its residents' carpet weaving.

Watchtower at Alghero, the azure Mediterranean Sea below

The **Capo Caccia** *(see pp122–3)* headland, with its vast horizons, will be appreciated by nature lovers for its wind-swept promontories and marvellous bird life. The

picturesque, sea-level Grotta di Nettuno with its limestone formations, accessible by way of a dizzy staircase, is also not to be missed.

To its south the attractive seaside town of **Alghero** *(see pp116–19)* is elegantly Spanish in character and architecture. A stroll along the broad seafront studded with photogenic watchtowers is a delight, as is a wander through the old streets fronted with craft boutiques – well known for jewellery and other pieces made from coral.

Further south down the coast is the tiny church of **San Giovanni di Sinis** *(see p131)*, gateway to an elongated peninsula, which hosts the evocative ruins of the ancient Phoenician city of **Tharros** *(see pp132–3)*, excavated to reveal a surprisingly evolved complex of buildings, roads and drains. In the vicinity it is not unusual to observe large flocks of beautiful **flamingoes** at home in the tranquil coastal lagoons such as Sale Porcus.

The most popular (and tourism-friendly) region of Sardinia has a mind-boggling choice of beach holiday destinations. If you want to socialize with the jet set aboard luxury yachts head to the exclusive resorts of the **Costa Smeralda**, which was successfully developed by the Aga Khan in the 1960s with the help of contemporary architects. Sailing enthusiasts will also appreciate the classy racing and facilities at **Porto Cervo** *(see p144)*.

A little quieter is the spread-out **Maddalena archipelago** *(see pp146–9)*, home to legendary national hero, Giuseppe Garibaldi. The island of **Santo Stefano** *(see p149)* will hopefully be open to visitors after the long-awaited closure of the controversial US base for nuclear submarines in 2008.

Anyone interested in culture should plan to see the string of beautifully preserved Romanesque churches in the Logudoro district west of **Sassari** *(see pp156–7)*. The highlight is **Santissima Trinità di Saccargia** *(see pp158–9)* with inspiring frescoes. Striking landscapes featuring unusual granite formations can be explored around the village of **Aggius and Valle della Luna** nearby *(see p152)*.

The Costa Smeralda, known for its exclusive resorts

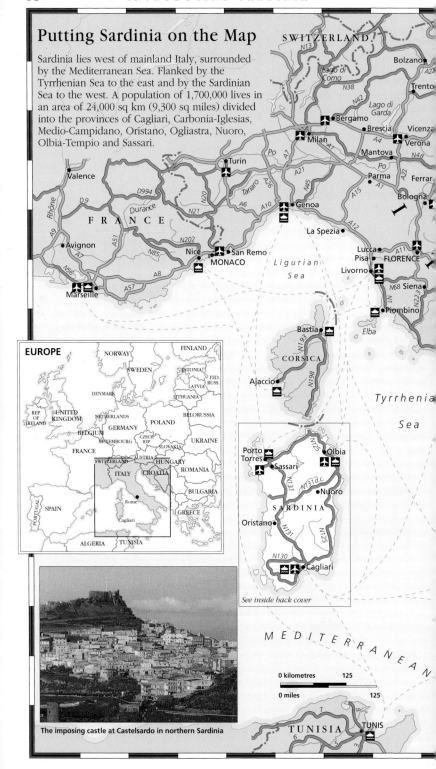

Putting Sardinia on the Map

Sardinia lies west of mainland Italy, surrounded by the Mediterranean Sea. Flanked by the Tyrrhenian Sea to the east and by the Sardinian Sea to the west. A population of 1,700,000 lives in an area of 24,000 sq km (9,300 sq miles) divided into the provinces of Cagliari, Carbonia-Iglesias, Medio-Campidano, Oristano, Ogliastra, Nuoro, Olbia-Tempio and Sassari.

See inside back cover

The imposing castle at Castelsardo in northern Sardinia

Satellite view over Northern Italy and Sardinia

KEY

☐ Area covered by this guide

⛴ Ferry port

✈ Airport

══ Motorway

▬▬ Major road

- - - Ferry routes

▬ ▬ International boundaries

A PORTRAIT OF SARDINIA

*T*he very isolation of this large island set in the middle of the Mediterranean has shaped its unique character. For thousands of years Sardinia has stood on the sidelines of mainstream Mediterranean historical events, remaining a singular world to itself. Even the Romans found it a difficult place to subdue.

Detail of a mural at Orgosolo

The experience of invasion from across the water over the centuries has left a legacy which is still evident today. The roads tend to follow valleys inland rather than tracing a scenic path along the beautiful coastline. There are yachting marinas and harbours, but fishing is not a mainstay of the economy and, even in peacetime, Sardinia has never really become a seafaring nation. Over the years Sardinia's shores have seen the arrival of Phoenicians, Romans, Genoans battling for supremacy with Pisans and Arabs, the Spanish, and finally the House of Savoy. The different cultures have all contributed to the art, architecture and cultural life of Sardinia and evidence is scattered throughout the island: prehistoric dwellings and fortresses from the earliest known inhabitants, ancient rock-cut tombs, and Romanesque churches which resemble those of Pisa or Lucca. Introduced artistic styles were often taken up and developed with distinctive Sardinian character – the altar paintings in the Spanish *retablo* tradition, for instance. In 1848 this untamed island became part of the newly created nation of Italy.

The 20th century brought with it dreams of industrialization and new-found prosperity, as well as the beginnings of a tourist industry.

However, the Sardinia that brings the visitors is a land of white beaches and deep blue sea, which does not really represent the essence of the place. The coastline is certainly beautiful, apart from some stretches

The stately procession of Sant'Efisio passing through Pula

◁ **The rugged cliffs of Punta Cristallo**

where random building has spoilt the views. But the interior is stunningly beautiful too, and deserves further exploration. The natural scenery is extremely varied, providing totally different environments and habitats for plants, animals and birds. In some areas there are fertile alluvial plains, in others steep mountains of granite and limestone where panoramas change from horizontal to vertical in the space of a few kilometres.

PEOPLE, LANGUAGE AND MUSIC

Human settlements have existed in the interior for thousands of years, and Sardinia is studded with the traces of ancient pastoral civilizations, further proof that the people have always tended to prefer to live in the comparative safety of the mountainous interior rather than along the coasts. The passing of the seasons is still marked by the stages in the agricultural year, and by celebrations of successful harvests. Ancient traditions – now deeply rooted in Catholicism

Hand loom at the Museo Etnografico in Nuoro

Fishermen at work on Isola Rossa

but showing traces of far older religions – are manifested in numerous festivals, which are often based on the very close relationship between the people of the island and their natural environment.

A number of very different dialects can be heard in the interior of the island, and the Sardinian language still has a clear Latin base – the word *domus* is used to mean a house, for instance, instead of the Italian *casa*. Years of Spanish rule mean that in Alghero, on the west coast, you can still hear Catalan spoken on the streets, and, on the island of Sant'Antioco in the southwest, the traditions and the cooking reflect a Ligurian heritage.

Music features strongly in Sardinian life, at feast days and weddings and even everyday events, especially in the interior, are always celebrated with music. Musicologists and musicians – such as Peter Gabriel, who recorded the music of the Tenores de Bitti group in his world music series – have described traditional Sardinian music as unique in Europe. Today it is undergoing something of a revival. There is a great deal of vocal and instrumental variety; based on the sound of the *launeddas*, a cane wind instrument, and polyphonic music for

Decanting ewes' milk after the morning milking

four voices. The most well-known exponents of the art are the Canto a Tenores, who perform regularly to growing numbers.

ECONOMIC DEVELOPMENT

In an uneasy position between the past and the future, the economy of Sardinia is complex. Agriculture and

Traditional bread from the Sulcis region

shepherding used to be the key factors in the economy, and there was also a mining boom in certain areas after unification, particularly around Sulcis, an abundant source of both coal and metals. But the Sardinian mining industry declined, especially after World War II, and is unlikely to recover. Other schemes for promoting industry have badly affected the environment, and have been abandoned. However, attempts in the 1950s to eradicate malaria, by treating marshy areas with pesticides, produced impressive results: in a short space of time the coast became habitable.

TOURISM IN SARDINIA TODAY

Interest in creating the facilities needed for tourism in Sardinia was initially subdued, and services were slow to take off. The gradual development of

tourism has, however, made the island famous, opening up Sardinia to the outside world, as well as increasing awareness of its history, local culture, arts and handicrafts.

The island's varied wildlife was perhaps bound to be affected by increasing numbers of visitors, and wildlife and marine reserves have now been established to protect unique habitats and their flora and fauna. The vast, wild Gennargentu range is also now a protected National Park. In recent years, the rare monk seal, thought to be extinct, has been sighted once again off the western coast, an indication that it is possible for tourism and ecology to co-exist in comfort. Sardinia possesses some of the most unspoilt scenery in Europe which, like its other special qualities, can only be fully appreciated by visiting the island.

The stacks on the Masua and Nebida coastlines

Marine Life of Sardinia

Marine prawn

The waters around Sardinia are considered to be the cleanest in Italy and are rich in flora and fauna. The generally healthy sea beds are havens for both scuba divers and naturalists. The sheer cliffs along the coast are home to dozens of species of nesting birds and birds of prey. Years of marine research in the Golfo di Orosei, on the eastern coast, have finally confirmed the return of the fabled monk seal, once so widespread in the area that caves and inlets were named after it. Dolphins and other large sea mammals, such as small whales, can occasionally be seen in the northwestern waters and the Straits of Bonifacio. In recent years the area has been declared an international marine reserve.

Neptune grass (Posidonia oceanica) *is a sea plant with shaggy leaves that grows down to a depth of 30–35 m (100–115 ft). Sea grass, as it is also known, has flowers, which is unusual for a marine plant.*

Rocks of volcanic origin

The striped sarago, quite a common fish in the Mediterranean, combs the sea bed in search of prey.

Rocks are covered with seaweed such as *Cystoseira*.

Sardinian coral *can be various shades of red or white and lives on the rocky sea bed, between 15–100 m (50–330ft) below sea level.*

The lobster *is a crustacean that lives mostly along the rocky shores, but can also be found at depths of up to 100 m (328 ft). The meat is a local delicacy.*

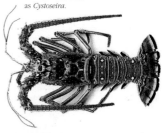

The sea anemone *attaches itself to rocks in shallow water. Its deceptively delicate tentacles contain stinging cells, enabling it to capture small fish and crustaceans.*

Gorgonian coral *survives because the water is so clean. The flexible branches may be white, yellow or red, and can grow to be 1m (3 ft) tall.*

BIRDS OF THE COASTLINE

The cliffs along the Sardinian coastline provide an ideal habitat for birds. Wild pigeons build safe nests here and raise their young without being disturbed. Herring gulls, Audouin's gulls and cormorants perch on the rocks between bouts of fishing. Further up the cliff edge, birds of prey such as the peregrine falcon, the red kite and the rare griffon vulture, build their nests.

Cormorants on the cliff ledges

Audouin's gull

Herring gull

Peregrine falcon

Red kite

UNDERWATER MEDITERRANEAN

The Mediterranean Sea has a rich and varied ecosystem, sustained by warm currents and clean waters. There is coral and myriad species of seaweed, a wide variety of fish, crustaceans and molluscs and marvellous rock formations for snorkellers and scuba divers to enjoy.

Cracks and crevices in the rocks make an ideal habitat for the moray eel.

Fronds

Brown meagres move in schools to defend themselves from predators by day. At night they hunt molluscs, small fish and prawns.

Dolphins *are frequently seen riding the waves at the bow of a boat in the warm waters around Sardinia, particularly in the clear seas around Maddalena along the northern shore.*

The moray eel *has powerful teeth and poisonous mucus. It also has an excellent ability to camouflage itself, making it one of the most dangerous creatures in the Mediterranean Sea.*

Monk seals, *once thought to be extinct, have returned to the Golfo di Orosei where they live in grottoes and solitary caves.*

The Sardinian Coastline

Grains of quartz on Is Arutas

Washed by the clear blue waters of the Mediterranean, Sardinia offers a varied coastline of sculpted cliffs and coves. Secluded inlets alternate with golden sand dunes, where wild lilies and cistus bloom, or rugged cliffs that plummet into the sea. The most well-known resort is the world-famous Costa Smeralda where visitors come to enjoy luxury villas and pretty, sandy beaches. Other popular areas are the coast south of Olbia, including the sheltered Cala Gonone, and the southeastern tip of the island, near Villasimius (easily accessible from Cagliari). Several stretches of coastline have remained untouched, such as the isolated coves between Orosei and Arbatax, and the south-western area between Baia Chia and Oristano.

At Capo Caccia, *sheer limestone cliffs, 168 m (551 ft) high, jut out from the sea.*

Isola dell'Asinara

GOLFO DELL'ASINARA

Porto Torres

THE NORTH AND THE COSTA SMERALDA

Between Bosa and Alghero *the spectacular coastline is punctuated by cliffs of volcanic origin, covered with mastic trees.*

Alghero

MAR DI SARDEGNA

THE WESTERN COAST

⑤ Bosa Marina

Around Piscinas *the coast is known for its impressive wind-carved sand dunes. The sand is an ideal habitat for juniper and tamarisk.*

Is Arutas
④

Oristano

③ Piscinas

② Cala Domestica

The cliffs on the island of San Pietro, *eroded by sea and wind, are of pink and grey trachyte. Crevices and ledges offer useful shelter to rare birds like Eleonora's falcon.*

Isola di San Pietro   CAGLIARI AND THE SOUTH

Isola di Sant'Antioco

Cagliari

GOLF CAGL

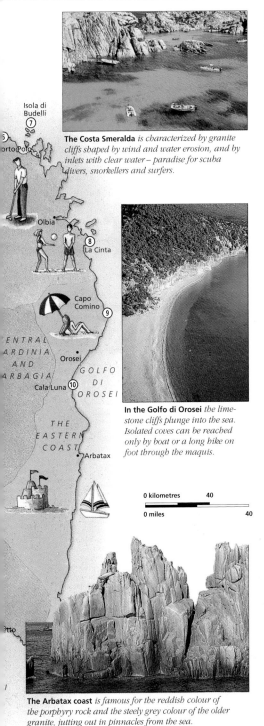

The Costa Smeralda *is characterized by granite cliffs shaped by wind and water erosion, and by inlets with clear water – paradise for scuba divers, snorkellers and surfers.*

In the Golfo di Orosei *the limestone cliffs plunge into the sea. Isolated coves can be reached only by boat or a long hike on foot through the maquis.*

0 kilometres   40

0 miles   40

The Arbatax coast *is famous for the reddish colour of the porphyry rock and the steely grey colour of the older granite, jutting out in pinnacles from the sea.*

SARDINIA'S TEN BEST BEACHES

Most lively ①
Il Poetto, just outside Cagliari, is the largest and liveliest beach on the island. Locals throng here at weekends and through the summer.

Most hidden beach ②
Cala Domestica, protected by a Saracen tower, is invisible from the sea. In World War II it was used as a German military base.

Best dunes ③
At Piscinas there are 9 km (5 miles) of sand dunes covered with maquis vegetation. Some are as high as 50 m (164 ft), the highest found in Europe.

Most tropical ④
The beach at Is Arutas is made of tiny "grains" of quartz. A forest of pine trees forms a green backdrop to the sand.

Cleanest sea ⑤
Bosa Marina, unchanged since the 1950s, has won medals for being the cleanest beach in Italy.

Best windsurfing ⑥
A strong and constant breeze from the mouth of the Liscia river makes Porto Pollo (*Porto Puddu* in Sardinian dialect) perfect for windsurfing.

Best coral beach ⑦
The beach on the island of Budelli consists of pieces of shells, coral and marine micro-organisms. Now, however, landing on the island is forbidden.

Best beach for young people ⑧
La Cinta, 1 km (half a mile) long, is a favourite with the trendy younger set. It is ideal for soaking up the sun and for windsurfing.

Most remote beach ⑨
Berchida, with its white beach and red rocks, can only be reached via a long sandy track through the shrubby maquis.

Most inaccessible beach ⑩
The secluded Cala Luna, with its white sand, pink oleanders and green mastic trees, is only accessible by boat or on foot.

The Flora and Fauna of Sardinia

Donkey at Gesturi

From the rugged Gennargentu massif to the Campidano plains, and from the Nurra hills to the wind-eroded rocks of the Gallura area, Sardinia offers a great variety of natural habitats for wildlife. The forests, especially in the north, are dominated by cork oaks, for centuries a useful source of raw material. The Mediterranean maquis is permeated with the scents of lentiscus, cistus, myrtle and strawberry trees. Despite decades of farming, the fauna is still varied and interesting. Deer and wild boar abound in the scrub and forests and the rocks are home to the moufflon. The small Monte Arcosu reserve retains a tiny population of rare Sardinian deer, and the island of Asinara is the home of wild donkeys. In the spectacular Giara di Gesturi plateau, unbroken horses graze freely. Assorted reptiles can also be found, but no vipers.

The moufflon *is an ancient inhabitant of the island. It has a thick coat and impressive curving horns.*

Sardinian deer *are stocky, with smaller horns than their mainland counterparts.*

Foxes *can still be seen on Monte Limbara and Gennargentu.*

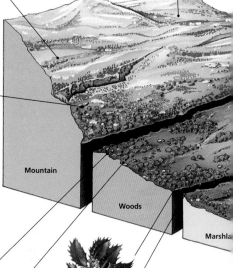

Mountain

Woods

Marshla

The Sardinian horse *is a compact animal native to the island. The horses roam on the Giara di Gesturi plateau and on the Capo Caccia headland.*

Sardinian boar *live in various parts of the island. They are smaller and stouter than species on mainland Italy.*

The Kermes oak (Quercus coccifera) *thrives mostly on the southern coastline.*

The cork oak (Quercus suber), *important to the economy, dominates the forest of Gallura (see p151).*

The holm oak (Quercus ilex) dominates in almost all medium-altitude woods.

THE MEDITERRANEAN MAQUIS

This thick, often impenetrable, shrubby vegetation (*macchia* in Italian) thrives in the coastal and mountainous regions of Sardinia. The shrubs – including myrtle, arbutus (strawberry tree) and blackthorn – flower in spring, rest in summer and revive again in autumn. Even in winter the island looks green, with splashes of colour from berries. In recent years the area of maquis has increased, as a result of forest fires which encourage plenty of new growth.

Myrtle in flower

The kite's *habitat is the wooded upland valleys.*

Strawberry tree

White cistus flowers

THE SARDINIAN TERRAIN

The southwestern corner of Sardinia began to emerge from the sea over 500 million years ago.

Turtles, *which may grow up to as much as 1 m (3 ft) in length, are dying out because their eggs are highly prized.*

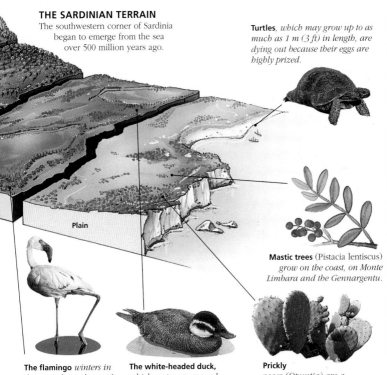

Plain

Mastic trees (Pistacia lentiscus) *grow on the coast, on Monte Limbara and the Gennargentu.*

The flamingo *winters in the coastal marshes and lagoons, and now nests on Sardinia.*

The white-headed duck, *which nests among reeds, is quite a rare sight on Sardinian marshland.*

Prickly pears *(Opuntia) are a characteristic feature every-where along the coastline.*

The Nuraghi

There are over 7,000 nuraghi in Sardinia, their distinctive truncated cones a familiar part of the landscape. Little is known about their builders, a civilization that flourished on the island from 1800 to 500 BC (in some areas the nuraghic peoples resisted the Romans long after this date). Initially a nuraghe consisted of a single tower made of huge blocks of stone laid without mortar. Later, more towers were added, with connecting ramparts, resulting in more complex structures such as the Losa nuraghe at Abbasanta, the Santu Antine at Torralba and the Su Nuraxi at Barùmini. Nuraghi served as both dwelling and fortress, and the towers were often surrounded by a village and wall. There is no trace of any written language, but over 1,500 bronze figures have been found in tombs and near holy wells. The figures, and other finds, are now on display in Sardinia's archaeological museums.

Bronze quiver

Tribal chief
This bronze figure comes from the nuraghic village of Santa Vittoria, at Serri, one of the largest in Sardinia. It is a portrait of a prince at prayer.

Simple nuraghe
This is the most commonly seen and simplest form of nuraghe, consisting of a single tower with a chamber made of inwardly stepped circular tiers of stones. At times these nuraghi had more than one storey.

The central tower is in the shape of a truncated cone.

The rampart incorporates three defence towers.

Outer defence wall

• Sassari

Nuoro

• Oristano

Cagliari

• Principal Nuraghic Sites

The Losa Nuraghe at Abbasanta
This nuraghe is in three parts and is surrounded by a rampart with small towers. The oldest tower dates from before 1500 BC. There is a fine panoramic view of the Gennargentu mountains from the terrace.

Maiori Nuraghe at Tempio Pausania
This ground-floor room of the Maiori nuraghe in northern Sardinia could only be illuminated by light filtering in from the outside.

NURAGHIC BURIALS

The nuraghic peoples built monumental tombs known as Tombe dei Giganti (Tombs of Giants) to bury their dead. Each tomb consisted of a long covered corridor constructed with huge slabs of stone. The shape represented the horn of the Bull God. A monolithic oval stele, with an opening at the base, formed the front face. Two rows of stones on either side, forming an arch, completed the burial chamber. The central, arched stele could sometimes be as much as 3 m (10 ft) tall. The area around a typical Tomba dei Giganti was often surrounded by long rows of menhirs.

The Tomb of Giants at Li Lolghi is one of the most famous prehistoric sites in Sardinia

The central tower had three superimposed chambers.

The side towers were built at a later stage, in the early Iron Age.

The rampart created a solid defence system.

SANTU ANTINE NURAGHE
The central tower of this roughly triangular nuraghe is surrounded by a three-sided rampart with three towers. It was built in different stages in the 9th–8th centuries BC. The huge complex was later dedicated to the Roman emperor Constantine.

This reconstruction *shows the original layout of Santu Antine. The central tower was the main fortress and dwelling, protected by the external towers.*

Arrubiu Nuraghe
This consists of a massive fortress built in red stone covering an area of about 3 hectares (7 acres) at the edge of a plateau dominating the Flumendosa valley. Imposing external ramparts with five towers protected the inner courtyard and the central nuraghic construction, which was 16 m (52 ft) high.

SARDINIA
THROUGH THE YEAR

Spring is by far the best season to visit Sardinia. Perfumed flowers are in bloom in the maquis thickets, the woods and meadows are still green and, although the weather is warm enough for swimming as early as May, it has not reached the scorching temperatures of summer. Easter, with its colourful processions, marks the religious high point of the island. During the rest of the year, towns and villages organize festivals to commemorate the feast day of the local patron saint and sanctuaries are enlivened by

Mask from Mamoiada

celebrations and banquets. The summer months are dedicated to activities along the island's stunning coast, such as bathing, sailing and windsurfing. Inland, it can get stiflingly hot in summer, but the higher mountainous areas provide a cool retreat from the crowds and an ideal place for walking. Grape harvesting begins in the autumn, and in early winter there is heavy snowfall on the Mount Gennargentu massif. At times snow can even fall on the lower areas covering the rocky landscape of the Supramonte.

Narcissus in bloom, a typical flower of the Mediterranean

SPRING

Once the warm spring weather sets in, the sheep and goats grazing on the hillsides will be moved to higher pastures. The aromatic plants and strongly scented flowers of the maquis are in full bloom, and bees abound. They produce the rather bitter honey used in many traditional Sardinian cakes.

In the flatlands and on the hills of the Anglona and Montiferru regions the fruit trees are in blossom, while in the countryside young artichokes are almost ready to be picked. These are shipped to vegetable markets on mainland Italy and are traditionally the first on the market.

MARCH AND APRIL

Holy Week and **Easter** (*Mar or Apr*) are a time of great religious celebrations, with colourful processions taking place throughout the island.

In Cagliari there is an important procession through the streets on Good Friday. A representation of the *Iscravamentu* and *Incontru* mystery plays is performed at Iglesias. At Oliena the costume procession known as *S'Incontru* takes place on Easter Sunday. *Su Concordu* in the town of Santu Lussurgiu features 15th-century psalms sung in Gregorian chant. On Holy Monday at Castelsardo, there is the *Luni Santu*, a religious feast of Spanish origin.
Sagra del Riccio di Mare (*early Mar*). A festival of the sea urchin in Alghero.
The **Livestock Festival** (*25 Apr*), at Ollastra Simaxis, is held in honour of St Mark.
Festa Patronale (*2nd Sat after Easter*). The island of Sant' Antioco celebrates its patron saint's feast day.

MAY

Sant'Efisio (*1-4 May*), in Cagliari, offers a grand procession commemorating the end of the plague in 1656. The saint's statue is carried through the city and is then taken to Nora on an ox-drawn cart. During this splendid display of religious feeling the faithful cast flowers onto the street as the statue passes by.
San Francesco's feast day (*second Sun*). Held at Lula, this is one of the most popular celebrations in the Baronie and Nuoro areas.
Festa dell'Annunziata (*third Sun*), at Bitti. A pastoral celebration of the Annunciation.
San Bachisio (*29 May*). This feast day consists of three days of *Ballu Tundu* (round dance) in the squares of Onanì.

The *S'Incontru* procession in the streets of Oliena on Easter Day

AVERAGE DAILY HOURS OF SUNSHINE

Hours

12 –
9 –
6 –
3 –
0 –

Jan Feb Mar Apr May Jun Jul Aug Sep Oct Nov Dec

Sunshine Chart
Summer is the sunniest, as well as the hottest time, and June has the maximum hours of sunshine daily. The least sunny month is January, but the weather varies a great deal between inland and coastal regions, and in general, coastal areas will be brighter.

The Ardia horse race in front of the Sant'Antine sanctuary at Sedilo

Cavalcata Sarda *(Ascension Day)*. Although this is a fairly new tradition, the "Sardinian Horseride" has become one of the island's major folk festivals. Handicraft stalls and general festivities fill the streets of Sassari's old town centre. People from all over the island crowd into the town on horseback or dressed in colourful costumes to hear traditional songs and poetry from the different towns and regions of the island.

SUMMER

The high temperatures and stunning coastline draw locals and visitors alike to the seashore during the summer months. The coastline is filled with bathers and windsurfers, and yachts and sailboats from all over Europe dock at the small, pretty harbours. For snorkellers and scuba divers there are underwater beds of posidonia to explore. Sailing, windsurf and scuba diving clubs organize lessons throughout the summer months *(see pp198-9)*. The

cooler temperatures on the slopes of Gennargentu make it excellent for hikers, and the climb down the gorges of Su Gorroppu is also popular.

This is the period of rural festivals, when small religious sanctuaries hidden among the valleys and hills come to life with pilgrimages and feasting. **Pani, Pisci, Pezza e Piricchittus** *(Jun-Sep)*, meaning bread, fish, pizza and almond pastry, is a food festival held in the restaurants of Quartu. Cagliari offers a programme of music, theatre and cinema during the summer. At San Gavino Monreale there are concerts and other cultural events as well as sports activities at night.

JUNE

Horse Festival *(2 & 3 Jun)*. Santu Lussurgiu holds an important agricultural festival with a handicrafts exhibition.
Sagra delle Ciliegie *(first Sun of month)*. Festival celebrating the cherry harvest at Villacidro, Bonarcado and Burcei.
San Leonardo *(11 Jun)*. An evening of music, dance and food in Villanova Monteleone.

JULY

Ardia *(5-8 Jul)*. This characteristic rural festival is held at San Costantino a Sedilo in front of the Santu Antine sanctuary. A lively horse race accompanies celebrations honouring the saint.
Sagra del Torrone *(second Sun of month)*. At Tonara, at the foot of the Gennargentu mountains, the festivities end with the preparation of the famous nougat *(torrone)*.
Sagra delle Pesche *(17 Jul)*, is a peach festival held at San Sperate on the feast day of the town's patron saint.
Estate Musicale *(Jul-Aug)*, at Alghero, with concerts in the Chiostro di San Francesco.
International Folklore Festival *(end of Jul)*, held in Tempio Pausania, during the summer Carnival.
Carpet Fair *(two weeks in Jul or Aug)* at Mogoro. This is one of the leading displays of Sardinian handicrafts, in particular carpets, tapestry and hand-made furniture.
Music in Antas Valley *(Jul-Aug)*. Classical music concerts held in the splendid setting of the Temple of Antas at Fluminimaggiore *(see p68)*.

Advanced sailing lessons off the Costa Smeralda

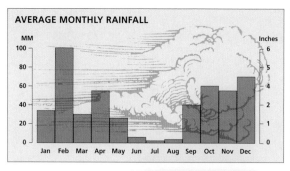

AVERAGE MONTHLY RAINFALL

Rainfall Chart
In Sardinia most of the rainfall occurs in the autumn and winter. The rainfall is heavier in the mountainous regions of the interior, with precipitation as high as 1,000 mm (39 inches) per year. The driest season is during the summer months, particularly in the coastal regions.

AUGUST

Mauretanian Wedding
(1–15 Aug) at Santadi. A ceremony dating back to the ancient traditions of the North Africans who inhabited the Sulcis region in Roman times.

Dieci Giorni Sulcitani
(1–15 Aug) in Sant'Antioco. This consists of ten evenings of traditional local entertainment, including plays in dialect, recitals of Sardinian poetry, traditional folk dances and local choral music.

Carpet Show *(first Sun of Aug)*. Traditional hand-made carpets and blankets are exhibited at Aggius.

Madonna della Neve feast day *(first Sun of Aug)*. The hardships of winter are exorcised in the Tascusì sanctuary at Desulo.

Sagra della Vernaccia
(first Sun of Aug). Festival of the local wine at Baratili San Pietro, near Oristano.

Sagra del Vino *(4 Aug)*. Wine festival at Jerzu with costume parades, dances, traditional songs and Cannonau wine.

Sagra del Pomodoro
(11 Aug). The tomato festival offers tomato-based dishes

A drummer playing at the Time in Jazz festival at Berchidda

served outdoors at Zeddiani. There is also an exhibition of local farm produce.

Faradda de li Candelieri *(14 Aug)*. Candles *(candelieri)*, weighing between 200–300 kg (440–660 lbs) are carried by members of the ancient guilds in Sassari. Each candle is decorated with the coat of arms of the guild and its patron saint.

Time in Jazz *(the week incorporating Ferragosto)*. Berchidda hosts an annual jazz festival.

Processione del Redentore
(29 Aug). Nuoro hosts one of Sardinia's most popular celebrations with a procession through the streets in honour

of Christ the Redeemer, and performances of local folklore.

Launeddas Festival *(fourth Sun)* at San Vito. This festival features performances by leading musicians of the traditional triple-piped wind instrument *(see p90)*. The music is accompanied by the *Ballu Tundu*, a circular dance.

Rassegna di Musica Leggera *(Aug–Sep)*. Performances of popular music and theatre in Piazza Peglia, Carloforte.

Regata Vela Latina *(end of Aug)*. A regatta for traditional Sardinian fishing boats held in Stintino *(see p120)*.

Mostra del Tappeto *(mid-Aug–late Sep)*. A carpet fair held at Nule.

AUTUMN

It is still possible to swim in the sea well into September, but the air becomes cooler in the evening. October is grape harvest time and autumn marks the beginning of the hunting season. The favourite game is wild boar, a tasty meat used in the strongly-flavoured Sardinian cuisine. The chestnut harvest in the mountains often ends with lively festivals.

SEPTEMBER

Pilgrimage to the Madonna di Gonare Sanctuary *(8 and 16 Sep)*. Departures to this hilltop church alternate between the centres of Sarule *(see p103)* and Orani.

Fiera del Bestiame *(third Sun of month)* at Serri. A livestock fair on the day of Santa Lucia.

San Cosimo *(27 Sep)*. The *Mamuthones (see p102)* parade through the streets of Mamoiada in sheepskins.

Traditional costumes worn for the Madonna della Neve festival at Desulo

AVERAGE MONTHLY TEMPERATURE

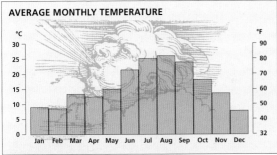

Temperature Chart

The summer months between June and September are hot and dry, with temperatures above 20° C (68° F), and at times reaching 30° C (86° F). In winter the temperatures are mild, rarely dipping below 5° C (41° F). January generally has sunny days and cold nights.

Masked figures *(Boes)* with cowbells during carnival at Ottana

OCTOBER

Santa Vitalia Festival *(first Mon of month).* A festival dedicated to agriculture held at Serrenti, with stalls selling local handicrafts.

Sagra delle Castagne e delle Nocciole *(last weekend).* Festival to celebrate the harvest of chestnuts and hazelnuts at Aritzo. There is also a handicrafts fair.

NOVEMBER

Festa della Madonna dello Schiavo *(15 Nov).* A statue of the Madonna is worshipped as it passes through the town of Carloforte. The statue is said to have been sculpted by citizens from Carloforte, who had been kidnapped by pirates and held in Tunis.

Santa Caterina *(25 Nov).* The saint's feast day is celebrated in Abbasanta.

WINTER

Winter is a fairly cold season throughout the island and snow covers the mountainous interior. Livestock is returned to its lower winter pastures

and pens, and the chill wind puts an end to fishing activity along the coast. As well as **Christmas**, which is very important in Sardinia, there are many other feast days and local festivals in the Carnival period before Lent.

DECEMBER

Sagra delle Salsicce *(first Sun of month)* held at Siligo. After the pig slaughter, preparation and curing of the meat, the sausage festival is an opportunity to taste the year's new delicacies.

Christmas is celebrated at home with presents and by preparing traditional sweets.

JANUARY AND FEBRUARY

Feast of Sant'Antonio Abate *(16–17 Jan)* is celebrated at Mamoiada and Flumini-maggiore *(see p68)* with huge bonfires.

Carnival *(the ten days before Shrove Tuesday)* is extremely popular in Sardinia, especially in the Barbagia region. Masked and costumed figures parade on Shrove Tuesday and the last Sunday of Lent. At Mamoiada, the *Mamuthones,*

men dressed in sheepskins with heavy bells strapped to their backs, are driven through the town by the *Issohadores (see p102)*. Similar festivals during carnival are the *Thurpos* at Orotelli, and the *Merdules* and *Boes* at Ottana *(see p101).* At *Sa Sartiglia* in Oristano, masked horsemen spear a silver star hanging from a tree. There are cakes and free wine at Iglesias *(see p68)* and food is served in the main square at Perfugas. At Tempio Pausania an effigy of "King George" is burned and at Santu Lussurgiu *(see p128)* there is the *Sa Carrela 'e Nanti* horse race.

Processo a Su Conte *(Ash Wednesday).* At Ovodda the stuffed figure of "Su Conte" is tried in the main square and burned at the stake.

PUBLIC HOLIDAYS

New Year's Day (1 Jan)
Epiphany (6 Jan)
Easter Sunday and Monday (Mar or Apr)
Liberation Day (25 Apr)
Labour Day (1 May)
Republic Day (2 Jun)
Ferragosto (Assumption Day, 15 Aug)
All Saints' Day (1 Nov)
Immaculate Conception (8 Dec)
Christmas Day (25 Dec)
Santo Stefano (26 Dec)

Snow-covered mountains of the Gennargentu in winter

THE HISTORY OF SARDINIA

The origins of Sardinian history go back thousands of years. The first people to settle are thought to have reached the island by crossing over a natural causeway which once linked Tuscany and Sardinia, perhaps between 450,000 and 150,000 years ago. A succession of different cultures led up to the rise of the nuraghic civilization. These tribes of shepherds and warriors lived in round stone dwellings called nuraghi, defended by walled fortresses, and their occupation left exceptional megalithic ruins across the island. Of the 7,000 nuraghi left in Sardinia, some are in an excellent state of preservation: the Su Nuraxi settlement at Barùmini, the Santu Antine complex and the nuraghi at Losa.

The Macomer Venus in the Museo Archeologico in Cagliari

The Phoenicians arrived in 1000 BC, settling along the coastline at Tharros, Nora, Bithia and Cagliari and, after winning the Punic Wars, the Romans occupied the island. Roman dominion lasted 700 years despite strong resistance from Sardinians, and evidence can still be seen in the many ruins. When the Roman Empire fell, Sardinia again fell prey to various conquerors. For centuries the Vandals, Byzantines and Arabs fought for possession of the strategic harbours, until the maritime republics of Pisa and Genoa made their appearance on Sardinian waters. A golden age of Sardinian Romanesque architecture was introduced, which gave way to Gothic when the House of Aragon conquered the island. After 400 years of Spanish rule, control of the island passed to Austria, which ceded it to the House of Savoy in 1718. The Kingdom of Sardinia survived up to the unification of Italy. A long period of neglect was ended only after World War II, with the reclamation of the malarial marshes. The scheme's success opened up possibilities for a tourist industry and the development of an autonomous, modern Sardinia.

Calaris, modern-day Cagliari, in a print dating from 1590

◁ The Roman Temple of Antas at Fluminimaggiore, built over a 6th–5th century BC Phoenician temple

Prehistoric Sardinia

Although some stone tools found at Perfugas show that Sardinia was inhabited from the Paleolithic period (150,000 years ago), it was only around 9000 BC that the island began to be settled by populations from Asia Minor, the African coasts, the Iberian peninsula and Liguria. The fertile, mineral-rich land and the obsidian mines at Monte Arci were a major factor in the island's prosperity. By around 3000 BC the Sardinians had grouped into tribes. They lived in villages with thatched-roof huts and buried their dead in rock-cut tombs called *domus de janas* (house of fairies). By about 1800 BC this rural society had evolved into the warrior nuraghic civilization, who built thousands of circular stone towers *(nuraghi)* across the island. Many of these remarkable prehistoric constructions are still visible.

Bronze figure from Teti-Abini

Necklace with Tusk
This ornament was found in a tomb dating from 2000–1800 BC, the bell-shaped pottery era.

Earthenware
These jugs and vases were everyday objects used to store water and grain.

The motifs on the prow have more to do with the land than the sea.

Monte d'Accoddi ruins
These traces reveal the ruins of a tiered, terraced construction, probably a temple, dating from the 3rd millennium BC. It looked remarkably similar to the famous ziggurat temples of Mesopotamia and the Aztec pyramids.

TIMELINE		
6000 BC Sardinian peoples make tools and weapons from the obsidian found at Monte Arci	*Obsidian arrowhead*	*A typical example of domus de janas*

6000 BC

4000 BC

Boar tusk, an ornament from the early Neolithic period

4000–3000 BC The age of the Bonu Ighinu culture - small communities living by raising sheep and goats. Distinctive, high quality grey pottery with incised decoration is produced

Bronze Artifacts from Abini

These spears were part of a hoard of 100 kg (220 lb) of objects hidden in large clay vessels, perhaps to conceal them from the Roman invaders.

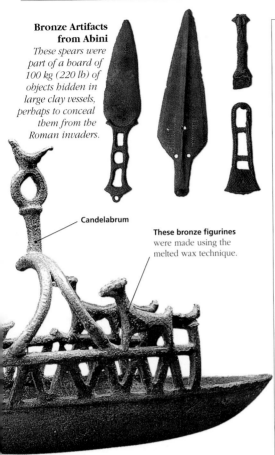

Candelabrum

These bronze figurines were made using the melted wax technique.

EX VOTO WITH DEER MOTIF

This ex voto lamp in the shape of a ship was one of 70 or so found at Is Argiolas near Bultei. It dates from the 8th–7th centuries BC, and is now in the Museo Archeologico Nazionale in Cagliari. In the nuraghic age, Sardinians had a love-hate relationship with the sea, which ended with the arrival of the Carthaginians, Romans and later conquerors, who forced the local inhabitants to live in the interior.

WHERE TO SEE PREHISTORIC SARDINIA

Pre-nuraghic ruins include a ziggurat at Monte d'Accoddi and rock-cut tombs (*domus de janas*) at Pranu Muteddu (Goni). Nuraghic villages survive at Su Nuraxi (*see pp64–5*), Serra Òrrios (*see p84*), Tiscali (*see pp104–5*) and Abini. Burial chambers, or "Tombs of Giants", can be seen at places such as Sa Ena 'e Thomes, and holy wells can be visited at Santa Cristina (Paulilàtino) and Santa Vittoria (Serri).

The nuraghic village of Serra Òrrios *is one of the best preserved in Sardinia. It consisted of about 70 dwellings (see p84).*

The Montessu necropolis *houses domus de janas of the Ozieri pre-nuraghic era.*

3000 BC Era of Ozieri or San Michele culture. Villages are established throughout the island and the dead are buried in the *domus de janas*

Replica of the goddess Mater Mediterranea of Senorbi

1800 BC Rise of nuraghic civilization, characterized by truncated cone-shaped buildings erected at the edges of upland plateaus

1000 BC Phoenician ships moor along coast

3000 BC	2000 BC	1000 BC

2000–1800 BC Civilization known for its bell-shaped pottery. Rectangular or round dwellings constructed

Dolmen at Luras

1500 BC The first simple forms of nuraghe appear

The Santa Barbara nuraghe at Macomer

The Phoenicians, Carthaginians and Romans

Around 1000 BC Phoenician ships began to use the inlets of the Sardinian coasts as harbours. When commerce intensified about 200 years later, they founded the cities of Nora, Sulcis, Tharros, Olbia and, later on, Bithia and Karalis (today's Cagliari). But good relationships with the local chiefs soon waned. After a brief period of peace, the nuraghic populations attacked the Phoenician settlements which, in 509 BC, asked Carthage for help. In 238 BC the Carthaginians, defeated in the first Punic War, ceded Sardinia to the Romans, who made it their province. For over a century the Sardinians put up fierce resistance, a situation which ended in 215 BC with the battle of Cornus *(see p129)*. The Romans never succeeded in subduing the entire island and rebellion in the interior continued for years. However, Roman civilization gave the island a network of roads, as well as baths, temples, aqueducts and amphitheatres.

Oil jar, 2nd century BC

Gold Bracelet
Decorated with palmettes, lotus flowers and a scarab beetle, this bracelet came from Tharros (pp132–3).

This shape of nose is typical of the Phoenicians.

Glass Vase and Perfume Bottle
In Roman times glass was used to make ornamental vessels as well as practical objects like cups, bowls and bottles. Numerous glass pieces have been found in burial grounds and examples can be seen in the Museo Archeologico Nazionale in Cagliari (p58).

Carthaginian Necklace
Carthaginian jewellery was often quite elaborate, as shown by this necklace with pendants carrying human and animal symbols.

Lines on the face imitate tattoos.

GRINNING MASK

This mask dates from the 4th century BC, when the island was under Carthaginian rule. Masks like these were used to ward off evil, to protect children or ensure the sleep of the dead. This mask was found in the settlement beneath the town of San Sperate *(see p62).*

TIMELINE

900 BC Nuraghic villages, bronze figures and stone sculptures

Phoenician ship

500–400 BC Sardinians flee to Barbagia after losing battles against Carthaginians

900 BC	750 BC	500 BC

730–700 BC First Phoenician harbours built: the future Nora, Tharros, Bithia and Karalis

ca. 550 BC The Carthaginians arrive and found the first Punic cities

509 BC The nuraghic peoples attack the coastal cities, who ask Carthage for help

**Statue of Drusus Junior
(13 BC–AD 23)**
*The portrait of the Roman
consul, son of the emperor
Tiberius, was found at
Sant'Antioco (see p72),
together with other busts
from the early Empire.*

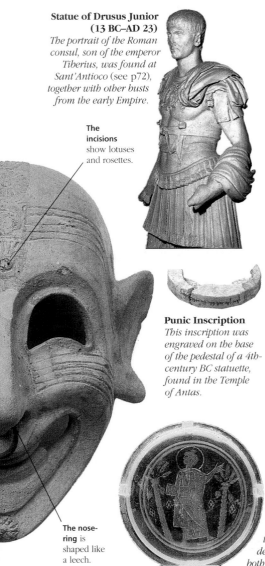

The incisions
show lotuses
and rosettes.

The nose-ring is
shaped like
a leech.

**WHERE TO SEE
PUNIC–ROMAN
SARDINIA**

The best preserved Punic-
Roman cities are Nora *(see
pp74–5)* and Tharros *(see
pp132–3)* . The ruins at Sulki,
present-day Sant'Antioco *(see
p72)*, are wholly Punic. Roman
ruins include the amphi-
theatre in Cagliari *(see p54)*,
near the Villa of Tigellio
(see p59), and baths at
Fordongianus *(see p136–7)*.

**Roman amphitheatre at
Cagliari**, *2nd century AD.*

The Roman theatre at Nora
*is still used for summer
cultural events.*

Punic Inscription
*This inscription was
engraved on the base
of the pedestal of a 4th-
century BC statuette,
found in the Temple
of Antas.*

**Glass Bowl with the Figure
of Christ**
*This beautiful early Christian
piece was found inside a
tomb near Ittiri. Christ is
depicted in the role of
both legislator and emperor.*

238 BC The
Carthaginians
lose the first
Punic War

227 BC Sardinia,
together with
Corsica, becomes
Roman province

*Mosaic
found
at Nora*

AD 200–300 Full of
disease, Sardinia becomes
a deportation site

250 BC | **AD 1** | **AD 250**

*Temple of
Antas
dedicated to
Sardus Pater*

27 BC Sardinia
is divided from
Corsica and
becomes a
senatorial
province

AD 66 Roman Sardinia
becomes an imperial
province and is
occupied by legions

The Middle Ages, from the Vandals to the Aragonese

Arborea's coat of arms

In AD 456 the Vandals conquered Sardinia. Shortly afterwards, liberated by Byzantium, the island became one of the seven African provinces of the Eastern Roman Empire. The subsequent power vacuum, aggravated by Arab invasions, gave rise to the four autonomous *giudicati*, or principalities, of Torres, Gallura, Arborea and Cagliari. Around AD 1000 the Pisans and Genoese, after fierce campaigns against the Arabs, took over parts of the island. The long relationship with Aragon was formalized in 1295, when Pope Boniface VIII signed the papal bull naming James II of Aragon as King of Corsica and Sardinia. On 12 June 1323 the Infante Alfonso landed in Sardinia with his army.

The Castello quarter, Cagliari
Built during the era of Pisan rule, the fortified Castello quarter in Cagliari was the heart of the city until the 1800s.

Eleonora of Arborea
This remarkable woman inherited Arborea from her father Mariano IV in 1383. After two wars against the Aragonese, Eleonora gained control of most of Sardinia in 1394. Known as the Giudica, she remains a symbol of Sardinian independence.

Papal coat of arms

Benedetto Caetani was the real name of Pope Boniface.

Barison I's seal
In 1038 the Pisans, after wresting Sardinia from the Arabs, helped Barison I of Arborea to take possession of its four giudicati (principalities).

BONIFACE VIII
In 1295, Pope Boniface VIII (depicted here while celebrating the Jubilee of 1300) signed the papal bull giving control of the *Regnum Sardiniae et Corsicae* to James II of Aragon, in exchange for relinquishing Sicily. The Aragonese continued to annexe Sicily, ignoring the agreement.

TIMELINE

534 Byzantium liberates Sardinia which, together with Corsica, becomes one of its seven African provinces

Pope Gregory the Great

AD 500	600	700	800

Earthenware from Vandal tombs

600 Pope Gregory the Great sets out to convert Sardinia to Christianity

711 Arab invasions begin

815 Sardinian diplomats ask France for aid in war against Arabs

Capo Falcone
This tower was part of a defence system which finally put an end to barbarian raids on Sardinia in the 16th century.

Pope
Boniface VIII

FACIO·VIII·Bene
·tani·nato ad Anagni·
morto 1303·Benedice il pe
Giubileo del 1300,

Boniface VIII, despite this serene pose, was a highly controversial pope.

Alghero city walls
The massive walls and their towers date from the 14th-century period of Catalan rule.

**WHERE TO SEE
MEDIEVAL SARDINIA**

The medieval conquerors often infiltrated the interior, influencing local architecture. San Saturnino in Cagliari *(see p59)* and San Gavino at Porto Torres *(see p120)* are two of the earliest medieval churches in Sardinia. Evidence of artistic contact with the mainland can be seen in the Romanesque churches of Logudoro *(see pp156–7)*, the cathedral of Oristano *(see pp134–5)* and the cathedral of Santa Maria in Cagliari *(see p55)*. Some castles remain: the Rocca at Castelsardo *(see p164)* and the Castello complex in Cagliari *(see pp56–7)*.

Santissima Trinità di Saccargia *is Pisan Romanesque (see pp158–9).*

The Castello Malaspina *dominates the town of Bosa (see pp126–7).*

1016 Pope Benedict VIII asks Pisa and Genoa to intervene in Sardinia	**1087** Guglielmo di Massa, in Cagliari, becomes the first non-Sardinian ruler	**1164** Frederick Barbarossa makes Sardinia a kingdom	**1257–9** Last years of the Cagliari and Torres principalities	*James II of Aragon*
1000	**1100**	**1200**	**1300**	
Frederick I Barbarossa		**1243** Frederick II crowns his son Enzo King of Sardinia	**1323** 12 June: Alfonso of Aragon lands in Sardinia	

Spanish Rule

Aragonese coat of arms

The Spanish conquest of Sardinia was slow: the rulers of Arborea waged a lengthy war against the invaders, there were determined revolts in Alghero and, in 1355, the Spanish crown was forced to grant a form of parliament to the six largest cities. The Aragonese took power definitively only in 1409, when the principality of Arborea was eliminated after the bloody battle of Sanluri and replaced by the marquisate of Oristano. Spanish domination of Sardinia was strengthened in 1479, with the marriage of Ferdinand of Aragon and Isabella I of Castile and Leon. The Spanish era also saw the founding of the first universities: Sassari in 1562 and Cagliari in 1620. Following the Peace of Utrecht in 1714, the island was ceded to Austria who then, in the Treaty of London, passed it over to King Vittorio Amedeo II of the House of Savoy.

The upper part shows scenes from the life of St Peter; below are the saints with St Peter in the centre.

Decorated border

Vittorio Amedeo II of Savoy

Vittorio Amedeo became king in 1718 when Austria gave Sardinia to him in exchange for Sicily. The Cagliari parliament swore allegiance to the new king on 2 August 1720.

VICTOR AMÉDÉE.

Four Moors Coat of Arms

Of Catalan origin, the coat of arms with four Moors first appeared in Sardinia after the arrival of Alfonso of Aragon in 1323. It has become one of the symbols of the island.

The Four Evangelists are depicted in the elaborately bordered predella. Sardinian artists put their own stamp on the Catalan *retablo* style.

TIMELINE

1355 Sardinian parliament established

1409 Battle of Sanluri; end of Arborea as a principality

1541 On his way to Tunis, Charles stops at Algh[ero]

| 1350 | 1400 | 1500 |

1402 *Anno de Sa Mortagia Manna*, the year of the great plague

Ferdinand of Aragon and Isabella of Castile

1509–1520 Repeated Arab pirate raids on Sardinia

Alghero Cathedral
The interior of the cathedral of Santa Maria, begun in the 16th century, is a splendid example of the Catalan Gothic style in Sardinia.

WHERE TO SEE SPANISH SARDINIA

The first Spanish building in Sardinia was the Gothic-Aragonese chapel in the cathedral in Cagliari *(see p55)*, followed by San Francesco in Iglesias, San Giorgio in Perfugas, and San Francesco and the cathedral in Alghero *(see p118)*. The cathedral in Sassari was built in the style known as "Colonial Baroque". Baroque influence is also evident in Àles cathedral. A notable school of *retablo* painting developed. There are 15th- and 16th-century paintings in the Art Gallery in Cagliari.

THE ST PETER *RETABLO*

The *retablo* is a religious panel painting that was quite often used as an altarpiece. It was one of the most important artistic genres in 16th-century Sardinia under Spanish rule. This work, *Madonna and Child with Saints Peter, Paul and George of Suelli*, is by Pietro and Michele Cavaro (1533–5). It is now in the church of San Giorgio at Suelli (Cagliari). The elaborate frame and wealth of decorative elements reveal its Flemish derivation.

This Aragonese house *at Fordongianus was built in the 15th–16th centuries.*

Retablos often combined painting, sculpture and carved decoration.

Philip V (1683–1746)
Forced to relinquish France and Sardinia, Philip tried to reconquer Sardinia in 1717 with the help of his chief minister Alberoni.

San Francesco *in Alghero (14th century) was rebuilt in the Gothic-Aragonese style.*

Charles V

1620 Under Philip III the University of Cagliari is founded

1688 Discontent and uprisings: the Spanish viceroy is assassinated

1600

1700

Cardinal Alberoni, Philip V's chief minister

1717 Philip V of Spain tries to reconquer Sardinia and Naples

1718 Treaty of London: Sardinia ceded to the House of Savoy

The Kingdom of Sardinia

One of the first acts of the Savoyard government was to reinstate the island's universities. However, a serious economic and social crisis led to unrest and the spread of banditry. After the Revolution of 1789, France made vain attempts to conquer Sardinia, but, by 1795, the island was overwhelmed by revolutionary fervour of its own and a "Sardinian revolution" broke out in Cagliari. In 1799 the Savoys took refuge on the island after losing their other territories to Napoleon. In 1847, in Cagliari and Sassari, huge crowds persuaded the Savoys to link the kingdom of Sardinia with Piedmont in "*fusione perfetta*". In 1861 both became part of the Kingdom of Italy.

The Harbour at Cagliari
The port was developed after the arrival of the Savoy rulers. Together with Porto Torres it became the island's principal harbour.

The University of Cagliari
The university was founded as part of a cultural reorganization and development policy adopted by Carlo Emanuele III (1730–73), who set up a committee for Sardinian affairs in Turin.

Carlo Emanuele IV
King of Sardinia from 1796 to 1802, Carlo Emanuele took refuge here after losing his mainland territories to Napoleon in 1798. His brother Vittorio Emanuele I became King of Savoy.

THE ABSOLUTIST VICEROY
Carlo Felice, seen here receiving the keys of Cagliari, was viceroy of Sardinia from 1799 to 1821, when he became king. Unchallenged, he nonetheless governed the island as an absolute monarch.

TIMELINE

1720 Filippo Pallavicino becomes the first Savoyard viceroy of Sardinia

Throne of the Kingdom of Sardinia in Turin

1793 Anti-Savoy rebellion

1720	1740	1760	1780

1764–5 Re-establishment of Cagliari and Sassari universities

1788 The court of the House of Savoy flees Turin and remains in Cagliari until 1815

Memorial Tablet
This tablet, embedded in Palazzo Viceregio in Cagliari, was dedicated to Carlo Felice by Vittorio Emanuele I, his brother, who abdicated in his favour in 1821.

Giuseppe Garibaldi
After years in exile because of his republican ideas, Garibaldi came to Caprera in 1857. He settled here permanently after conquering the Kingdom of Two Sicilies for the House of Savoy with his army of 1,000 volunteer soldiers, the Redshirts (see p148).

House of Savoy Coat of Arms
Dating back to the 11th century, the dynasty first ruled Savoy and Piedmont, then the Kingdom of Sardinia and finally the Kingdom of Italy.

WHERE TO SEE SAVOYARD SARDINIA

Important Savoy buildings are the theatres in Cagliari, Sassari and Alghero, the provincial administration buildings and Cagliari Town Hall *(see p58)*. Many of Sardinia's railway lines were laid down in this era. Statues of prominent Savoy figures, like the one of Garibaldi at Caprera, were put up everywhere. The Villa Aymerich at Làconi was one of many country houses to be rebuilt.

The Galleria Comunale d'Arte di Cagliari, *the capital's art gallery.*

Monument to Carlo Emanuele III *at Carloforte, the town he founded.*

Vittorio Amedeo III, king of Sardinia (1773–89)

1847 Sardinia and Piedmont join forces

1857 Garibaldi settles on Caprera and then buys part of the island

1820	1840	1860

Tomb of Carlo Emanuele IV of Savoy, Cagliari

1826 Alberto La Marmora's *Voyage to Sardinia* published

Alberto La Marmora

1861 Sardinia, together with Piedmont, becomes part of Kingdom of Italy

Sardinia and a United Italy

Ashes, by Grazia Deledda

Industrialization in Sardinia began to make progress after unification: in 1871 the first railway line was built and the mines in Sulcis and Iglesiente became fully operational. The first daily newspapers were founded and Nuoro became the centre of a cultural movement that included the Nobel Prize-winning novelist Grazia Deledda. In World War I the heroism of the Brigata Sassari emerged as a symbol of the island's new confidence, and led to the foundation of the Partito Sardo d'Azione political party in 1921. Between the wars the mining industry continued to develop, and the town of Carbonia was founded in 1938. A wide-ranging programme of land reclamation and artificial lakes – such as Lake Omodeo, created by a dam on the Tirso river – was carried out, significantly altering the health of previously malarial areas. On 31 January 1948 the island became an autonomous region of Italy.

The Monteponi mine
A 19th-century print shows the huge plant at this important Sardinian lead and zinc mine.

The crowd consisted of the social groups suffering most from the high cost of living.

Carbonia
In 1938 Mussolini himself inaugurated the newly-built town of Carbonia (see p71). The town was meant to become the leading mining centre in Sardinia.

Brigata Sassari
The brigade consisted entirely of Sardinians. They distinguished themselves in World War I by their heroism, winning two gold medals of honour.

Emilio Lussu (1890–1975) *This author recorded his World War I experiences in the Brigata Sassari in* Un anno sull'alto-piano *(One Year on the Plateau).*

TIMELINE

1871 Writer Grazia Deledda is born

1889–1899 Arrival of army task force to combat rampant banditry in Sardinia

1897 First ever special restrictive laws passed in Sardinia

1870	1880	1890	1900

Quintino Sella, Minister of Finance in 1862, 1865, 1869–73

1889 The first daily newspaper in Sardinia, *Unione Sarda*, is founded

1891 Political writer Antonio Gramsci born in Ales

Antonio Gramsci

The Cagliari-Arbatax Railway
As part of a unified Italy, Sardinia embarked on a programme of modernization. The first railway lines were laid in 1871; by 1881 Cagliari and Sassari were linked by rail. The line connecting Cagliari and Arbatax passes through lovely scenery and is now an attractive tourist route (see pp92–3).

The strikers attacking the customs and excise office to protest against the bread tax.

The Dam on the Tirso River
This dam, 70 m (230 ft) high, with a 40-m (130-ft) drop, was begun in 1918, creating Lake Omodeo. At 20 km (12 miles) long, it was the largest artificial lake in Europe of its time.

The Cabras Marsh
The marsh, extending over 20 hectares (49 acres), is one example of the wide-ranging land reclamation schemes carried out in Sardinia. These public works freed the island from malaria, paving the way for the development of a tourist industry.

THE STRIKE IN CAGLIARI
At the turn of the century, social conflict and tensions were so strong in Sardinia that the first special restrictive laws were enacted. The unrest of miners at the Buggerru mine on 3 September 1904 led to the first general strike in Italy. In 1906, distress at the high cost of living led to a wave of riots in Cagliari which were brutally repressed; ten people died and many others were injured.

Flag of the Region of Sardinia

1915–18 The Sardinians make a significant contribution to the war effort

1924 The "billion lira law" finances vast public works programme in Sardinia

1943 Allied bombings seriously damage Cagliari

10   1920   1930   1940

1921 Partito Sardo d'Azione founded

1926 The Sardinian writer Grazia Deledda wins Nobel Prize

1938 Mussolini founds mining town of Carbonia

1948 Sardinia declared an Autonomous Region

Modern Sardinia

**Burgee of the
Costa Smeralda
Yacht Club**

The reclamation of Sardinia's coastal marshes was crucial to the modern development of the island. Sardinia's lovely coastline, abandoned and shunned for millennia, could now be developed and seaside resorts built. New luxury villas and holiday villages sprang up, and the Costa Smeralda, or Emerald Coast, became world-famous as an exclusive holiday area. Reclaimed land could also be used for agriculture for the first time, and market gardens and orchards could be planted. The economy has started to shift as a result. Sheep-rearing is on the decline, while industry and services are developing, sometimes adversely affecting the environment. Sardinia today appears to be at a crossroads: modern life competing with the most precious resource: unspoilt nature and habitat diversity.

1972 The first mines are abandoned, signalling the decline of the Sardinian mining industry

1980 The Capre... National Park founde...

1971 The Cagliari football team of star striker Gigi Riva wins the Italian championship for the first time

1962 Antonio Segni, a Christian Democrat from Sassari, is elected President of the Italian Republic

1979 Revolt of terrorists in maximum security prison on island of Asinara

1950	1960	1970

1950	1960	1970

1956 Sardinia starts receiving television broadcasts from RAI, the Italian state TV

1970 Pope Paul VI visits Sardinia

1971 Industrial workers outnumber farmers for the first time

1974 The oil crisis in the Middle East damages the Sardinian petrochemical industry

1953 First island kidnapping at Orgósolo, marking the beginning of one of Sardinia's most serious postwar problems, one which has fortunately decreased in recent years. Vittorio de Seta's film on Sardinian banditry was awarded a prize at the 1961 Venice Film Festival

1962 Creation of the Costa Smeralda syndicate, promoted by Karim Aga Khan (above), which triggers development in the Costa Smeralda and a consequent tourist boom in north-eastern Sardinia. That same year a law is passed with the aim of stimulating all business sectors

1979 Cases of kidnapping increase: well-known Italian singer/ songwriter Fabrizio De André and his wife Dori Ghezzi kidnapped

1950 No Sardinian cases of malaria, for the first time. The American Rockefeller Foundation's public health programme eliminates the *Anopheles maculipennis* mosquito, which transmits the disease

1972 Enrico Berlinguer from Sassari (centre) elected secretary of the Italian Communist Party, a post he holds until his death (1983), promoting a "third way to socialism" and the "historic compromise" between Communists and Christian Democrats

2000 Together with tourism, the livestock industry (cattle breeding, dairies, tanning) is the leading force in the island's present-day economy

2004 Renato Soru, founder of successful ISP Tiscali SpA, is elected president of Sardinia

1989 Fires, mostly cases of arson, kill ten tourists on the northeastern coast

1990 Sardinia struck by a terrible drought

2006 Luxury tax on second homes, yachts and private aircraft introduced for non-residents

1990	2000	2010

1990	2000	2010

1995 The mining industry crisis worsens; the Sulcis coal mines are put up for sale

2002 The Euro replaces the Lira, becoming Italy's new currency

1985 Francesco Cossiga from Sassari, former Prime Minister and Home Secretary, is elected President of the Italian Republic

2001 Gold Mines of Sardinia and the Homestake Mining Company of California agree to open up Sardinia's gold deposits. The metal was first detected in the 1980s, when traces were discovered in streams

SFIDA
ITALIANA
AMERICA'S
CUP 1983

2000 The island's marinas, especially those at Porto Cervo, are rated among the best in the entire Mediterranean

1983 The first Italian participation in the America's Cup, with the yacht *Azzurra*, is promoted by the Costa Smeralda Yacht Club

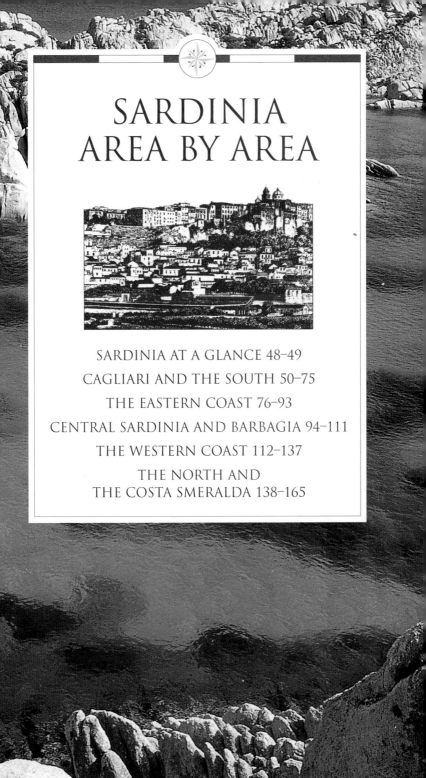

SARDINIA
AREA BY AREA

Sardinia at a Glance

Famous mostly for its sea and coastline, Sardinia also abounds in spectacular natural scenery and numerous archaeological ruins. Prehistoric nuraghi are scattered throughout the island, from Su Nuraxi to Orroli, Santu Antine and Silanus. Besides the Costa Smeralda, northern Sardinia is dotted with Romanesque churches in the Logudoro and Gallura countryside. In the Barbagia region and the eastern coast, which are dominated by the large Gennargentu National Park *(see pp82–3)*, the maquis vegetation reigns in the isolated valleys and on inaccessible hilltops. The south and west have interesting Punic ruins (Nora, Sant'Antioco, Tharros), as well as a relatively wild and undiscovered western coastline.

Ardara's Romanesque church, Santa Maria del Regno *(see p156)*

Flamingoes wintering in the marshes around Oristano *(see pp134–5)*

The impressive ruins of Tharros *(see pp132–3)*

THE WESTERN COAST

● Oristano

The rugged coast near Buggerru *(see p68)*

```
0 km          20
0 miles       20
```

CAGLIARI AND THE SOUTH

◁ **The clear emerald water and granite cliffs of the Costa Smeralda**

Capo Testa lighthouse near Santa Teresa di Gallura, on the north coast *(see pp144–5)*

Wild moufflon in the woods of central Sardinia *(see pp22–3)*

THE NORTH AND THE COSTA SMERELDA

• Olbia

• Nuoro

CENTRAL SARDINIA AND BARBAGIA

• Arbatax

THE EASTERN COAST

Part of the route followed by the narrow-gauge train, the Trenino Verde *(see pp92–3)*

Cagliari

View of Cagliari, the ancient Roman city of Kàralis, capital of the region of Sardinia *(see pp54–61)*

CAGLIARI AND THE SOUTH

*S*outhern Sardinia has a varied landscape with tall sand dunes along the coast, marshland where pink flamingoes build their nests and abundant maquis where the rare Sardinian deer still survive. It is also an area of interesting prehistoric sites, such as Nora and Su Nuraxi, and it was once the mining heartland of the island.

The mining history of the area dates back to 5000 BC, when the island's inhabitants discovered how to extract and smelt copper and silver. The Phoenicians used the area as a base for trade and shipped local ores across the Mediterranean. In the Middle Ages the Pisans brought new wealth to the region with expansion of the silver mines. During the Fascist era, Mussolini exploited the island's coal in an attempt to make Italy self-sufficient.

Today, after years of decline, the industrial buildings of the Sulcis and Iglesiente areas are being converted into tourist attractions with mines and museums to visit. The area's natural beauty merges with the 19th-century mining buildings, which look like Gothic castles among the maquis.

The island's capital, Cagliari, was founded by Phoenician sailors, but it was the Aragonese who left the most enduring mark. The Spanish fortification, or Castello district, still dominates today's city.

North of Cagliari lies the Campidano plain, bordered by prickly pears and eucalyptus. This has long been Sardinia's "bread-basket", but farm labour now combines with factory work, especially around Cagliari.

In the uplands to the east are the ruins of Sardinia's largest prehistoric site, Su Nuraxi, chosen for its vantage point over the surrounding plains.

The islands of San Pietro and Sant'Antioco are separate from the mainland culturally as well as geographically: the towns of Calasetta and Carloforte are inhabited by the descendants of Ligurian coral fishermen who were held hostage in North Africa by Muslim pirates and, once freed, were offered a home on the islands. Today, their dialect, cuisine and traditions remain little changed.

Volcanic rock framing Cala Fico (Fig Bay)

◁ The elegant boulevard Via Roma lined with arcaded 19th-century buildings

Exploring Cagliari and the South

The southwestern coast is one of the most
unspoiled on the island, with undisturbed
coves and beaches. Few roads run along the
coast, so the best way to explore is by sea or
on foot. Inland, the wild maquis of the rugged
Iglesiente and Sulcis terrain contrasts with the
derelict 19th-century industrial buildings of this
former mining area. In the north, excavations
at Su Nuraxi have revealed a complex nuraghic
settlement. Cagliari offers the city's sights and
a wildlife sanctuary in the salt flats, and is
also a good base for the ancient site of Nora.

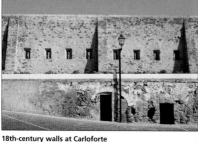

**18th-century walls at Carloforte
on the island of San Pietro**

SIGHTS AT A GLANCE

KEY

▭▭	Major road
──	Secondary road
═══	Minor road
──	Scenic route
─•─	Main railway
────	Minor railway
△	Summit

Map labels:

Capo della Frasca

Sant'Antonio di Santadi

Marina di Arbus

Monte Arcuentu 785m

Montevecchio

PISCINAS DUNES ❽

GÙSPINI ❾

ARBUS ⑩

Ingurtosu

Gonnosfanadiga

Capo Pecora

Monte Linas 1236m

Portixeddu

Fluminimaggiore

⑫ **BUGGERRU**

⑪ **TEMPLE OF ANTAS**

Masua

Domusnovas

COSTA DI MASUA ⑭

IGLESIAS ⑬

Fontanamare

Gonnesa

Villamassargia

Coróngiu

Terras

Portovesme

Fluert. . .

SAN PIETRO

Monte Sirai

⑯ **CARBONIA**

⑮ Carloforte

Perdàxius

La Caletta

San Giovanni Suergiu

Punta d. Colonne

⑰ **CALASETTA**

⑲ **TRATALÌAS**

SANT'ANTIOCO ⑱

Giba

Isola di Sant'Antioco

Porto Botte

Cannai

Golfo di Palmas

Is Pillónis

Capo Sperone

Stangno di Porto Botte

Punta di Cala Piombo

Capo Teulada

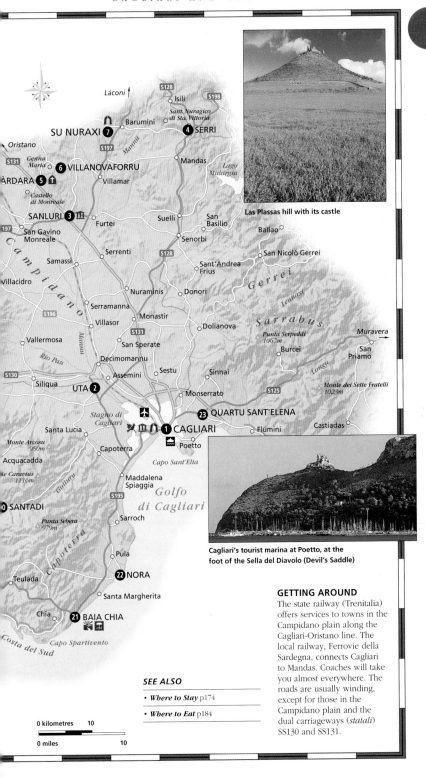

Láconi

S128
Isili
S198

Sant' Nuragico
di Sta. Vittoria

Barumini

SU NURAXI 7

4 SERRI

Oristano

Genna
Mariá

S131

6 VILLANOVAFORRU

Mandas

Lago
Mulargia

ÁRDARA 5

Villamar

Castello
di Monreale

SANLURI 3

Furtei

Suelli

San
Basilio

Ballao

197

San Gavino
Monreale

Senorbi

San Nicolò Gerrei

Serrenti

S128

Samassi

Sant'Andrea
Frius

Gerrei

Villacidro

Nuraminis

Donori

Serramanna

Sarrabus

Leunaxi

Villasor

Monastir

Dolianova

Punta Serpeddi
1067m

Muravera

S131

Burcei

San
Priamo

Vallermosa

San Sperate

Rio Pau

Decimomannu

Longu

S130

Assemini

Sestu

Sinnai

Monte dei Sette Fratelli
1023m

Siliqua

S125

UTA 2

Monserrato

Stagno di
Cagliari

23 QUARTU SANT'ELENA

Santa Lucia

1 CAGLIARI

Flúmini

Castiadas

Monte Arcosu
950m

Capoterra

Poetto

Capo Sant'Elia

Acquacadda

e Caravius
1116m

Maddalena
Spiaggia

Golfo
di Cagliari

S195

0 SANTADI

Punta Sebera
979m

Sarroch

Pula

Teulada

22 NORA

Santa Margherita

Chia

21 BAIA CHIA

Costa del Sud

Capo Spartivento

Las Plassas hill with its castle

Cagliari's tourist marina at Poetto, at the
foot of the Sella del Diavolo (Devil's Saddle)

GETTING AROUND

The state railway (Trenitalia)
offers services to towns in the
Campidano plain along the
Cagliari-Oristano line. The
local railway, Ferrovie della
Sardegna, connects Cagliari
to Mandas. Coaches will take
you almost everywhere. The
roads are usually winding,
except for those in the
Campidano plain and the
dual carriageways (*statali*)
SS130 and SS131.

SEE ALSO

• *Where to Stay* p174

• *Where to Eat* p184

0 kilometres   10

0 miles   10

Cagliari ❶

Lion on a pulpit in the Cathedral

The city's sheltered position, tucked into the Golfo di Cagliari, has long made Cagliari an important harbour. The Phoenicians chose the eastern shore of Santa Gilla lagoon in the 8th–6th centuries BC, as a stopover for trade ships en route between the Lebanon and the Iberian peninsula. Kàralis ("rocky city") soon became one of the leading Mediterranean centres of trade. The city's present appearance was the work of the Pisans, who developed the Aragonese Castello district. Local inhabitants, who could only enter the city during the day, lived in the walled villages of Stampace and Villanova. These fortifications were demolished in 1862 and the areas are now part of the city. Modern-day Cagliari, capital of the region, is flanked on three sides by sea and marshes and has only expanded northwards.

Sala del Consiglio Comunale, Palazzo Comunale

Arcaded 19th-century buildings on Via Roma

Exploring Cagliari

For those arriving by sea, the elegant boulevard of Via Roma, parallel to the quay and lined with 19th-century buildings and long arcades, is the first view of the city. During the day crowds throng along this busy shopping street, stopping at the cafés to relax and chat. Stretching out behind are the narrow streets and alleys of the old Marina district. Formerly inhabited by fishermen and merchants, this area is now filled with traditional trattorias and rustic taverns as well as shops selling antiques and local food and handicrafts. Heading northeast from Via Roma, Largo Carlo Felice is a wide, tree-lined avenue dating from the mid-1800s, with a statue of Carlo Felice, the viceroy of Sardinia (see pp40–41).

City's coat of arms

🏛 Palazzo Comunale
Via Roma. **Tel** 070 67 71.
📷 Call 070 677 72 35/6.
At the corner of Via Roma and Largo Carlo Felice is the Palazzo Comunale (town hall). Built in the early 20th century in Neo-Gothic style, the building was restored after World War II. Its façade is decorated with double lancet windows and turrets. Paintings by Filippo Figari and Giovanni Marghinotti hang in the Sala della Rappresentanza, and in the Sala del Consiglio Comunale depicting key moments in Sardinain history.

🏛 Bastione San Remy
Terrazza Umberto I.
Built in the late 19th century over the Spanish ramparts, the bastions can be reached from Piazza Costituzione up a stairway that leads to a wide terrace, Terrazza Umberto I (also accessible from Porta dei Leoni if the stairway is closed). From here, there is a magnificent view over the seafront to the surrounding marshes.

🏛 Roman Amphitheatre
Viale Fra Ignazio. **Tel** 070 65 29 56.
Apr–Oct: 9:30am–1:30pm, 3:30–5:30pm Tue–Sun; Nov–Mar: 9:30am–1:30pm Tue–Sat, 10am–1pm Sun.
www.anfiteatroromano.it
Northwest of the city centre is the most significant evidence of Roman Cagliari. The 2nd-century AD amphitheatre was hewn out of the rock, in the style of Greek theatres. Circus acts with wild beasts were performed here, as well as *naumachiae*, popular recreations of naval battles. A canal system made it possible to fill the arena with water. Much of the brick masonry collapsed during the Middle Ages and stone was taken from the tiers to build the Castello district. Still visible are the *cavea*, the pit that held the wild beasts, the corridors behind the tiers and underground passageways, as well as some of the tiers where the spectators sat.

The ruins of the 2nd-century AD Roman amphitheatre

⚘ Orto Botanico

Viale Fra Ignazio 13. **Tel** *070 675 35 12.* ◯ *Apr–Oct: 8:30am–1:30pm, 3–7pm daily; Nov–Mar: 8am–1:30pm.* 🎞 ✂ *(070 675 35 22).* ♿

South of the amphitheatre, the Botanic Gardens extend over an area of about 5 hectares (12 acres). Founded in 1865, the gardens contain over 500 species of tropical plants from America, Africa, Asia and the Pacific, as well as from the Mediterranean region.

The Orto Botanico is full of small caves such as the Grotta Gennari, used to cultivate ferns because of its ideal temperature and high levels of humidity. There are also remains of Roman tunnels, constructed to improve the water supply to the gardens, a Roman gallery and a well.

🔒 Cathedral

Piazza Palazzo. ◯ *8am– noon, 4–7pm daily.* **Museo Capitolare Tel** *070 66 38 37.* ◯ *by appt.*

The Baroque marble interior of the Cathedral of Santa Maria

Cagliari's Cathedral of Santa Maria was built by the Pisans in the 11th and 12th centuries. Gradually transformed over the centuries, particularly with 17th-century additions, today's façade is the result of

Holy water basin detail

radical restoration in the 1930s, which reinstated the original Romanesque style. Four lions guarding the entrance date from this period. Inside, Santa Maria retains much Baroque decoration, as well as some original detail. Close to the entrance are two pulpits by Mastro Guglielmo, sculpted in 1162 for the cathedral of Pisa and donated to Cagliari by the Tuscan city. A marble basin for holy water is decorated with the image of an angel. A crypt under the altar houses the tombs of the

princes of the House of Savoy. In the chapterhouse a collection of paintings includes a *Flagellation of Christ* attributed to Guido Reni. The **Museo Capitolare** (Treasury) displays precious church items such as chalices and amphoras, as well as a large gilded silver cross.

VISITORS' CHECKLIST

Road map C6. 🏛 *177,000.* ℹ *Piazza Matteotti 9 (070 66 92 55); Piazza Deffenu 9 (070 60 42 41).* 🚌 *(Sun, Sant'Elia district (general).* 🎉 *1 May: Sant'Efisio Feast Day.* **www**.comune.cagliari.it

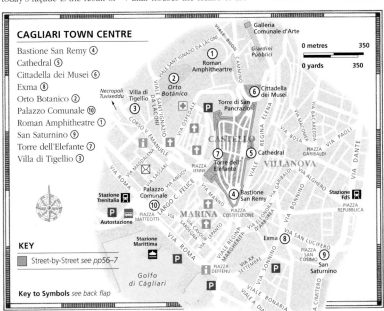

CAGLIARI TOWN CENTRE

Bastione San Remy ④
Cathedral ⑤
Cittadella dei Musei ⑥
Exma ⑧
Orto Botanico ②
Palazzo Comunale ⑩
Roman Amphitheatre ①
San Saturnino ⑨
Torre dell'Elefante ⑦
Villa di Tigellio ③

KEY

▮ Street-by-Street *see pp56–7*

Key to Symbols *see back flap*

Street-by-Street: Castello

Torre dell'Elefante detail

The Castello district, the oldest part of Cagliari, was built by the Pisans and Aragonese. Positioned at the top of a hill, and protected by ancient city walls, it consisted of aristocratic mansions and the city's Cathedral. With time its function as a centre of power waned, and the elegant buildings gradually deteriorated. At the centre of the district is Piazza Palazzo with the Palazzo Arcivescovile (Archbishop's Palace) and the Cathedral. Surrounding the ancient citadel, imposing watchtowers dominate the entrance gates, and parts of the fortifications have been transformed into a museum complex and an esplanade.

★ Cathedral
Santa Maria Cathedral, re-built several times, combines Pisan, Aragonese and Baroque features. The multi-coloured marble interior has fine sculptures (see p55).

★ Cittadella dei Musei
This modern complex, converted from the former Savoyard arsenal, houses the city's most important museums (see p58).

Palazzo Arcivescovile

PIAZZA
PAL

VIA MARTINI

PIAZZA
ARSENALE

VIA DEI G

Torre di San Pancrazio
The northern gate of the Castello district was built in 1305 by Giovanni Capula. It is dressed on three sides with limestone ashlar, while the inner face is open, exposing the stairs and wooden balconies of the interior.

Via La Marmora
A number of craft workshops and antique shops line the characteristic Via La Marmora.

★ **Bastione San Remy**
In the early 1900s the Spanish defensive walls were transformed into the bastions of San Remy, opening out onto a wide esplanade with spectacular views.

Porta dei Leoni
The gate that leads into the lower Marina district owes its name to the two Romanesque lions' heads (leoni) *above the arch.*

BASTIONE SAN REMY

VIA CANNELLES

VIA LA MARMORA

PIAZZA CARLO ALBERTO

VIA VIVALDI

VIA UNIVERSITA

Palazzo Boyl
Overlooking the bastions of San Remy, this palazzo was built in 1840. It incorporates the remains of the Torre dell'Aquila (Eagle's Tower), one of the large Pisan towers that stood over the entrance gates of the ancient city.

Torre dell'Elefante
The "Elephant's Tower" was built by local architect Giovanni Capula in 1307. The mechanism for opening the gates is still visible and an elephant statue, after which the tower was named, can be seen on the façade.

STAR SIGHTS

★ Cittadella dei Musei

★ Cathedral

★ Bastione San Remy

KEY

– – Suggested route

0 metres	50
0 yards	50

Cittadella dei Musei, the modern complex in the Castello district

Cittadella dei Musei
Piazza Arsenale.

At the northern end of the Castello district is this modern museum complex. Fashioned from the former royal arsenal which had been built on the site of the Spanish citadel, the complex houses the Museo Archeologico Nazionale, the Museo Civico d'Arte Orientale Stefano Cardu and the Pinacoteca Nazionale.

🏛 Museo Archeologico Nazionale
Cittadella dei Musei, Piazza Arsenale. **Tel** 070 65 59 11. 🕐 9am–7pm Tue–Sun.

The National Archaeological Museum is devoted to the history of Sardinia. The ground-floor exhibits are arranged in chronological order, from the Neolithic era to the Middle Ages; the other floors are organized by archaeological site. In the Neolithic hall are fine alabaster statues of female divinities, including one in the shape of a cross from Senorbì. Objects from the late Bronze Age include axes with raised edges. There is an exceptional collection of nuraghic bronze figurines *(see pp32–3)*, found in the Tempio di Teti at Abini. The collection includes votive swords decorated with the head of a deer, a tribal chief or a warrior. In the third hall is a statuette of a musician playing the Sardinian flute, the *launeddas (see p90)*.

The Phoenician and Roman periods are represented by objects found mostly at sites around Cagliari, Tharros and Nora. These include jewellery and amulets, small coloured glass heads and terracotta votive statuettes. Among the loveliest pieces of jewellery are an embossed golden bracelet and gold earrings from Tharros.

The Early Christian pieces, such as jugs, lamps and gold jewellery, give an insight into the island's medieval culture, and influences from Byzantine, Vandal and Moorish invaders.

🏛 Museo Civico d'Arte Orientale Stefano Cardu
Cittadella dei Musei. **Tel** 070 65 18 88. 🕐 9am–7:30pm Tue–Sun. 🎫

The Museum of Oriental Art has on exhibition most of the 1,300 objects donated to the city in 1917 by Stefano Cardu, a Sardinian who served at the court of the King of Siam. The collection includes imperial gold and silver objects, ivory statues and vases, mostly dating from the 11th century.

🏛 Pinacoteca Nazionale
Cittadella dei Musei. **Tel** 070 67 40 54. 🕐 9am–8pm Tue–Sun. 📷 🎫 *(buy ticket at the Museo Archeologico).*

The entrance to this three-storey gallery is on the upper floor. Here, 15th- and 16th-century paintings include Catalan and Sardinian altar-pieces, like the *Annunciation* by Juan Mates (1391–1431), *Sant'Eligio* by the Master of Sanluri (early 16th century), and *Nostra Signora della Neve* (1568) by Michele Cavaro.

The middle floor houses a collection of 17th- and 18th-century paintings and reveals the original Spanish fortification wall (1552–63). The lower floor features the restored *Retablo di San Cristoforo*, rescued from the Chiesa di San Francesco di Stampace, which was damaged by lightning in 1871.

🏛 Galleria Comunale d'Arte
Giardini Pubblici, Viale Regina Elena. **Tel** 070 49 07 27. 🕐 9am–1pm, 5–9pm (Oct–Apr: 3:30–7:30pm) Mon, Wed–Sun. 🎫

The Municipal Art Gallery has a collection of significant works by Sardinian artists from the late 19th century to the 1970s. On the ground floor are works by Francesco Ciusa. The first floor features contemporary art.

🏛 Necropoli Tuvixeddu
Via Falzarego. 🕐 Mar–Sep: 8am–sunset.

The hundreds of underground burial chambers of the Punic necropolis, west of the Botanical Gardens, are overgrown with brambles. The funerary paintings on the tombs, however, are worth a visit, especially the *Tomba del Guerriero* (Warrior's Tomb) and the *Tomba dell'Ureo*.

🏛 Grotta della Vipera
Viale Sant'Avendrace. **Tel** 070 41 108 or 070 6771. 🕐 9am–5pm Tue–Sun.

One of the tombs in the necropolis is that of Atilia Pomptilla, wife of Cassius Philippus, exiled here in the 1st century AD. Two snakes adorn the façade of the "viper's cave" and on the walls are inscriptions in Greek and Latin.

Marble sarcophagus (4th century AD) from the Archaeological Museum

For hotels and restaurants in this region see p174 and p184

The early Christian church dedicated to San Saturnino, patron saint of Cagliari

🏛 Subterranean Cagliari

Viale Fra Ignazio. *Tel 070 66 30 52.*
🚫 *to the public.*

Northeast of the city centre, in the area below the Roman amphitheatre, the hospital and the Orto Botanico, there are underground chambers and passageways cut out of the rock by the Phoenicians. The most spectacular of these is the vast chamber named after King Vittorio Emanuele II. From the Casa di Riposo in Viale Fra Ignazio, it is accessed via a dingy stairway which leads into the eerie chamber. The walls, around 2,500 sq m (26,900 sq ft), are covered with thick facing to protect them from the humidity.

The Phoenician underground chamber, "Vittorio Emanuele II"

🏛 Villa di Tigellio

Via Tigellio. 🚫 *to the public.*

Situated southeast of the Botanical Gardens, Villa di Tigellio is a group of three aristocratic Roman villas and baths dating from the Imperial era. The first house has a *tablinum*, the room used to receive guests, which opens onto the central atrium.

🏛 Exma

Via San Lucifero 71. *Tel 070 66 63 99.* ⬜ *10am–1pm, 5–10pm Tue–Sun (Oct–Apr: 9am–1pm, 4–8pm).*
📷♿🖥

On the eastern side of the Castello district stands the former municipal slaughterhouse, built in the mid-19th century and closed in 1964. The dark red building, decorated with sculpted heads of cows, has been restructured to house the city's arts centre.

The centre's cultural calendar offers temporary exhibitions of photography, painting and sculpture, as well as courses for children and adults. Classical music concerts are held in the courtyard in the summer and in the auditorium in the winter.

A cow's head on the Exma building

🔒 San Saturnino

Piazza San Cosimo. *Tel 070 201 01.*
⬜ *9am–1pm Tue–Sat.*
🚫 *public hols.* ♿

East of the Exma building is the church of San Saturnino, also known as Santi Cosma e Damiano. Reopened after 18 years of restoration, and still not completely refurbished, this simple church is one of the oldest Christian buildings on the island. It was begun in the 5th century to commemorate the martyrdom of Saturno, the city's patron saint.

In the Middle Ages, San Saturnino, together with its adjacent monastery, became an important religious and cultural centre. The Greek cross plan of the church was enlarged in the 11th century by French Victorine friars from Marseille, who built three aisles with barrel vaults. Inside, a marble ex voto holds the oldest representation of San Saturno.

Glass windows have been placed in the sturdy tufa construction to prevent further damage and decay from humidity and air, and this has given the church a rather modern appearance. Nonetheless, it is still a fascinating place to visit.

The Marshes and Salt Flats

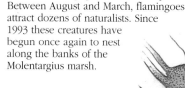

A yellow-bellied toad from the marshes

A network of marshes and lakes extends around the outskirts of Cagliari, particularly along the western shore of the bay. The vast lagoon of the Santa Gilla marsh stretches over 4,000 hectares (9,800 acres), including the ancient Macchiareddu salt flats. These saltworks are now the only ones in operation in the area. After years of neglect and environmental deterioration, the marshy areas around Cagliari have finally become reserves, and the area once again has a rich and varied fauna. To the east of the city, the Molentargius marsh is a favourite refuge for migratory birds. At least 170 species have been identified here, which is one-third of the entire bird population of Europe. Between August and March, flamingoes attract dozens of naturalists. Since 1993 these creatures have begun once again to nest along the banks of the Molentargius marsh.

A Naturalist's Paradise
In autumn the marshes are filled with migratory birds and are a favourite with bird-watchers.

The Saltworks
Of the numerous saltworks that once operated around Cagliari, only those in the Macchiareddu industrial area are still active.

Macchiareddu Salt Flat

Fishing port of Giorgino

GOLFO
CAGLIA

Stagno di Santa Gilla

Nesting Grounds
In recent years, flamingoes have begun to use the marshes as a nesting ground again.

VISITORS' CHECKLIST

Road map C6. P from Via Roma for Poetto; 8 for Santa Gilla. Piazza Matteotti (070 66 92 55). The best period for bird-watching is August–March.

WILDLIFE OF THE MARSHLANDS

Many migratory and endemic bird species populate the marshes around Cagliari. These feed upon the small creatures, such as the brine shrimp *Artemia salina*, which thrive in the salt-rich water. As well as the colony of flamingoes, which sometimes exceeds 10,000, you will also see many other species of water birds such as blackwinged stilts, avocets, cormorants and teals. The waters of Macchiareddu salt flats, on the other hand, are populated by mallards, coots and pintail ducks, which hunt peacefully among the islets and inlets.

Flamingo

Blackwinged Stilt

Avocet

Cormorant

Teal

Cat's-tail flowers

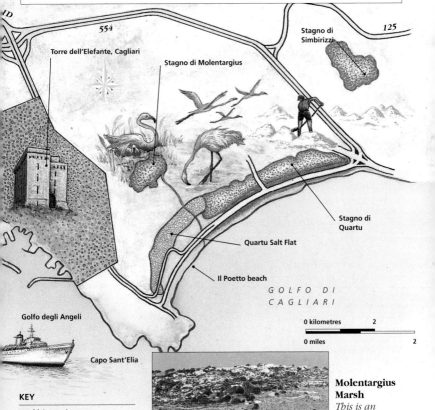

Stagno di Simbirizzi

554

125

Torre dell'Elefante, Cagliari

Stagno di Molentargius

Stagno di Quartu

Quartu Salt Flat

Il Poetto beach

GOLFO DI CAGLIARI

Golfo degli Angeli

Capo Sant'Elia

0 kilometres 2

0 miles 2

KEY

Major road

Minor road

Salt flat

Marsh

Molentargius Marsh
This is an ideal stopping place for migratory birds from Africa.

The Romanesque church of Santa Maria at Uta

Uta ❷

Road map C6. 🚶 *7,000.* 🚌 🚉
ℹ️ *Via Umberto I (070 96 66 02 01).*
📅 *26–31 Aug: Santa Lucia.*

The flourishing agricultural town of Uta is situated at the edge of the Campidano plain, a vast fertile corridor that stretches northwards from Cagliari to Oristano. On the outskirts of town is the church of **Santa Maria**, built in 1140 by French Victorine friars from Marseille. The façade is made of light-coloured stone, with blocks of a darker hue, and is decorated with blind arches and a small bell gable. Sculptures of human heads, deer, calves and geometric patterns adorn the arches.

Environs: The village of **San Sperate**, 8 km (5 miles) north-east of Uta, is a living museum with murals, and sculptures by local artist Pinuccio Sciola.

🛕 **Santa Maria**
Via Santa Maria. **Tel** *070 96 81 57.*
⭕ *by appt only.*

Sanluri ❸

Road map C5. 🚶 *9,000.* 🚌 🚉
ℹ️ *Piazza Mazzini 74 (070 937 05 05).* 📅 *10 Aug: San Lorenzo*
www.*prolocosanluri.it.*

An important town in the Campidano plain, Sanluri developed around the 14th-century castle of Eleonora d'Arborea *(see p36)*. This stronghold changed hands several times before it was taken by the Aragonese in 1709. The massive square

structure has towers on its four corners and an ornate wrought-iron gate.

Today the castle is owned by the Villasanta family and houses the **Museo Risorgimentale Duca d'Aosta**. The historical exhibits include fine furniture such as a 16th-century bed. A sculpture of San Michele (St Michael) stands in the entrance hall. On the upper floor is the **Museo della Ceroplastiche** in which there are 343 pieces of wax from 1500 to 1800.

In the restored 16th-century Convento dei Cappuccini (still a working monastery), on a hill overlooking the town, the **Museo Storico Etnografico** displays a collection of tools and archaeological finds.

🏛 **Museo Risorgimentale Duca d'Aosta**
Castello di Eleonora d'Arborea. **Tel** *070 930 71 05.* ⭕ *9:45am–1pm, 3–7pm Sun, Easter Mon, 25 Apr & 1 May (1 Jul–20 Sep: 4:30–9pm Tue, Wed & Fri; 9:45am–1pm Sun).* 📷 🎫

🏛 **Museo Storico Etnografico**
Via San Rocco 6. **Tel** *070 930 71 07.* ⭕ *8am–noon, 3pm–7pm daily.*
📷 🎥 🎫 ♿

Serri ❹

Road map C4. 🚶 *810.* 🚌 🚉 ℹ️
Via Municipio 1 (0782 80 50 09); Pro Loco, Via Roma 36 (0782 80 61 93).
📅 *Third Sun of Sep: Santa Lucia.*

This sheep-farming centre lies on the edge of a rocky plateau dominating the Trexenta hills. Right on the spur of the promontory is the **Santuario Nuragico di Santa Vittoria**, one of Sardinia's most fascinating nuraghic sites. The archaeological ruins here have yielded some important bronze votive statuettes, now housed in the Museo Archeologico Nazionale in Cagliari *(see p58)*.

Pilgrims came here to worship the God of Water at the sacred well. The temple well, which is in an excellent state of preservation, is reached via 13 amazingly precise basalt steps. A short walk from the entrance leads to the *Recinto delle Feste* (festivities area). This elliptical building has a porticoed court-yard surrounded by rooms for the pilgrims. This is possibly a predecessor of the many rural sanctuaries *(cumbessias* or *muristeni)* found today in Sardinia's country churches.

Wax statue in Sanluri's Museo della Ceroplastica

🛕 **Santuario Nuragico di Santa Vittoria**
7 km (4 miles) NW. **Tel** *0782 80 51 42/43.* ⭕ *by appt only.*

A modern mural in the village of San Sperate

The 16th-century parish church of the Beata Vergine Assunta at Sàrdara

Sàrdara **❺**

Road map C5. 👥 5,000. 🚗
ℹ️ Town Hall (070 93 45 02).
📅 22 Sep: Santa Maria is Acquas.

Situated at the northern edge of the Campidano plain, the town of Sàrdara lay on the border between the medieval principalities of Arborea and Cagliari (see pp36 – 7). Stone houses from this period, with large arched doorways, have been preserved in the district around **San Gregorio**. This Romanesque church was built in the 6th century. Its tall, narrow façade, however, shows the initial influence of Gothic architecture. On the western outskirts of town is the 16th-century parish church of **Beata Vergine Assunta**, interesting for its sculpted columns and arches, and vault patterned with stars.

Near the Assunta church are the remains of a nuraghic well-temple. This underground chamber, from the 9th–10th centuries BC, has walls of basalt and limestone and a domed ceiling. Also known as the *Funtana de is Dolus* (fountain of pain), it is where worshippers came to take the curative spring waters. The source of the temple water was an ancient underground well, and a canal carried the mineral water from the spring to the temple. Decorated earthenware votive objects found in the temple are now in the Museo Archeologico Nazionale in Cagliari (see p58).

Sàrdara is also famous for its carpet-weaving and woollen and cotton tapestries. These are colourfully embroidered with traditional animal and floral decorative motifs.

Environs: Ruins of the medieval **Castello di Monreale**, a fortification of the principality of Arborea, stand on a hill 1 km (half a mile) southwest of town. A little further west are the remains of the **Aquae Neapolitanae**, Roman baths, and nearby is the Gothic church of **Santa Maria is Acquas**, where a festival takes place in September.

Villanovaforru **❻**

Road map C5. 👥 730. 🚗 ℹ️
Piazza Costituzione (070 93 45 11).
📅 15 Jul: Santa Marina
www. comunevillanovaforru.ca.it

This agricultural centre was founded in the 1600s by the Spanish and has retained much of its original layout. Many houses have kept their decorative features. Today, the Monte Granatico building (formerly a grain store), in the town's central square, houses a small but well-run **Museo Archeologico**. Finds from the nearby nuraghic site of Genna Maria are on display here, including bronze, iron and ceramic objects from the 9th century BC on the ground floor. On the first floor are votive objects dedicated to Demeter and Persephone from the Roman era.

Environs: On the road to Collinas, 1 km (half a mile) west of the town, is the nuraghic village of **Genna Maria**. Discovered in 1977, the site, which is still being excavated, is on a prominent hilltop. This nuraghe has a typical design (see pp36 – 7). Thick walls with three towers form a triangle which encloses a central tower and courtyard with a well. Another wall with six corner towers surrounds the entire village area.

🏛 **Museo Archeologico**
Piazza Costituzione. **Tel** 070 930 00 50. ⏰ 9:30am–1pm, 3:30–6pm (Apr–Sep: to 7pm) Tue–Sun. 📷 ♿ &

🏛 **Genna Maria**
1 km (half a mile) W. **Tel** 070 930 00 48/50. ⏰ 9:30am–1pm, 3:30–7pm (Oct–Mar: 6pm) Tue–Sun. 📷 📷 call in advance. 📷

THE SAFFRON OF SARDINIA

Stigma

The production of Sardinian saffron, prized through-out Europe, is based around San Gavino in the Campi-dano plain. Saffron is obtained by drying the dark red stigma of *Crocus sativus,* a purple flower that carpets the barren fields in autumn. The harvest, however, is very brief as the stigmas must be collected the day the flower comes into bloom. Saffron, once considered as precious as gold, was used to make dyestuff for fabrics and rugs, as a colouring agent for sweets and as a spice for savoury dishes. It is still used in today's cooking (see p180).

Crocus flowers

Su Nuraxi ❼

Excavations east of Barùmini have brought to light the largest nuraghic fortress in Sardinia, Su Nuraxi. The original settlement dates from 1500 BC, during the Middle Bronze Age. Built on a hill, the 19 m (62 ft) high fortress occupied an excellent vantage point, with clear views over the surrounding plains. In the 7th century BC, with the threat of Phoenician invasion, the central section of the fortress, consisting of a tower connected to four external nuraghi, was further protected by a thick outer wall with turrets and a sentinel's walkway. The village gradually developed outside the main fortifications with single- and multi-room dwellings, including a flour mill and bakery. The area was inhabited for almost 2,000 years although, after the Carthaginian conquest, the upper parts of the fort were demolished and the site lost its strategic importance.

Single dwellings
The oldest living quarters were circular with a single room.

Defences
In order to defend themselves from Carthaginian invasions, the Nuraghic inhabitants built an outer bulwark. This consisted of seven towers connected by a wall with a walkway for sentinel patrols.

The circular assembly hall was built against the outer wall. During meetings the elders sat on a long stone bench that ran along the inside of the wall. Objects found here are held in Cagliari's archeological museum *(see p58).*

Multi-room Dwellings
These living areas were made up of seven or eight square or trapezoidal rooms which opened onto a courtyard or vestibule, often with a well.

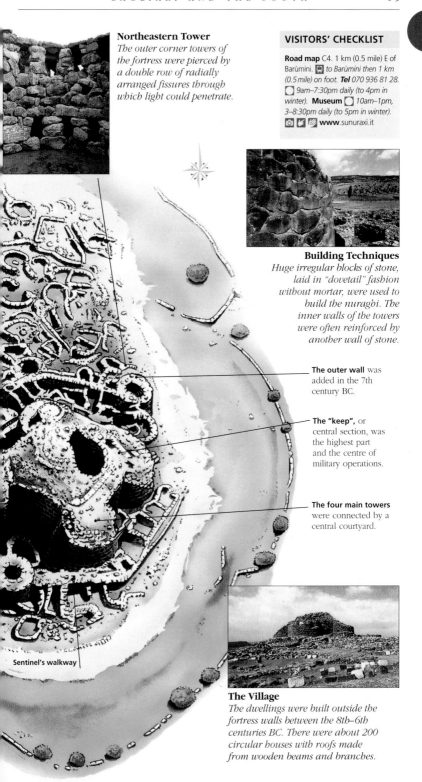

Northeastern Tower
The outer corner towers of the fortress were pierced by a double row of radially arranged fissures through which light could penetrate.

Building Techniques
Huge irregular blocks of stone, laid in "dovetail" fashion without mortar, were used to build the nuraghi. The inner walls of the towers were often reinforced by another wall of stone.

The outer wall was added in the 7th century BC.

The "keep", or central section, was the highest part and the centre of military operations.

The four main towers were connected by a central courtyard.

Sentinel's walkway

The Village
The dwellings were built outside the fortress walls between the 8th–6th centuries BC. There were about 200 circular houses with roofs made from wooden beams and branches.

The Piscinas Dunes ❽

The hills of sand at Piscinas and Is Arenas ("the sands" in Sardinian) are "moving" dunes, sometimes as much as 50 m (164 ft) high, that rise up around the estuary of the River Piscinas. Wind erosion by the mistral, the cold north wind that blows in from France, continually changes the landscape, while strongly rooted pioneer plants work their way across the sand. The robust roots of marram grass (*Ammophila arenaria*) gradually stabilize the dune slopes, which are then covered by other salt-resistant plants such as juniper and lentiscus. This unique ecological niche is also the habitat for many animals, and footprints of foxes, wild cats, partridges and rabbits are a common sight on the sand. Remains of the 19th-century mines that were once the mainstay of the Sulcis regional economy are also still visible.

Piscinas beach
The sandy beach at Piscinas is 9 km (5 miles) long. Exposed tNhe strong mistral wind in winter, the shape of the beach is continually changing.

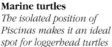

Marine turtles
The isolated position of Piscinas makes it an ideal spot for loggerhead turtles to lay their eggs.

The Sardinian partridge favours sunny habitats. It was introduced from North Africa by the Romans.

The sand, shaped by the wind, is an ever-changing landscape.

Tracks of wild animals can often be seen in the sand, particularly in the morning.

Le Dune Hotel
This hotel overlooking the sea shore occupies an old restructured mine building (see p174).

The wild lily, though slim and delicate, manages to bloom and survive even in arid environments.

VISITORS' CHECKLIST

Road map B6.
🚌 to Arbus then private car along rough road via Ingurtosu. Spring and autumn are the best seasons to visit.

Mine railway
A section of the 19th-century narrow-gauge railway, once used to transport material from the mines to the sea, has been reopened near the beach.

Marram grass
This strongly rooted, perennial plant, Ammophila arenaria, *is typical of sandy environments.*

Wild rabbits are a common sight on the dunes. You may also come across other small animals such as foxes and lizards.

The sand dunes
Areas of the dunes are covered in thick maquis vegetation.

San Nicola di Mira, at Gùspini

Gùspini ⑨

Road map B5. 🏠 14,000. 🚌
ℹ Town Hall, Via Don Minzoni 10 (070 97 601). 🎪 15–31 Aug: Santa Maria. **www**.comune.guspini.ca.it

Overlooking the flat and fertile Campidano plain, Gùspini is surrounded by olive groves and backed by the gradually rising foothills of Monte Arcuentu. The 16th-century church of **San Nicola di Mira**, in the main square, boasts a large rose window and is the hub of local life. The feast day of Santa Maria is celebrated with a procession and a horse race.

The rose window of San Nicola di Mira

The **Montevecchio mine**, 8 km (5 miles) west, was one of the largest in Europe until the 1950s. Despite the state of abandon, the miners' houses, headquarters, church, school and hospital are worth a visit. There are guided tours of the mine and the office building as well as an exhibition on the life of the miners in the past.

🏭 Montevecchio mine
8 km (5 miles) W of Gùspini.
Tel 335 531 41 98. ⭕ Easter–Oct.
🎟 tours leave every 30 minutes from the Piazzetta di Montevecchio.

Arbus ⑩

Road map B5. 🏠 8,000. 🚌
ℹ Town Hall, Via XX Settembre (070 975 94 44). 🎪 13 Jun: Sant'Antonio; 21 Aug: Santo Lussorio Palio (horse race) **www**.arbus.it

Granite houses characterize the village of Arbus, set on the slopes of Monte Linas. Arbus is known for the production of traditional knives with curved blades, *arrasoias*.

Southwest down the N126 for 7 km (4 miles), then due west across a winding mountain road, is the mining village of **Ingurtosu**, built by the French firm Pertusola. Once home to over 1,000 mine workers, the houses, office building and church are now abandoned. The pine forest surrounding the dilapidated buildings was planted by the mine workers.

A dirt road runs among the old mines, abandoned buildings and former dumping area as far as Naracauli, where there are ruins of a more modern mine complex built shortly after World War I. A train once transported the extracted lead and zinc to the sea, where it was loaded onto ships. Certain sections of the narrow-gauge track and some carriages can be seen on the Piscinas beach.

Stretching northwards from the dune beach of Piscinas is a maquis-covered coast aptly called the Costa Verde. A quiet, scenic road follows the coastline, offering spectacular views of the sea. The road goes as far as the resort of Marina di Arbus, with easy access to sandy beaches.

The large tanks at the Montevecchio mine

Temple of Antas ⓫

Road map B5. 🚃 *to Fluminimaggiore (0781 58 09 90).*

First discovered in 1966, the ancient Temple of Antas is believed to have been a sacred nuraghic site. It was adopted by the Carthaginians in the 4th century BC and dedicated to the deity Sid Addir Babài. A century later the Carthaginians restructured the building with an atrium and a central chamber. The temple was decorated with Egyptian and Ionic symbols.

In the 3rd century AD, the Romans rebuilt the temple using some of the existing material, such as the Ionic capitals of the columns. This temple was dedicated to the god and "creator of Sardinians", Sardus Pater. Although only six of the columns remain standing today, the temple's isolated position amid the wild maquis makes it an enchanting place to visit.

Environs: Set in the fertile valley of the River Mannu, 9 km (5 miles) north, is the small agricultural village of **Fluminimaggiore**, founded in the 18th century. Turning west towards the sea for 9 km (5 miles), the road proceeds to **Portixeddu beach**, protected by extensive sand dunes. The headland of Capo Pecora offers stunning views of the sea and coast.

The old mining community of Buggerru, now a tourist resort

Buggerru ⓬

Road map B5. 🏘 *1,500.* 🚃 *(0781 540 23/93).*

Situated in a valley opening out onto the sea, Buggerru was founded in the mid-18th century in an area rich in mineral deposits. It soon became a flourishing mining town with a small theatre where opera singers used to perform, and the headquarters of the French *Société Anonyme des Mines de Malfidano*. The mines have now closed and the town is surrounded by slag heaps. In the lower part of the town, sculpture by Pinuccio Sciola *(see p62)* is dedicated to the miners who died in the strikes of 1904.

Today, the town has been reclaimed as a harbour for pleasure boats, the only one between Carloforte and Oristano. The docks, where boats were once loaded with local minerals for export, now serve as a port for visitors to the wild western coast of the island and its long stretches of sandy, sheltered beaches. To the south is the long and secluded **Cala Domestica**, a rocky bay overlooked by a Spanish watchtower.

Iglesias ⓭

Road map B5. 🏘 *30,000.* 🚃 🚉 *(0781 417 95).* 🎭 *Easter Week* **www**.comune.iglesias.ca.it

Iglesias, or Villa Ecclesiae, was founded in the 13th century by Count Ugolino della Gherardesca (mentioned in Dante's *Inferno* XXXIII). The Pisans had conquered the area in 1257 and reopened mines abandoned in Roman times. Silver was extracted, and the city had the right to mint its

---

TEMPLE OF ANTAS

This plan shows how the later Roman temple incorporated the 3rd-century BC Carthaginian temple. The rectangular plan and six columns of the pronaos, the enclosed portico leading to the temple chamber, are still visible. An architrave above the entrance supported a triangular pediment and steps led up to the temple.

The columns, 8 m (26 ft) high, were made of smooth limestone blocks placed on bases about 1 m (3 ft) wide.

The capitals were in the Ionic style but are atypical, lacking the abacus and volutes.

Pronaos

Columns

Steps

The Roman temple was built over the Carthaginian temple.

The Easter procession during Holy Week at Iglesias

own coins. In the mid-19th century Iglesias grew into an important mining centre.

Today, the ruins of the mine buildings, most of which have been abandoned, create a striking contrast with the well-preserved historic centre. The elegant pedestrian shopping street, Corso Matteotti, leads to Piazza del Municipio and the Palazzo Vescovile (Bishop's Palace), built in 1785. On the west side is the 19th-century Palazzo del Comune (Town Hall) and opposite is the cathedral of **Santa Chiara**. Completed in the late 17th century, the cathedral has a Romanesque façade dating from 1288.

Romanesque portal of Santa Chiara, Iglesias

The narrow, winding streets around the cathedral are lined with two-storey buildings adorned with wrought-iron balconies. **San Francesco** on Via Don Minzoni was built between the 14th and 16th centuries and has side chapels dedicated to noble families. Half an hour's walk from Piazza Sella is the **Castello di Salvaterra**, built in 1284 as part of the city's medieval defensive walls. A part of these walls is also visible in Via Eleonora d'Arborea.

During Easter week, holy processions and performances of mystery plays take place in the town (see p26).

THE SULCIS MINES

The history of Sardinia's mines is inextricably linked with the island's economic development. Ancient rock formations, particularly in the southwestern region of the island known as Sulcis, have left rich mineral deposits of silver, copper, lead, iron and zinc. Nuraghic people are known to have had metalworking skills and there is evidence of Phoenician and Roman

Entrance to an abandoned mine

mines. In the short-lived boom of 19th-century industrial-ization, the mines stood like citadels in a predominantly agricultural country. Today, the dream of prosperity through mining is vanishing, and all that remains is a rich heritage of mining architecture and culture.

The area around Iglesias is the mining heart of Sardinia, and the landscape descending to the sea has been deeply scarred by mine working. At Monteponi the industrial plants, mine shafts and miners' houses look as though they were only recently abandoned, while at Masua, tunnels and railways are still visible. At Buggerru, the Malfidano mine, exploited for eight centuries, opens onto the sea front.

Environs: At Case Marganai, 10 km (6 miles) northeast of Iglesias, the **Linasia Botanical Gardens** extend over an area of 9 sq km (3 sq miles) with several examples of plants from the maquis. The **Museo Casa Natura** here also has a collection of local plants and an exhibit of pieces from the local mine shafts.

Guided tours of local mines are organized by the **Società Igea**. One tour takes in the lead and zinc Monteponi mine, with the elegant Bellavista building and Sella shaft. The Santa Barbara mine is also worth visiting; the shaft has unusual crenellated walls, which make it look like a medieval castle.

🌼 **Linasia Botanical Gardens**
Località Marganai. **Tel** 0781 200
61. ☐ Oct–Apr: 9:30am–1pm
Sat & Sun; May–Sep: 9am–noon,
4:30–7:30pm Tue, Thu, Sat & Sun.
🔲 🔲 **Museo Casa Natura** phone
in advance.

📮 **Società Igea**
Località Campo Pisano.
Tel 0781 49 13 00 or 348 154 95
56. 🔲 🔲 phone in advance.
www.igeaminiere.it

Costa di Masua ⓮

Road map B5. 🛈 (0781 46 801).

The corniche road between Fontanamare and Masua, 12 km (7 miles) north, follows a wild and splendid coastline. At Masua, the little beach of Porto Flavia is over-looked by pillars of eroded limestone and, offshore, the unmistakable profile of Pan di Zucchero ("sugarloaf") island. This sheer rock rises 132 m (433 ft) from the sea. At Nebida you can see the abandoned mines of the industrial archaeological area.

A panoramic path along the coast leads to the abandoned remains of La Marmora mine buildings and shafts.

The island of Pan di Zucchero jutting out from the sea

Island of San Pietro ⑮

Named after the apostle Peter, who is said to have taken refuge here during a storm, the island of San Pietro was virtually uninhabited until 1736, when Carlo Emanuele III offered it to a community of Ligurian coral fishermen whose ancestors had been exiled to the island of Tabarca, off the Tunisian coast. San Pietro's Ligurian origins can be seen in the architecture, dialect and cuisine, which also bears traces of North African influences. The rugged coast, inhabited by the rare Eleonora's falcon, has spectacular coves that can be reached only by sea. The island is covered in thick maquis vegetation.

La Punta
In September, for a couple of days only, local fishermen open their homes and feed visitors.

Cala Fico
Walls of silver rock on one side and brown rock on the other enclose this sheltered inlet.

Cala Vinagra

Montagna di Ravenna

Carloforte

Capo Sandalo
The westernmost point of the island, dominated by a lighthouse, is frequently exposed to the mistral wind.

Eleonora's falcon, so named because Eleonora d'Arborea *(see p36)* passed a law forbidding falcon hunting, is protected in this reserve. The conservation area has observation points and marked footpaths.

Monte di Gasparro

La Cletta

Stango dello Vinagra

0 kilometres   2

0 miles   2

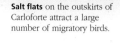

Salt flats on the outskirts of Carloforte attract a large number of migratory birds.

La Caletta
Protected from rough seas by Punta Spalmatore, the sheltered bay of La Caletta has a white, sandy beach.

KEY

▬	Major road
═	Minor road
▦	Salt flat
▬	River

*Isola
Piana*

Carloforte
*The only town on the island,
Carloforte overlooks the port,
with alleys and stairways
descending to the water.
The centre of social life is
Piazza Carlo Emanuele III.
The San Pietro feast day
procession of boats is also
worth watching.*

Punta delle Colonne
*The name, Cape of Columns,
refers to the trachytic stacks
that jut out from the sea.*

Carbonia's Piazza Roma, a typical example of Fascist architecture

Carbonia ⓰

Road map B6. 34,000. Pro Loco, Via Marconi 12 (0781 67 16 27). **www**.comune.carbonia.ca.it

Carbonia, located in the mining region of Sulcis, was founded by Mussolini in 1936. The town has retained its Fascist town planning and architectural conception, with imposing buildings and broad streets that converge at the central Piazza Roma. The town's most important public buildings are found here, including the Town Hall, the Torre Civica tower and the parish church of San Ponziano.

Villa Sulcis, the former residence of the director of the mines, has become the **Museo Archeologico**. On display are earthenware and bronze statuettes and jewels from local *domus de janas*, and finds from the archaeological sites at Monte Sirai.

The **Museo Martel** has a collection of fossils dating back 600 million years.

Environs: West of Carbonia along the SS126, a signposted road leads to the imposing hill occupied by the Monte Sirai archaeological site. The stunning view alone is worth the visit, as you can see the islands of Sant'Antioco and San Pietro. The fortified **Parco Archeologico Monte Sirai** was built by the Phoenicians in 750 BC. The thick outer wall protected the acropolis and the surrounding garrison town, which could house 500 foot soldiers and 100 mounted soldiers. The ruins of this ancient military camp were discovered in 1963 and excavations are still under way.

The necropolis, northwest of the main citadel, is mainly Carthaginian, but there is a Phoenician section with common graves, as well as an area of Punic tombs with underground burial chambers.

🏛 **Museo Archeologico**
Villa Sulcis, Via Napoli 4. **Tel** 0781 69 11 31. ◯ 9am–1pm, 3–7pm (Jun–Sep: 4–8pm) daily. 🚫 📷 ♿

🏛 **Museo Martel**
Via Campania 61. **Tel** 0781 69 10 06. ◯ 9am–1pm, 3–6:30pm Tue–Sun. 📷 ♿

⋔ **Parco Archeologico Monte Sirai**
3 km (2 miles) S of Carbonia. ◯ 9am–5pm daily (Jun–Sept: 9am–1pm, 4–8pm). 📷 📷 📷 compulsory. 📷

Underground burial chambers in the necropolis of Monte Sirai

Calasetta ⓱

Road map B6. 2,800. 0781 885 34.

The second largest village on the island of Sant'Antioco *(see p72)* and a trading port for Carloforte, Calasetta was founded in 1769 to house the Ligurian fishermen arriving from the Tunisian island of Tabarca. The straight streets with their two-storey houses lead to the main square. Here, the parish church has a bell tower of Arab derivation. The road heading south along the western coast offers a panoramic view of alternating cliffs, coves and beaches.

Urns that held the ashes of babies in the Tophet outside Sant'Antioco

Sant'Antioco ⑱

Road map B6. 🏛 *13,000.* 🖼 🛈
*Town Hall (0781 80 301); Pro Loco,
Piazza Repubblica 41 (0781 82 031).*
🗓 *2nd Mon after Easter:
Sant'Antioco; 29 Jun: San Pietro*
www. *comune.santantioco.ca.it*

Sant'Antioco is the main
town on the island of the
same name. The island is
connected to Sardinia by a
causeway and remains of a
Roman bridge are still visible
from the road. The *faraglioni*,
two large menhirs, stand on
one side. According to legend
these are the petrified figures
of a nun and a monk, turned
to stone as they tried to elope.

The town was founded by
the Phoenicians in the 8th
century BC and named Sulki.
It soon became a major port
in the Mediterranean, due to
the trade in minerals, including
gold, extracted from the area.
Ptolemy, the Greek astronomer,
gave it the name of *insula
plumbaria* (island of lead).
The Carthaginians used the
port during the second Punic
War *(see p34)*, but this alliance
was harshly punished by the
victorious Romans. Under
the Roman Empire the town
flourished, until continuous
pirate raids during the Middle
Ages led to its gradual decline.

The picturesque town centre
climbs away from the sea and
its characteristic houses have
small wrought-iron balconies.
The main street, **Corso
Vittorio Emanuele**, is shaded
by an avenue of trees. Above
the town is the church of
Sant'Antioco, built in the 6th

century with a Greek cross
plan and central dome, but
modified in the 11th century.
According to tradition the
remains of the island's patron
saint, Sant'Antioco, are buried
in the catacombs,
reached via the
transept. The body of
the martyr is said to
have floated here after
he was killed by the
Romans in Africa.
Some catacombs are
open to the public.
The chambers are less
than 2 m (6 ft) high
and some are deco-
rated with frescoes.

The newly built
Museo Archeologico contains
Phoenician and Roman
earthenware, jewels and other
objects found in the area,
including urns from the
nearby Tophet necropolis.

The **Museo Etnografico**
is housed in a former wine-
making plant. The large
central hall contains kitchen
equipment used to make
cheese and cultivate grape-

vines. The weaving section has
spindles and looms on show,
once used for the processing
of wool and *byssus,* a fine
filament taken from the *Pinna
nobilis,* the largest bivalve
mollusc in the Mediterranean.
Under the arcade outside,
original wine-making equipment and implements used for
raising livestock are on display.

Dominating the town is the
red stone **Castello Sabaudo**,
rebuilt by the Aragonese in
the 16th century. Just outside
town, on a cliff overlooking
the sea, the bleak **Tophet** is
a Phoenician sanctuary and
necropolis. This burial ground
was used for the ashes of still-
born babies, or those who
died shortly after birth.
Nearby is the Carthaginian
Necropolis with about 40
underground family tombs.

Fresco in the catacombs of Sant'Antioco

This area was later used by
the Romans for the ashes of
their dead. The tombs occupy
the upper part of town and
were used as catacombs during
the Early Christian period.

🛈 **Sant'Antioco**
Via Necropoli. **Tel** *0781 830 44.*
Catacombs ⏰ *9am–noon, 3–6pm
daily.* 📷 📷 **www**.*basilica
santantioco.com*

Cala Domestica, north of Sant'Antioco *(see p68)*

🏛 **Museo Archeologico**
Via Regina Margherita 113.
⏲ 9:30am–1pm, 3:30–7pm
daily. 🖼 ✏ ♿

🏛 **Museo Etnografico**
Via Necropoli.
⏲ 9:30am–1pm, 3:30–7pm
daily (summer: 9am–8pm).
🖼 ♿

⋔ **Tophet**
Via Castello. 🔧 Archeotour
(0781 835 90). ⏲ 9:30am–1pm,
3:30–7pm daily. 🖼

Tratalìas ⓲

Road map B6. 🏘 1,182. 🚉

This village in the Sulcis
region was the seat of the
diocese until 1413. The
façade of the Pisan
Romanesque cathedral of
Santa Maria, consecrated in
1213, is divided horizontally
by a row of little arches
surmounted by a rose
window. The tympanum is
curious, in that the last
section of a stairway
juts out from it.
 The sides
and apse are
decorated with
pilasters and
blind arches.
Inside, the three
naves are sepa-
rated by large,
octagonal
pillars. An altar-   **Cathedral of Santa Maria, Tratalìas**
piece from 1596
depicts St John the Baptist
and St John the Evangelist
with the Madonna and Child.

Santadi ⓴

Road map C6. 🏘 4,100. 🚉 🔧
0781 94 201. 🎪 first Sun in Aug:
Matrimonio Mauritano. **www.**
comune.santadi.ca.it

Built on the banks of the
River Mannu, Santadi's
old town sits on the higher,
north side. Some traditional
architecture made from rough
volcanic rock is still visible in
the medieval centre. Evidence
that the area has been inhabited since the nuraghic age
can be seen in the copper,
bronze, gold and earthenware
objects found here, which are
now on display in the Museo
Archeologico in Cagliari (see
p58). Local tools and furniture
can be seen at the **Museo
Etnografico Sa Domu
Antigua**. The shop here sells
typical Sulcis handicrafts.

Environs: On a plateau southwest of the town is the 7th-
century BC Phoenician
fortress, **Pani Loriga**.
Continuing south for
5 km (3 miles)
are two caves,
**Grotta Is
Zuddas**, with
splendid forma-
tions of sta-¬
lagmites and
stalactites,
and **Grotta
Pirosu** (now
closed) where
archaeological finds such as
a votive lamp and a Cypriot
style tripod were found.

The necropolis at Montessu

North of Villaperuccio, the
Montessu Necropolis has
typical domus de janas (see
p33) tombs, some of which
still have traces of the original
yellow and red wall facing.
Other tombs were probably
used for worship.
 The August festival, Matrimonio Mauritano (Mauretanian
Wedding), is a ceremony that
may have started with the
North Africans who settled
here during the Roman era.

🏛 **Museo Etnografico Sa
Domu Antigua**
Via Mazzini 37. **Tel** 0781 94 201.
⏲ 9am–12:30pm, 3–7:30pm daily.

🎪 **Grotta Is Zuddas**
Benatzu. 🔧 Cooperativa Monte Meana
(0781 95 57 41). ⏲ Jun–Sept: 9:30am–
noon, 2:30–6pm daily; Oct–Mar: tours
only, noon & 4pm daily. 🖼 ✏ compulsory. **www.**grotteiszuddas.it

⋔ **Montessu Necropolis**
Località Peruccio. 🔧 0781 94 201.
⏲ 9am–1pm, 3–7pm daily. 🖼 ✏

MONTE ARCOSU

The mountains in the Sulcis region are covered with forests
of cork oak, holm oak, strawberry trees and heather, from
which the granite peaks seem to emerge. This area extends
for about 7,000 hectares (17,300 acres), interrupted only by
a rough road that connects Santadi and Capoterra along the
Mannu and Gutturu Mannu river valleys. There are plans to
make the area into a National Park: the World Wide Fund
for Nature (WWF) has purchased 300 hectares (741 acres)
of land on the slopes of Monte Arcosu to protect the
Sardinian deer, which roamed the entire island until 1900,
but is now restricted to a few isolated areas. Other forest
mammals include fallow deer, wild cats, boar and martens.
Among the birds found here are the golden eagle, peregrine
falcon and goshawk. This nature reserve is open all year   **Stag in the Monte Arcosu reserve**

and visitors can stay overnight in refuges. There are well-marked nature trails as well as
unmarked wild walks, although an official WWF guide is obligatory in some areas. The Cagliari-
based Cooperativa Quadrifoglio (070 96 87 14) has information regarding accommodation
and trekking. To reach the reserve, take the road east from Santadi along the Gutturu river.

The sheltered beach at Baia Chia

Baia Chia ㉑

Road map C6. ℹ️ *070 923 50 15.*

The Southern Coast (Costa del Sud) is an area of high sand dunes and white beaches that extend as far as the Capo Spartivento headland. Junipers grow in the sand and there is marshland frequented by egrets, purple herons, grebes and other migratory aquatic birds. There are plans to turn the area into the centre of a regional nature reserve.

Along the coastal road, the hamlet of Chia is a popular tourist destination set among orchards and fig trees. A rough road leads to the sheltered bay of Chia, flanked on one side by the 17th-century **Torre di Chia**, and on the other by red cliffs covered with maquis vegetation. At the foot of the tower it is possible to visit the remains of Phoenician **Bithia**. This ancient city, mentioned in the writings of Ptolemy and Pliny the Elder, had been covered by the sea for centuries and has not yet been completely excavated.

Remains of a Punic and Roman necropolis are visible, as are the ruins of a temple probably dedicated to the god Bes. Earthenware pots and amphorae from the 7th century BC have been discovered in the sand, and traces of Roman wall paintings and mosaics decorate porticoed houses. Ancient Punic fortifications can be seen near the base of the watchtower and an elliptical cistern has also been found.

🏛 **Bithia**
Domus de Maria, Località Chia.
⭕ *at all times.*

Environs: Along the coast as far as the promontory of Capo Spartivento, where there are spectacular views, is a series of bays, dunes and pine forests that can be reached on foot.

The Roman theatre at Nora

Nora ㉒

Road map C6. ℹ️ *070 920 91 38.*
⭕ *9am–sunset daily.* 🎟 *combined ticket with Museo Archeologico.*
📷 ♿ 💻 www.nora.it

Founded under Phoenician rule in the 9th–8th centuries BC, the ancient city of Nora was built on a spit of land jutting out to sea. The town became the island's main city, a role it continued to enjoy under the Romans.

Repeated Saracen raids and the lack of fertile land finally forced the inhabitants to abandon the city in the Middle Ages; the three ports were gradually covered up by the incoming sea, resulting in the legend of the submerged city.

The ruins extend to the headland of Capo di Pula, dominated by the Spanish **Torre del**

The promontory of Capo Spartivento overlooking the southern coastline

Coltelazzo. An impressive vestige of the Carthaginian city is the Temple of Tanit, goddess of fertility. Little else remains of the Punic period, although rich findings in the tombs testify to active trading.

Left of the entrance are the 2nd–3rd-century AD Terme di Levante, Roman baths decorated with mosaics. Nearby is a 2nd-century AD theatre, the only one in Sardinia, and the large rectangular Forum behind it. South of the theatre, the mosaics in the *frigidarium* and *caldarium* of the baths are decorated with white, black and ochre tesserae. Paved roads and the city's sewage system are also still visible.

Many finds, including Punic inscriptions in which the name of the island of Sardinia is first mentioned, are kept in Cagliari's Museo Archeologico Nazionale *(see p58)*.

Some earthenware objects found at the site are on display in the small **Museo Archeologico Patroni**. The nearby Romanesque church of **Sant'Efisio**, built by French Victorine monks in the 11th century, is the site of an annual procession from Cagliari *(see p26)*.

🏛 **Museo Archeologico Patroni**
Corso Vittorio Emanuele 67. *Tel* 070 920 96 10. ◗ Apr–Oct: 9am– 7:30pm daily; Nov–Mar: 9am– dusk daily. 🎫 combined ticket with Nora. 📷 (no flash). 🚻

The popular resort of Poetto, between Quartu Sant'Elena and Cagliari

Quartu Sant'Elena ㉓

Road map C6. 🏘 66,000. 🚌 🚉 Cagliari. ✈ Elmas. 🛈 070 860 11. 🎉 14 Sep: Sant'Elena

Situated on the outskirts of Cagliari, Quartu Sant'Elena has grown to become one of the island's largest cities. It lies at the edge of the salt flats and marsh of the same name which are a favourite breeding and nesting ground for flamingoes.

The medieval church of **Sant'Agata** stands in the town's main square, Piazza Azuni. From here Via Porcu leads to the **Casa Museo Sa Dom 'e Farra**, literally "the house of flour". This large country house, converted into a museum, features over 14,000 traditional farm and domestic tools and equipment collected over the years by Gianni Musiu, a

Golden pen found at Nora

former shepherd. Each of the museum's rooms is dedicated to different farm activities: displaying saddles and leather harnesses to wagons and blacksmiths' bellows. One of the more curious objects is the snow-cooled icebox. Gathered in the Barbagia region, the snow was taken to Cagliari on muleback and kept cold in large straw-lined containers stored underground.

The farmstead consisted of the owner's home and living quarters for farm labourers. Other rooms around a large courtyard were used for various domestic and farm activities such as milling, bread-making and tool repair.

A bus ride southwest of Quartu Sant'Elena brings you to the beach resort of Poetto, a favourite with local people.

🏛 **Casa Museo Sa Dom 'e Farra**
Via Eligiu Porcu 143. *Tel* 070 81 23 40. ● for restoration.

FORESTA DEI SETTE FRATELLI

The Forest of the "Seven Brothers" was named after the seven peaks that can be seen from Cagliari and which tower over the holm oak forests and maquis. Run by the *Azienda Foreste Demaniali (070 279 91)*, the forest covers an area of 4,000 hectares (9,800 acres), replanted with pine, eucalyptus and cypress trees, and reaching an altitude of 1,023 m (3,355 ft). It is also one of the few areas inhabited by the rare Sardinian deer, now almost extinct. The mountain has many mule trails, once used by coal merchants; one of these footpaths begins at the forest headquarters at Campu Omo on the SS125. To drive into the mountains take a right turn past the Arcu 'e Tidu pass on the SS125.

Densely wooded Foresta dei Sette Fratelli, which extends over seven hills

THE EASTERN COAST

*M*ile after mile of pastures and rocks characterize the interior of eastern Sardinia, falling away to inaccessible cliffs on the coast, refuge for the rare monk seal. The coastline of the Golfo di Orosei is now part of the Parco Nazionale del Gennargentu, a vast nature reserve founded to protect golden eagles and moufflon.

There are no towns of any great size along the Eastern coast but there are some good seaside resorts around Arbatax and Villasimius. Except for a few stretches, the road runs inland, so that most of the beaches can be reached only after walking a long way or by driving on dirt roads. The largest towns are Orosei, Muravera and Dorgali, also situated in the interior at a certain distance from the coast. The historical reasons for this go back to the endemic malaria that afflicted the island until after World War II and, before that, the constant pirate raids which plagued the coasts for centuries. This is still unknown Sardinia, the interior the domain of shepherds and their flocks, and the southeast yet to be discovered by tourism. Until recently the region of Sarrabus was isolated because of the absence of negotiable roads. The only way of reaching it was via a narrow-gauge railway from Cagliari, which followed the contours of the valleys. It is still in operation, and offers a delightful opportunity to take a trip back into the past. Sarrabus today attracts visitors who prefer to stray from the beaten track. Further north, the Ogliastra region, with its sandy beaches which vary from pearly grey to a startling reddish colour, has rugged mountains and hills where time seems to have stood still, pastoral life has not been invaded by the 21st century and strong traditions survive. The Baronie region, in contrast, has the towns of Siniscola and Orosei, with good public transport systems and a fast modern motorway, making the area more accessible.

The alluvial plain around Posada, seen from the Castello della Fava

◁ Steep limestone cliffs on the Golfo di Orosei

Exploring the Eastern Coast

Splendid natural scenery and prehistoric
archaeological sites around Dorgali and
Orroli are the main attractions of the Eastern
Coast. The cliffs along the coast are steep,
and the most secluded coves in the Golfo di
Orosei (Cala Sisine, Cala Luna, Cala Goloritze) are most easily reached by boat. The
alternative is a lengthy walk, best tackled in
hiking boots. The countryside is marvellous
however, and the trek rewarding. The main road
winding through the region is the Orientale Sarda.
There is a proposal – supported by the local people
but vehemently opposed by environmentalists – to
widen this road into a fast access motorway.

A glimpse of the Golfo di Orosei, near Baunei

SIGHTS AT A GLANCE

0 kilometres   10

0 miles   10

KEY

▬▬	Major road
▬	Secondary road
▬	Minor road
▬	Scenic route
—	Minor railway
✕	Pass

Panoramic view of the foothills of Mount Gennargentu

Rocky outcrops of reddish granite at Arbatax

Golfo Orosei

Capo di Monte Santu

Baunei
SANTA MARIA NAVARRESE ③
tzorai
ARBATAX ②
Tortolì
S125
S198
BARÌ SARDO
LANUSEI ② ⑮ Torre di Barì
Cardedu
GAIRO
Ulassai Marina di Gairo
JERZU ⑬
Capo Sferracavallo
Tertenia
Melisenda
PERDASDEFOGU ⑲
Salto di Quirra
Escalaplano Quirra
Flumendosa S125
Ballao Villaputzu Porto Corallo
Villasalto MURAVERA ⑯
San Priamo
Cagliari Capo Ferrato
Camisa Costa Rei

Casa della Marina
Castiadas Cala Sinzias
Isola Serpentara
Solánas VILLASIMIUS ⑰
Capo Carbonara

One of the rocky coves on the Eastern Coast near Cala Luna

GETTING AROUND

The Orientale Sarda road (SS125) was once famous for being winding and slow to drive. In 2007, works totalling nearly 50 million euros were completed. There is now a direct dual-carriageway link from Cagliari to Arbatax/Tortolì. There is also a north-south coach service. The Ogliastra plain (Tortolí and Arbatax) is connected to Cagliari by the Ferrovie Complementari della Sardegna narrow-gauge train; the trip takes about eight hours. It is slow, but the line goes through wonderful scenery.

Pisan tower at Orosei

The Orientale Sarda Road ❶

Along the eastern peaks of the Gennargentu
National Park *(see pp82–3)*, the SS125, or the
"Orientale Sarda" route, connects Olbia to Cagliari.
The most spectacular stretch is between Dorgali and
Baunei, 63 km (39 miles) of winding road hewn out
of the rock by Piedmontese coal merchants during the
mid-1800s. These "foreigners" carved a road through
the remote mountain valleys and felled trees that were
sent to the mainland. The deforestation
that resulted has proved irreversible.

Flumineddu River Valley ②
This stretch of the SS125 road goes
through rugged terrain with cliffs
and a fine view of the Flumineddu
river valley under the peaks of
Monte Tiscali. There are many
places where you can stop
to enjoy the
wonderful
scenery.

Dorgali

*GROTTA DEL BUE
MARINO*

*GOLFO
DI
OROSEI*

Flumineddu

N125 (Orientale Sarda)

Codula di Luna

Codula di Sisine

*GENNARGENTU
NATIONAL PARK*

Genna Silana Pass ③
This is the highest point of
the tour at 1,017 m (3,336 ft).
Stop here to get a dramatic
view of the Gorroppu ravine.
A footpath from Pischina
Urtaddalà descends to the
Flumineddu river bed.

Urzulei ④
Built on different levels
on the slopes of Punta
Is Gruttas, Urzulei was
once an isolated town
difficult to reach. The
stone church of San
Giorgio di Suelli dates
from the 15th century.

KEY

▬▬ Major road

▭▭ Minor road

▬ River

Baunei ⑤
The white houses of this mountain village
stand out under the limestone crags.

TIPS FOR DRIVERS

Length: *63 km (39 miles).*
Stopping-off points: *at Dorgali, Genna Silana, San Pietro and Santa Maria Navarrese there are cafés and restaurants. Allow a full day to take into account the winding roads and opportunities to stop.*

Cala Gonone ①

A 400-m (1,300-ft) tunnel cut out of the limestone rock leads to the popular seaside resort of Cala Gonone. A winding road, with fabulous views of the sea, white rocks and the maquis, continues to the Grotta del Bue Marino where there have been sightings of the rare monk seal *(see p19).*

```
0 kilometres        4

0 miles             4
```

San Pietro ⑥

A rough track with precipitous hairpin bends climbs to a wooded plateau where wild pigs graze. At the end is the Golgo ravine, 295 m (967 ft) deep. A little further along is the 18th-century church of San Pietro. Shepherds still make offerings here and a rural festival takes place from 28–29 June.

The holiday resort of Cala Moresca, at Arbatax

Arbatax ②

Road map D4. 🏛 *1,100.* 🚂 🚌 🚢
🛈 *Pro Loco (0782 62 28 24).* 🎭 *2nd Sun in Jul: Madonna di Stella Maris*

The small town of Arbatax lies on the northern tip of the Bellavista promontory, a red porphyry cliff that plunges into the sea. The port, guarded by a Spanish tower, is the terminus for the narrow-gauge trains arriving from Cagliari. Ferries from Cagliari, Olbia and the Italian mainland also dock here.

This stretch of coast has clear, clean water and enticing coves such as **Cala Moresca**, south of Arbatax. Several tourist resorts now cover this small promontory, such as the popular *Vacanze Club* village, built to resemble a typical Mediterranean village. The solid wood doors and wrought-iron grilles on the

windows were taken from the abandoned village of Gairo *(see p89)*. Further south is Porto Frailis, also protected by a Spanish tower, and the long, sandy Orrì beach. From Arbatax footpaths lead up to the lighthouse high on the Bellavista promontory.

Santa Maria Navarrese ③

Road map D4. 🏛 *1,500.* 🚌 🚢
🛈 *0782 61 08 23.* 🎭 *15 Aug: Festa dell'Assunta.*

This seaside resort was named after the lovely country church around which it developed. It is said that this three-aisle construction, with a semicircular apse, was built in the 11th century by the daughter of the king of Navarra after she had been saved from a shipwreck.

In the church courtyard is a gigantic wild olive tree that is reputed to be over a thousand years old.

The beautiful beach at Santa Maria Navarrese is bordered by a pine forest and protected by a Spanish watchtower. Opposite this is the huge Agugliastra (or Sa Pedra Longa) rock, a slim limestone pinnacle that rises up 128 m (420 ft) from the sea. Boat services from the little port of Santa Maria Navarrese will take visitors to the stack, as well as to Cala Luna, Cala Sisine and Cala Goloritzè, further up the coast.

The Aragonese tower at Santa Maria Navarrese

The rocky Ogliastra island viewed from Capo Bellavista

Gennargentu National Park ❹

The park extends over 59,102 hectares (146,000 acres) of some of the wildest, most mountainous landscape in Sardinia, and includes the island's highest peak, Punta La Marmora. Established in 1989, most of the park lies in the province of Nuoro. There are 14 towns in this protected area, but few tarmac roads, and the steep-sided valleys and bare peaks give the area an isolated air. The unspoilt nature of the park makes it fascinating for walkers, geologists and naturalists alike. The climb up Punta La Marmora (1,834 m, 6,015 ft) is rewarding, and the limestone desert of Supramonte is one of Italy's spectacular sights. Monte Tiscali hides the prehistoric rock village of Tiscali *(see pp104–5)*, and the ravines of Su Gorroppu and the Su Gologone spring are unmissable. The coast to the east, home to the endangered monk seal, is one of Europe's loveliest. When walking, it is advisable to take an up-to-date map and plenty of water.

Peonies in flower

The Wild Cat
Larger than the domestic cat, the wild cat lives on Gennargentu and Supramonte.

Bearded vulture

Moufflon

Refuge

FONNI

N389

DE...

ARI...O

Marten

Flumendosa

Punta La Marmora

SE...

Griffon vulture

0 kilometres   15

0 miles   15

The Mount Gennargentu Massif
In winter the barren peaks and the lower slopes, carpeted in oak and chestnut trees, are sometimes covered by snow.

THE HIGHEST PEAK IN SARDINIA: PUNTA LA MARMORA

The massif of Gennargentu, whose name means "door of silver", reaches its peak in Punta La Marmora which, at 1,834 m (6,015 ft) above sea level, is the highest point on the island. The landscape here is quite barren and wild. The sky is populated by raptors circling around in search of prey and with a bit of luck you might be able to see, in the distance, small groups of moufflons, or mountain sheep.

Hikers on the top of Punta La Marmora

The Crests of Supramonte

The peaks rise to the east of Gennargentu and their slopes descend towards the sea.

VISITORS' CHECKLIST

Road map D4.
🛈 0784 323 07 or 0784 300 83; Pro Loco Dorgali, Via La Marmora 181 (0784 93 305); Desulo Town Hall (0784 61 92 11); WWF Cagliari (070 67 03 08)
www.wwf.it/sardegna

The Monk Seal

The monk seal (Monachus albiventer), *thought to be extinct, has been sighted in recent years in the Golfo di Orosei. Tourism has been blamed for the fall in population.*

KEY

━━ Major road

══ Minor road

▬ River

TIPS FOR TRAVELLERS

Ascending Punta La Marmora
From Desulo, follow the road to Fonni for about 5 km (3 miles) until you come to the S'Arcu de Tascusi pass, then take the asphalt road on the right until you reach a fork. Follow the dirt road on the right for 100 m (328 ft) and then take the right-hand road leading to the Girgini holiday farm. Skirt around it by keeping to the left. In a little less than 4 km (2 miles), take the right-hand fork and continue for 5 km (3 miles) until you reach the control cabin for an aqueduct. Leave your car here and follow the road on the right on foot until you reach the end, then proceed up the valley floor on the left until you reach the crest. From here you can continue up to the summit (an hour and a half on foot).

Refuge

🏔 DORGALI

DESOLO

CODULA DI LUNA

URZULEI

N 125

BAUNEI

N 389

Lago Alto Flumendosa

ARZANA

Eagle

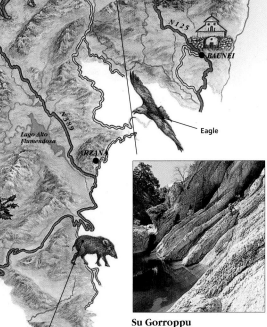

Su Gorroppu

This wild gorge, with its steep sides, can only be scaled by expert climbers.

Wild Boar

Displays of exhibits at the Museo Archeologico in Dorgali

Dorgali ❺

Road map D3. 🏠 8,500. 🚶 Pro Loco (0784 933 05). 🎭 16–17 Jan: Sant' Antonio Abate **www**.dorgali.it

The charming town of Dorgali lies on a ridge that descends from Monte Bardia and is 30 km (19 miles) from Nuoro and a little less than 10 km (6 miles) from the sea at Cala Gonone. Dorgali is predominantly an agricultural centre, but it is also important

Santa Caterina parish church in the centre of Dorgali

for locally produced crafts such as leather, ceramics and filigree jewellery, as well as rug- and carpet-weaving.

In the old part of town the buildings are made of dark volcanic stone. These include several churches: Madonna d'Itria, San Lussorio and the Maddalena. The central square, Piazza Vittorio Emanuele, is dominated by the façade of the parish church, Santa Caterina, home to a large carved altar.

Dorgali's **Museo Archeo- logico** contains an important collection of objects from nuraghic sites, as well as finds from sites dating back to Punic and Roman times. Some of the finest nuraghic pieces come from the nearby site of **Serra Òrrios**. The museum also provides information on visits to the rock village of Tiscali, another major nuraghic site *(see pp104–5)*. The town is known

for its wine, and the local wine-making cooperative can be visited. The local dairy is also of interest.

Nuraghic dwelling at Serra Òrrios

🏛 **Museo Archeologico di Dorgali**
Cooperativa Ghivina, Scuola Elemen-tare, Via La Marmora. 🚶 338 834 16 18. ☐ Sep–May: 9:30am–1pm, 3:30–6pm; Jun–Aug: 9am–1pm, 4–7pm. 🎫 ♿

🏠 **Serra Òrrios**
🚶 0784 93 696. ☐ daily. 🎫 compulsory, on the hour. ♿

THE NURAGHIC VILLAGE OF SERRA ÒRRIOS

At Serra Òrrios – about 10km (6 miles) to the north-west of Dorgali and 23 km (14 miles) east of Nuoro – lies one of Sardinia's best preserved nuraghic villages, which dates from the 12th–10th centuries BC. The 70 round dwellings, each with a central hearth, are arranged in at least six groups around large central spaces with a well. Small places of worship have also been found in the village.

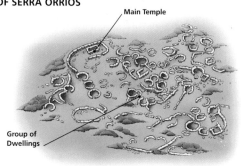

Main Temple

Group of Dwellings

Codula di Luna ➏

A four-hour walk down the "Valley of the Moon" will take hikers from the Supramonte to the sea. The path is straightforward but strenuous, with little shade. The track runs through aromatic maquis scrub, and passes shepherds' huts, as well as the entrances to enormous caves, many of which have not yet been fully explored. It is highly advised that you do not attempt this walk without a local guide.

The beautiful, secluded beach of Cala Luna, backed by a small lake

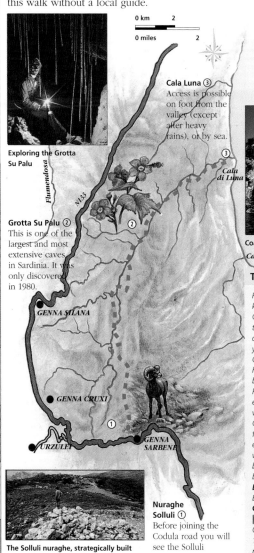

0 km 2
0 miles 2

KEY

▪ ▪ Tour route
▬ Major road
═ Minor road
— River

Exploring the Grotta Su Palu

Cala Luna ③
Access is possible on foot from the valley (except after heavy rains), or by sea.

Cala di Luna

Grotta Su Palu ②
This is one of the largest and most extensive caves in Sardinia. It was only discovered in 1980.

Coast near the Grotta del Bue Marino

Cala Sisine

Flumendosa

N133

GENNA SILANA

GENNA CRUXI

URZULEI

GENNA SARBENE

Nuraghe Solluli ①
Before joining the Codula road you will see the Solluli nuraghe to the right.

The Solluli nuraghe, strategically built on a ridge with views around

TIPS FOR TRAVELLERS

From the SS125 main road, also known as Orientale Sarda (at the Giustizieri fork, not far from the turn-off for Urzulei), take the road down the Codula valley and leave your car where the tarmac ends. Cross the river bed to begin the hike. About one hour's walk brings you to the entrance to Su Palu cave (on the right, for experienced cavers). Further along, the valley widens and opens out onto Cala Luna bay (a further two to four hours' walk). This walk is for experienced hikers only. In good weather the bay is accessible by boat from Cala Gonone (see p81); boats also go to the **Grotta del Bue Marino** *(mooring facilities). Bring plenty of drinking water.*
Grotta del Bue Marino
ℹ 0784 933 05. ⬚ 1 Apr–15 Oct. 🎫 (11am, 3pm; groups of 10 people or more: 10am, noon, 4pm).

The Chiesa delle Anime at Orosei

Orosei ❼

Road map D3. 🏃 *6,000.* 🚌
🛈 *Pro Loco (0784 99 83 67).* 🎿
Easter Week, 26 Jul, San Giacomo.
www.proloco-orosei.com

The historic capital of the Baronia region is situated about 5 km (3 miles) inland, and has a bustling, well-kept historic centre with churches, archways and small, white-washed stone buildings over-looking flowered courtyards.

The town of Orosei was probably founded in the early Middle Ages and its golden age occurred under Pisan domination, when it was ruled by the barons of the Guiso family. Orosei developed into an important harbour with moorings alongside the Cedrino river. After yielding to Aragonese rule, the town began to decline as a result of malarial disease, repeated pirate raids and the gradual silting up of the river.

The portal of Santa Maria 'e Mare

A labyrinth of alleys leads to the central Piazza del Popolo, where three churches stand. At the top of a flight of steps is **San Giacomo Maggiore** with an 18th-century façade and terracotta-tiled domes. Opposite is the **Chiesa del Rosario**, with a Baroque façade, and the **Chiesa delle Anime**, founded by the brotherhood of monks that participates in the Easter Week ceremonies.

Sant'Antonio Abate, once an isolated rural sanctuary, is now surrounded by the expanding town. Local handicrafts are on display in the Pisan tower inside the precincts of Sant'Antonio. The 17th-century Sanctuary of the Madonna del Rimedio, also once isolated, is now part of the outskirts and is surrounded by *cumbessias*, the houses used by pilgrims each September.

Monte Albo Tour ❾

The massive white limestone ridge that gave this mountain its name (*albo* means white) extends like a bastion between the Barbagia and Baronia regions. There are magnificent panoramic views from the maquis-covered slopes of the mountain. The area is destined to become a reserve to protect 650 plant species as well as moufflons, wild boar and raptors. Part of this tour follows a narrow road along the base of the limestone cliffs.

Lodè ②
This small town amid olive trees and maquis is the home of the Annunziata sanctuary, with its whitewashed, red-roofed *cumbessias*. On 22–23 May the sanctuary becomes a pilgrimage site.

Bitti ③
This lively town *(see p100)* lies in pretty countryside surrounded by clusters of oak and wild olive trees.

The Annunziata Sanctuary, Lodè

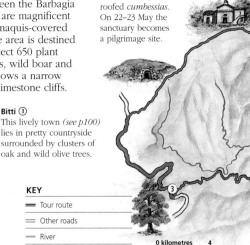

KEY

━━ Tour route

═══ Other roads

━━ River

0 kilometres   4

0 miles   4

Environs: Near the mouth of the Cedrino river is **Santa Maria 'e Mare**, founded in the 13th century by Pisan merchants. The church is full of ex votos, and on the last Sunday in May it is the focus of a pilgrimage, when a statue of the Madonna is taken down the river on a boat, followed by a flotilla of boats.

At the mouth of the estuary the river divides into two. The northern part flows into an artificial canal, the southern half feeds the Su Petrosu marsh. This is where to find coots, moorhens, mallards and purple gallinules. The shallows are home to avocets, stilts, grey heron and egrets.

Galtellì **8**

Road map D3. 2,400. 0784 90 150; Pro Loco, Via Garibaldi 2 (0784 904 72). 16–17 Jan, Sant'Antonio Abate; 2nd Sat in Aug, Festa dell'Immigrato/Turista.

Lying on the slopes of Monte Tuttavista, Galtellì was the most important town in the region during the Middle Ages. Until 1496 it was the regional bishopric, as can be seen in Romanesque San Pietro, the former cathedral built in the 12th century. After this era the town began to decline thanks to the ravages of malaria and frequent pirate raids, but traces of its glorious past have been preserved in the parish church of Santissimo Crocifisso.

The historic centre is pretty, with its whitewashed buildings and well-kept houses. In August, the town throws a party for all foreigners and tourists living or staying there.

Environs: One of the most interesting sights in this area is Monte Tuttavista. A dirt road and then a footpath take you to Sa Pedra Istampada ("the perforated rock"), a wind-sculpted arch 30 m (98 ft) high. There are splendid views from the summit.

Near the village of La Traversa, 12 km (8 miles) from Galtellì, is the Tomba di Giganti (giants' tomb) of **Sa Ena 'e Thomes**, a very impressive prehistoric monument with a 3-m (10-ft) stele hewn out of a single block of granite.

The Sa Ena 'e Thomes "giants' tomb" near La Traversa

Sant'Anna ①
This pass is 624 m (2,050 ft) above sea level, and offers splendid scenic views. The road winds up among cliffs, euphorbia bushes and cluster pines.

TIPS FOR DRIVERS

Length: 76 km (47 miles). This tour takes about two hours by car, but allow half a day to include the stops.
Stopping-off points: the Sant'Anna roadman's house and the town of Bitti (see p100)

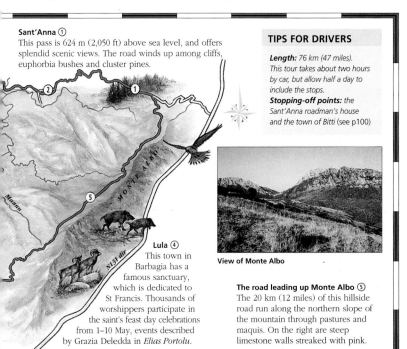

View of Monte Albo

Lula ④
This town in Barbagia has a famous sanctuary, which is dedicated to St Francis. Thousands of worshippers participate in the saint's feast day celebrations from 1–10 May, events described by Grazia Deledda in *Elias Portolu*.

The road leading up Monte Albo ⑤
The 20 km (12 miles) of this hillside road run along the northern slope of the mountain through pastures and maquis. On the right are steep limestone walls streaked with pink.

Siniscola ⑩

Road map D2. 🏠 *11,000.*
🚉 ℹ️ *0784 87 08 00.*
🎭 *18 Aug: Sant'Elena.*
www.comune.siniscola.nu.it

Set at the foot of Monte
Albo, the once agricultural
town of Siniscola was an
important trading centre in
the 14th century under the
principality of Gallura *(see
p36)*. Since then, the town has
grown in a haphazard manner
around the medieval centre.
On the lively main street,
Via Sassari, the 18th-century
parish church of **San Giovanni
Battista** is decorated with a
fresco cycle representing the
life of St John the Baptist. The
town is also well known for
its local pottery studios.

Environs: A straight
road northeast
from Siniscola
leads to **La Caletta**,
a small tourist port
with a wide sandy
beach, 4 km
(2 miles) long.
Heading south-
wards, the SS125
passes the fishing
village of **Santa
Lucia**. Probably
founded by
emigrants from
the island of
Ponza, the
village is guarded
by a Spanish watchtower.
Today Santa Lucia is a popular
summer resort, with a pine
forest that extends behind the
beach. Continuing southwards,
a long walk along the shore

The church at Santa Lucia

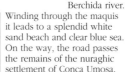

Spanish tower at Santa Lucia

will take you to the white sand
dunes and juniper bushes of
Capo Comino (also accessible
from the SS125).

The headland of Capo
Comino consists of rounded
rocks and pebble beaches and
is overlooked by a lighthouse.
A two-hour walk along the
seashore and pine forest will
take you to **Berchida
beach**, where there is a
huge rock called
*S'incollu de sa
Marchesa* (The
Marquise's
Throat). Eels
and grey mullet
populate an
area of marsh-
land here.

An alternative
excursion is to
take the rough
track that turns
right from the
SS125 after the
Berchida river.
Winding through the maquis
it leads to a splendid white
sand beach and clear blue sea.
On the way, the road passes
the remains of the nuraghic
settlement of Conca Umosa.

Posada ⑪

Road map D2. 🏠 *2,600.* 🚉 ℹ️
Via Vittorio Veneto (0784 87 05 00).

Perched on top of a lime-
stone bank covered with
euphorbia and lentiscus, this
village is dominated by the
ruins of **Castello della Fava**.
The castle was built in the
12th century by the rulers
of Gallura, who were later
conquered by the principality
of Arborea before passing
under Aragonese dominion
(see p36) . In the Carthaginian
era this place was known as
the colony of Feronia.

The town still retains its
medieval character, with
winding alleyways connected
by steep stairways, arches and
tiny squares. The castle has
had a face-lift, and wooden
steps lead to the top of its
square tower, where there is
a panoramic view of the sea,
the mouth of the Posada river
and the surrounding plain,
covered with fruit orchards.

Environs: Inland, 9 km
(5 miles) west of Posada, is
the artificial lake of Posada.
The pine forests and fine views
make this a popular spot.

Lanusei ⑫

Road map D4. 🏠 *5,800.* 🚉 🚉 🚉
🚉 ℹ️ *Via Roma 98 (0782 47 311).*
🎭 *22 Jul: Santa Maria Maddalena.*

This large, austere-looking
town, situated on a hillside
at 600 m (1,926 ft), overlooks
the plain that descends to the

The white sand dunes at Capo Comino

The village of Posada and the Castello della Fava

sea. It was once a health retreat due to its excellent climate, high altitude and the many walking trails in the surrounding forest. The town was built on various levels and still has some aristocratic buildings of interest.

Jerzu ⓭

Road map D4. 🏘 *3,600.* 🚌
🛈 *0782 700 23.* 🎎 *13 Jun: Sant'Antonio; 25 Jul: San Giacomo; 4 Aug: Sagra del Vino.*

Tall, sharp pinnacles of rock, known locally as *tacchi* (high heels), are an impressive sight as they emerge from the maquis on the approach to Jerzu. This modern town is built on several levels up the hillside with houses of two storeys or more overlooking the main street. Steep

Wine labels from Jerzu

side streets in the lower quarter lead to older houses with many original features.

Jerzu's economy is based mainly on viticulture and small vineyards cling to the steep slopes around the town. The area produces about 10,000 tonnes of grapes from which the local wine cooperative makes the good red wine Cannonau DOC, one of the most famous in Sardinia.

The most important holiday is the feast day of Sant'Antonio da Padova, on 13 June. One of the town's churches is dedicated to the saint.

Environs: At Ulassai, 7 km (4 miles) northwest of Jerzu, is the limestone **Grotta Su Màrmuri**. Steps descend to reveal spectacular pools and stalagmites. Wear warm clothes and sturdy shoes.

🐾 **Grotta Su Màrmuri**
🛈 *Piazzale Grotta Su Marmuri (0782 798 59).* 📷 📹 *compulsory: 11am, 2:30pm (& more in summer).* 📷

Gairo ⓮

Road map D4. 🏘 *2,000.* 🚌 🚌
🛈 *0782 76 00 00.* 🎎 *third Sun in Sep: Nostra Signora del Buoncammino.*

Gairo Sant'Elena lies in the Pardu river valley, a deep ravine with limestone walls. The present-day village was built after 1951, when Gairo Vecchio had to be evacuated after excessive rain caused a series of landslides. All that remains of the abandoned village are gutted houses without doors and windows. The entire area has spectacular scenery.

Environs: On the coast, the bay of Gairo is protected by a headland covered with maquis. From here you can go to Coccorocci, the only beach with black sand in Sardinia. The coast road runs along the seashore, which is characterized by sandy inlets and cliffs of pink rock.

Barí Sardo ⓯

Road map D4. 🏘 *4,500.* 🚌
🛈 *0782 295 23/93.* 🎎 *29 Aug: San Giovanni Battista; 8 Sep: Nostra Signora di Monserrato.*

This agricultural centre is set in fertile countryside filled with vineyards and orchards. The name of the town is derived from the Sardinian word for marshes, *abbari*. In the oldest part of town, around the district of San Leonardo to the southwest, original stone houses are still visible. Here, the parish church, **Beata Vergine del Monserrato**, has a Rococo bell tower dated 1813. The town is also known for its textiles: tapestries, rugs and linen cushions and bedcovers.

Environs: On the coast, east of Barí Sardo, **Torre di Barí** is a pleasant seaside resort that developed around the 17th-century Spanish tower built to defend the town from pirates. It has a sandy beach and small pine forest. During the festivities for San Giovanni Battista, known here as *Su Nenneri*, grain and vegetable seedlings are cast into the sea to encourage a good harvest.

The vineyards at Jerzu produce Cannonau, Sardinia's best-known wine

The basalt rock promontory at Capo Ferrato, south of Muravera

Inland, the route towards Cagliari along the SS125 offers spectacular scenery, with red rock among myrtle, juniper and strawberry trees. A trip down the Flumendosa river valley, beyond San Vito, also offers spectacular scenery.

Castiadas is a hamlet behind the Costa Rei, set around a 19th-century prison amid vineyards and citrus trees. From the late 19th century to the 1950s the area was occupied by a prison farm, where prisoners worked on the land.

Muravera ⓰

Road map D5. 🏚 4,500. 🚌 070 99 00 01. 🚏14–15 Aug: l'Assunta. **www**.comune.muravera.ca.it

Muravera lies at the mouth of the Flumendosa river, in the middle of an area of fruit orchards. It is a modern tourist town, catering to the resort complexes that have grown up along the coast. In ancient times this was the Phoenician city of Sarcapos. Today, the only building of any historical interest is the church of **San Nicola**, off the main street, which retains its original 15th-century chapels.

Environs: Muravera is an ideal starting point for trips along the coast and into the valleys of the interior. To the east, the beach around **Porto Corallo** is long and sandy, interrupted by small rocky

headlands. Near this tourist port is another **Spanish tower** which, in 1812, was used as a stronghold in one of the rare victories of the Sardinians over the Muslim pirates.

Northwards, 11 km (7 miles) along the SS125, also known as the Orientale Sarda road *(see p80)*, are the remains of the **Castello di Quirra** and the small Romanesque church of **San Nicola**, the only church in Sardinia built of brick.

To the south, the coast around **Capo Ferrato** is also beautiful, with basalt rocks, small white sandy coves and pine trees. Past the headland of Capo Ferrato is the **Costa Rei**, a stretch of straight coastline with beaches and tourist villages. The sea bed at the bay of **Cala Sinzias** further to the south consists of long slabs of rock, giving the water a strikingly clean and transparent look.

Villasimius ⓱

Road map D6. 🏚 3,000. 🚐 🚌 070 793 02 08. 🚏 Jul: Madonna del Naufrago. **www**.comune. villasimius.ca.it

With its hotels, residences and second homes, this modern town is the leading seaside resort on the southeastern coast. Villasimius lies on the northern edge of a promontory that extends to **Capo Carbonara**. At the centre of the headland is the **Notteri marsh**, separated from the sea by Simìus beach, a long stretch of sand. In the winter the marsh is a popular stopping-off point for migratory flamingoes. On the very tip of the promontory the lighthouse offers a sweeping view of the coast and the tiny islands of **Serpentara** and **Cavoli** in the distance. The stretch of water between the

THE TOWN OF THE LAUNEDDAS

Northeast of Muravera is San Vito, an agricultural town that thrived in past centuries thanks to the silver mines on Monte Narba. In the centre of town, the parish church with its twin bell towers over the façade is worth a visit. San Vito is known for its tradition of craftmanship, in particular the flute-like instrument, the *launeddas*, which was originally played by shepherds *(see p25)* . Luigi Lai, Sardinia's most famous player of this ancient instrument, lives here and makes the instrument himself. Other crafts at San Vito include fine embroidery and basket-weaving with juniper twigs.

Luigi Lai, one of Sardinia's most famous *launeddas* players

The long beach separating the sea from Notteri marsh, south of Villasimius

two islands is shallow and has witnessed many shipwrecks over the years. Off the island of Cavoli, at a depth of 10 m (33 ft), is the statue of the *Madonna dei Fondali* (Our Lady of the Sea Floor) by local sculptor Pinuccio Sciola. Excursions by glass-bottomed boat leave from the quay at Porto Giunco to view the submerged statue. This port is protected by the **Fortezza Vecchia**, a star-shaped fortress built in the 17th century. The sea around the headland is rich in fauna and flora and is popular with scuba divers.

Orroli ⑱

Road map C4. 🧍 *3,300.* 🚌
ℹ️ *0782 84 70 06.* 📅 *30 Jun: Santa Caterina* **www**.comuneorroli.it

The town of Orroli lies in the rather barren Pranemuru plateau, at the edge of the Flumendosa valley. The area is

dotted with archaeological sites, such as the necropolis of **Su Motti** where *domus de janas* tombs are cut out of the rock.

Other archaeological sites in the area include the ruins of the **Arrubiu Nuraghe**, 3 km (1.8 miles) southeast of Orroli. This complicated, pentagonal site is larger than the one at Su Nuraxi *(see pp64–5)*. The complex, made of red stone, was built around a 14th-century BC central tower which, according to experts, was 27 m (88 ft) high. Five towers, probably dating from the 7th century BC, connected by tall bastions, were built around the complex, and an outer defensive wall was added in the 6th century BC. The ruins of the nuraghic village, consisting of round and rectangular dwellings, lie around the nuraghe.

Another interesting site is the nearby **Su Putzu** nuraghe, which has numerous dwellings in excellent condition.

🏛 **Su Motti**
4 km (2 miles) SE of Orroli. **Tel** *0782 84 72 69.* ⏰ *by appt only.* 🏷 📷

🏛 **Arrubiu Nuraghe**
Tel *0782 84 72 69.* ⏰ *9:30am–1pm, 3–8:30pm (Oct–Apr: 9:30am–5pm).* 🏷

The Arrubiu Nuraghe near Orroli

Perdasdefogu ⑲

Road map D4 & D5. 🧍 *2,500.* 🚌 ℹ️
0782 94 614. 📅 *12 Sep: San Salvatore.*

An isolated mountain village in the lower Ogliastra area, Perdasdefogu lies at the foot of the striking *tacchi*, vertical limestone walls that tower over the maquis *(see p89)*. The road that meanders northeast towards Jerzu is one of the most scenic in Sardinia. It runs along a plateau at the base of these dolomitic walls, offering a spectacular view of the sea and Perda Liana peaks in the distance. Along the way is the rural church of **Sant'-Antonio**, set in a meadow at the foot of Punta Coróngiu, one of the most impressive of the limestone *tacchi*.

View from the headland of Capo Carbonara, south of Villasimius

A Trip on the Trenino Verde ⑳

It takes almost five hours to travel 160 km (99 miles) on the narrow-gauge *trenino verde* (little green train), but the reward is a trip backwards in time through some of the wildest landscapes in Sardinia. The line passes through the softly rolling hills of Trexenta, carpeted with almond and olive trees, to the rugged mountains of Barbagia di Seui, where the train runs along the foot of a magnificent *tònnero*, with a broad view of its vertical limestone walls. This particular route – one of several across Sardinia – follows the craggy contours of the mountain and there are so many bends that it is easy to lose your sense of direction. The train makes two hairpin turns through the town of Lanusei in order to get over a steep slope. The only drawback is the timetable: travellers cannot make the return trip on the same day.

Lake Alto Flumendosa, on the southern side of Gennargentu

Villanovatulo ⑥
This isolated shepherds' village has a view of the Flumendosa river basin. The walls of the houses have murals by Pinuccio Sciola.

Flumendosa

The Trenino Verde
This picturesque train skirts the hillsides, well away from the road amid unspoilt scenery. As well as the timeless landscape, you can appreciate the atmosphere of a forgotten age.

Lago di Flumendosa

N198

VISITORS' CHECKLIST

🛈 Cagliari (070 57 93 03 46).
Trenino Verde Tel 070 58 02 46. @ treninov@tin.it
www.treninoverde.com
Train timetable Jun–Sep: from Arbatax, 8am and 2:30pm daily; from Mandas, 8:15am and 3pm daily; mid-Jul–Aug: from Mandas, 4:44pm daily. For other Trenino Verde routes, check the website. The train is also available for private hire all year round.

Mandas ⑧
69 km (43 miles) from Cagliari, Mandas is the leading agricultural town in the area. The church of San Giacomo, with statues of San Gioacchino and Sant' Anna, is worth a visit.

Orroli ⑦
Surrounded by oak forests, the town of Orroli lies on a basalt tableland crossed by the Flumendosa river. Look out for the Arrubiu nuraghe *(see p91)*.

Montarbu Forest ③
This is one of the best preserved forests in Sardinia, where moufflons live among ash, holm oak and yew trees. A striking feature here are the *tònneri*, massive vertical limestone walls.

Lanusei ②
This village lies on the slope of a hill commanding a fine view of the sea *(see p88)*.

Tortolì ①
The capital of the Ogliastra region is 3 km (2 miles) from the sea, on the edge of a large marsh which attracts thousands of migratory birds in winter. Watch out for the ruins of Castello di Medusa.

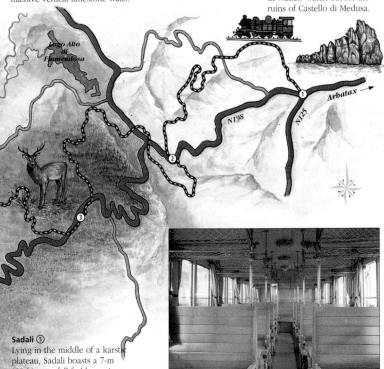

Lago Alto di Flumendosa

N198

N125

Arbatax →

Sadali ⑤
Lying in the middle of a karstic plateau, Sadali boasts a 7-m (23-ft) waterfall fed by springs that flow into an underground chasm. There are numerous caves, such as Is Janas, 205 m (672 ft) long with an underground lake and impressive stalagmites and stalactites.

Interior of the Trenino Verde

Seui ④
The village of Seui, on the side of a steep valley, retains some traditional stone houses. The 17th-century Spanish prison is now occupied by the Civic Museum of Rural Culture with displays of traditional farm utensils and reconstructions of an 18th-century kitchen and bedroom.

0 kilometres 4

0 miles 4

KEY

🚂 Train route

▬ Major road

▭ Minor road

— River

TIPS FOR TRAVELLERS

Refreshments are not served on the train and the few stations en route are not equipped to offer restaurant facilities, so it is advisable to take along something to eat and drink.

Going towards Mandas, the best views can be appreciated from the left-hand side of the train (and vice versa).

The "normal" train, called TL, is superior to the AT (single-unit rail diesel car), which is noisier and less comfortable.

The train passing near Orroli

CENTRAL SARDINIA AND BARBAGIA

The central region of Sardinia is the area that most vividly reflects the ancient character of the island. Rugged mountains are marked by shepherds' trails and villages perch over steep valleys. The inhabitants of this isolated region are known as hardy and proud and have retained many aspects of their traditional way of life.

The name Barbagia derives from the Latin word *barbària*, used by the Romans to designate the inaccessible regions of the interior inhabited by "barbarians" (any culture that did not share the values and beliefs of the Roman civilization). Inhabited since prehistoric times and rich in archaeological sites, such as the nuraghic village of Tiscali *(see pp104–5)*, the heart of Sardinia resisted Roman invasions for many centuries and preserved its nuraghic religious rites up to the advent of Christianity.

Getting to know this rugged land requires some effort, since the roads are slow and winding, road signs are sometimes missing and many sights can be reached only via rough dirt tracks. The people, however, are often hospitable and tradition is still an essential part of local life. The churches and villages come to life during the colourful folk festivals, the patron saints' feast days and at religious festivities. At Mamoiada the *Mamuthones* lead the Mardi Gras processions wearing forbidding masks, cow bells and sheepskins *(see p102)*.

The mountainous landscape dominates central Sardinia. Trekkers can enjoy walks from the rocks of Supramonte di Oliena to the dense forests of holm oak on the slopes of Monte Novo San Giovanni *(see p107)* and the chestnut woods along the old railway near Belvì *(see p109)*.

The local cuisine is flavoured with herbs from the maquis, such as rosemary and thyme, while the handicrafts draw inspiration from pastoral life. Woven carpets, baskets and pottery with traditional motifs can be seen in Nuoro's Museo Etnografico *(see p99)*.

A shepherd and his flock in the high summer pastures at Pietrino

◁ Wind-battered cork oak, a common sight in the Barbagia

Exploring Central Sardinia and Barbagia

Nuoro is the capital of Sardinia's interior region: to the east lies the Supramonte mountain range, with Oliena, Orgòsolo and Dorgali at its feet, while to the west the valleys descend towards Lake Omodeo and Macomer. In this landscape of hills and steep limestone walls (the *tònneri* formations) are some of the most important towns in the region: Mamoiada, Bitti and Sarule. To the south is the Gennargentu massif, carpeted with dense forests, on the slopes of which are typical mountain villages such as Gavoi and Fonni. Heading northeast and skirting the slopes of Monte Ortobene, which towers above the city of Nuoro, the road descends among almond trees and vineyards towards the Baronia region.

Rebeccu

Monte Rasu 1258m

Foresta di Bùrgos

BON

Bonorva

BURGOS **4**

S131

Padru Mannu

Cat. d. Marghine

Punta Palai 1202m

Bolotana

S129

Macomer

OTTANA

Dualchi

Tirso

Sedilo

S131d

Abbasanta

Toloro

Lago Omodeo

Sorradile

Neoneli

Ortueri

Atz

Mea San

Asuni

Araxisi

LÀCONI

Nureci

Flumin

Nura

Nuragus

Giara di Gesturi

S197

Sanluri

Barren slopes on the Gennargentu mountain range

SIGHTS AT A GLANCE

A mural painted on rocks near Orgòsolo

A dwelling in the nuraghic village of Tiscali

GETTING AROUND

Public transport in the interior of Sardinia is slow and unreliable if it exists at all, and is not the best way to visit the area. If you have a car, the main roads are the SS131 from Siniscola to Nuoro up to Lake Omodeo; the SS125, the Orientale Sarda road, which skirts Supramonte and links Orosei to Arbatax, and the SS389, which also goes to Arbatax from Nuoro, passing Gennargentu on the east. For sights such as Tiscali and Punta La Marmora, you have to hike up fairly steep footpaths.

A pleasant alternative mode of transport is the little narrow-gauge train on the Cagliari-Sòrgono line (*see p109*).

SEE ALSO

• *Where to Stay* pp175–6

• *Where to Eat* pp185–6

KEY

▬▬	Major road
▬▬	Secondary road
▬▬	Minor road
▬▬	Scenic route
▬	Minor railway
△	Summit

Nuoro ●

Nùgoro, as the locals still call their city, is one of Sardinia's most important centres. The city began to expand in the 14th century, but by the 18th century there was social unrest and riots erupted. In 1746 the Piedmontese prefect, De Viry, described the city as "a hotbed of bandits and murderers". A decree in 1868 that put an end to the common use of farmland culminated in a popular rebellion known as *Su Connottu*.

Traditional costume   At the beginning of the 20th century Nuoro became the heart of the island's cultural life, producing political and social writers such as Grazia Deledda. The city became the provincial capital in 1926, and today it is the commercial heart of Barbagia.

Santa Maria della Neve

to medieval objects, including the skeletons of an ancient hare, *Prolagus sardus*, and a collection of cave finds. Also of interest are nuraghic bronze statuettes. Finds from the Roman era include belt buckles and other everyday household objects.

The huge granite blocks in Piazza Sebastiano Satta

Exploring Nuoro

The city is set in spectacular surroundings on a granite plateau beneath Monte Ortobene. Its isolated position and relatively recent exposure to tourism have helped to preserve local culture, traditions and costumes.

The modern city retains many picturesque streets and buildings in the old centre. Corso Garibaldi, once known as Bia Maiore, leads up to the quarter of San Pietro and the city's Neo-Classical cathedral, **Santa Maria della Neve** (1836). Near Corso Garibaldi is the whitewashed Piazza Sebastiano Satta, paved in 1976 with large granite blocks.

Nuoro is the birthplace of some of Sardinia's most notable men and women of letters, who at the end of the 19th century injected new life into the island's culture. Apart from Grazia Deledda, other native literary figures are politician and essayist Attilio Deffenu (1893–1918) and poet Sebastiano Satta (1867–1914).

⛫ Civico Museo Speleo-Archeologico

Via Mannu 3. **Tel** 0784 316 88.
⬜ 9am–1pm Tue–Sat (also 3–5:30pm Tue & Thu). ♿
This museum combines the collections of fossils and fossil plants of the *Gruppo Speleologico Nuorese*, with archaeological finds excavated over many years in the area. Exhibits range from Neolithic

⛫ Museo Deleddiano

Via Grazia Deledda 28. **Tel** 0784 25 80 88. ⬜ 9am–1pm, 3–7pm daily (mid-Jun–Sep: 9am–8pm). 📷 📵
Grazia Deledda's birthplace retains the atmosphere of a mid-19th-century Sardinian home. The newly refurbished house has been arranged according to her own description, set out in her novel *Cosima*, with objects marking the stages of her career. The courtyard leads to what was the kitchen garden (now the venue for cultural events), while the upper floors are given over to displays of the covers of her books, programmes for her plays, and a copy of the diploma for the Nobel Prize for Literature.

GRAZIA DELEDDA (1871–1936)

Grazia Deledda won the Nobel Prize for Literature in 1926 in recognition of her perceptive portrayal of the power and passions in the primitive communities around her. Born in Nuoro in 1871, she has become a symbol of Sardinian culture and an example of the island's prolific artistic production. The eventful and difficult years of her early career are described in the auto-biographical novel *Cosima* (1937). Her world of fiction revolves around Barbagia, with its mysteries and strong sense of identity. Among her best-known novels are *Elias Portolu* (1900), *Cenere* (1903), and *Canne al Vento* (1913). She died in Rome in 1936.

The author Grazia Deledda

For hotels and restaurants in this region see pp175–6 and pp185–6

The whitewashed Museo Etnografico in Nuoro

VISITORS' CHECKLIST

Road map *D3.* 🏘 *38,000.*
ℹ *0784 300 83.* 🚌 *19 Mar:
San Giuseppe; 6 Aug: San
Salvatore; last Sun in Aug:
Processione del Redentore*
www.*provincia.nuoro.it*

solemn procession known as
the *Processione del Redentore*
in which representatives from
almost every town in Sardinia
take part *(see p28)*.

Traditional costume from Dèsulo,
Museo delle Tradizioni Sarde

🏛 Museo Etnografico

Via Antonio Mereu 56. **Tel** *0784 24
29 00.* ☐ *Jun–Sep: 9am–8pm daily;
Oct–May: 9am–1pm, 3–7pm daily.*
🖼 📷 www.isresardegna.org

The Museum of Sardinian life
and popular traditions was
designed in the
1960s by
architect
Antonio
Simon
Mossa. The
aim of the
project was to
recreate a typical
Sardinian village,
with courtyards,
alleys and stairways, as a
setting for artifacts, objects
and costumes representing
Sardinian daily life.

Chest and cover in the
Museo Etnografico

On display in this popular
ethnographic museum are
traditional pieces of furniture,
such as a 19th-century chest
and cover and silver jewellery
used to adorn aprons or hand-
kerchiefs. Characteristic costumes worn daily or on special
occasions by women are also
on show, as are different types
of traditional bread moulds,
looms and hand-woven car-
pets. One room is dedicated to
carnival masks and costumes.

The museum also has a
library specializing in
anthropological literature, an
auditorium and an exhibition
centre. Every other October,
the museum features a festival
of ethnographic and anthropological films.

Environs:
🏔 Monte Ortobene

East of Nuoro.
Nuoro was founded on the
granite slopes of this mountain
and the inhabitants have
always held it in high regard.
To reach its
wooded areas,
take the SS129
Orosei road
east out of the
city. The road
passes the
church of **Nostra
Signora della
Solitudine**, where
Grazia Deledda is
buried. At the summit is a
statue of the Redentore (Christ
the Redeemer) that overlooks
the city below and next to it
is the church of **Nostra
Signora di Montenero**. On
the last Sunday in August this
church is the focus of the

🕳 Necropoli di Sas Concas

SS128. **Tel** *0784 300 83.* ☐ *daily.* 🖼
To visit this necropolis, take
the SS131 15 km (9 miles)
west out of Nuoro and then
the SS128 southwards for 3
km (2 miles) towards Oniferi.
The complex consists of a
series of *domus de janas*,
some decorated with bas
reliefs, such as the *Tomba
dell'Emiciclos* (Tomb of the
Hemicycle). The area is
unattended, so a torch for
the tombs may be useful.

The Sagra del Redentore procession on Monte Ortobene

Su Tempiesu well-temple near Bitti

Bitti ❷

Road map D3. 🏛 *3,800.* ℹ *Town Hall, Piazza G Asproni (0784 41 51 24).* 🎎 *23 Apr: San Giorgio*

This pastoral village has recently become known thanks to the *Tenores de Bitti* musical group, whose interpretations of traditional Sardinian close harmony songs have won them acclaim throughout Europe *(see pp24–5)* . Experts say the local dialect is the one that most resembles Latin.

The 19th-century church of **San Giorgio Martire** stands in the central Piazza Giorgio Asproni. In the nearby parish home is a fine small collection of local archaeological finds.

Environs: Not far from Bitti on the road to Orune (watch out for the signs, which can be difficult to follow) is the **Su Tempiesu** well-temple. This consists of several chambers made of large square basalt stones, and houses the sacred well. The well water was used

in nuraghic rituals. A little way east of Bitti are five churches, Santo Stefano, Santa Maria, Santa Lucia, San Giorgio and *Babbu Mannu* (Holy Ghost). These become lively during religious festivities.

Bono ❸

Road map C3. 🏛 *4,100.* ℹ *Town Hall, Corso Angioj 2 (079 79 169).* 🎎 *31 Aug: San Raimondo Nonnato*

Set at the foot of the Gocèano mountain range, Bono is an ideal starting point for trips to the wooded Monte Rasu and the Foresta di Burgos. In the centre of town is the parish church of **San Michele Arcangelo**, which has been rebuilt several times over the years. Inside is a curious clock driven by the weight of four cannonballs, shot at the town during the 1796 siege, when the government troops were driven out by the city's inhabitants. This episode is re-enacted every year during the traditional festival held on 31 August. On this day the largest pumpkin from the local kitchen gardens is awarded to the person who comes in last in the festival horse race as a facetious sign of recognition of the "valour" of the routed army. Until recently, this pumpkin was

rolled down the mountain to the valley to symbolize the government troops escaping from the local inhabitants.

In early September Bono plays host to the colourful *Fiera dei Prodotti Tipici Artigiani del Gocèano*, a fair featuring typical handicrafts from the Gocèano region.

Environs: From the Uccaidu pass, northwest of Bono, you can hike up the ridge to the summit of Monte Rasu at an altitude of 1,258 m (4,125 ft). From here there are magnificent sweeping views of the Foresta di Burgos and surrounding mountain range as well as most of Sardinia.

The countryside between Bono and Burgos

Burgos ❹

Road map C3. 🏛 *1,100.* ℹ *079 79 31 34.*

The hamlet of Burgos lies below a cone-shaped peak in the Gocèano mountains. The town was founded in 1353 by Mariano d'Arborea and is

The village of Burgos, dominated by the 12th-century castle

Small Giara horses in the Foresta di Burgos

dominated by the ruins of **Burgos Castle**, built in 1127. The castle was the scene of many battles between the Sardinian principalities and mainland colonists during the Middle Ages. It was from here that in 1478 Artaldo di Alagon's troops marched from the castle to the battle of Macomer, marking the start of Aragonese dominion. Inside the outer defensive walls, further fortifications surround a restored tower. The entrance to the tower was once through a wooden stairway that could be raised in case of a siege.

Environs: The **Foresta di Burgos**, 5 km (3 miles) northwest of Burgos, is a well-kept forested area with holm oak and cork oak trees, cedars, conifers and some chestnut trees. The area is also known for the small Sardinian Giara horses that graze in fenced-off pastures.

Ottana ❺

Road map C3. 🏘 *2,700.* 🏢 *Town Hall (0784 75 623).* 🎭 *Carnevale*

Ottana lies in the valley of the river Tirso, not far from the slopes of the Barbagia di Ollolai region. In the Middle

Ages the town was an important religious centre. On the southern outskirts of town is the church of **San Nicola**, once the cathedral of the regional diocese. It was built in 1150 in austere Romanesque style, with black and purple trachyte ashlars showing strong Pisan influence. Inside is a 14th-century polyptych showing the Madonna flanked by the bishop of Ottana and Mariano d'Arborea, count of Gocèano. In the apse is a 16th-century wooden crucifix.

San Nicola, near Ottana

Almost abandoned in the 16th century due to an outbreak of malaria, Ottana was chosen in the 1970s as an industrial development site,

Typical masked figures dressed for the Carnival at Ottana

promoted by ENI, the National Hydrocarbon Corporation. The industries have not produced the expected profits, however, and the ecological problems are so serious that the entire project is to be abandoned.

Carnival is a popular festival in Ottana, when locals dress in sheepskin and bells and wear bull-like masks *(see p29)*.

Ollolai ❻

Road map C3. 🏘 *1,800.* 🏢 *Town Hall (0784 51 051).* 🎭 *24 Aug: San Bartolomeo*

Asphodel, used in traditional basket-weaving at Ollolai

The village of Ollolai was once the medieval administrative centre of the Barbagia di Ollolai region, an area that included the northern part of Barbagia and still retains the name today. The town's decline began in 1490 after a terrible fire destroyed most of it and today it is a small hamlet.

Some original houses decorated with dark stone doorways are visible in the old centre and there are still a few craftsmen who weave the traditional asphodel baskets in their courtyards.

Environs: A short distance west of Ollolai is the church of **San Basilio**. A traditional rural religious festival is held here on 1 September. A rough road climbs up to S'Asisorgiu peak to an altitude of 1,127 m (3,700 ft). From here there are fabulous views of the surrounding mountain range and the summit is popularly known as "Sardinia's window".

Sarule seen from the nearby hills

Sarule ❼

Road map C3. 👥 *1,840.* 🛈 *Town Hall (0784 760 17).* 🎉 *8 Sep: Madonna di Gonare.*

Sarule is a village of medieval origin which has preserved its tradition of carpet-weaving. Along the main street you can still see the workshops where these vividly coloured carpets with stylized figures are woven on antique vertical looms and then sold on the premises.

Perched on a spur overlooking the village is the sanctuary of **Nostra Signora di Gonare**, one of the most sacred shrines in Sardinia. The church was built in the 13th century for the ruler of the principality, Gonario II di Torres, and by the 16th century it had already become a famous pilgrimage site. The sanctuary was enlarged in the 17th century with a dark stone exterior and austere buttresses.

To reach the sanctuary, a rough road heads east from Sarule and climbs up Monte Gonare for 4 km (2.5 miles). This granite rock mountain is interspersed with layers of limestone and outcrops of schist covered in vegetation. The mountain slopes are populated by many species of birds, including partridges, turtle doves, woodpeckers, shrikes and various birds of prey. The forest has holm oaks and maples, while in the spring the undergrowth is enlivened by brightly coloured cyclamen, peonies and morning glory. The road ends at an open space with pilgrims' houses *(cumbessias)*, and a winding footpath up the bluff through the holm oak forest leads to the sanctuary. From here there are marvellous views of Monte Ortobene towering over Nuoro, Monte Corrasi near Oliena, and the Gennargentu mountains in the distance.

From 5–8 September a lively festival takes place at the sanctuary for the Madonna di Gonare, to which pilgrims travel on foot from all of the neighbouring villages. As well as religious festivities, a horse race is held, and the square resounds with poetry readings and sacred songs sung in traditional dialect.

The sanctuary of Nostra Signora di Gonare at Sarule ❼

Mamoiada ❽

Road map D3. 👥 *2,700.* 🛈 *Town Hall (0784 560 23).* 🎉 *17 Jan, Carnival Sun & Shrove Tue: Mamuthones procession.*

Some old buildings, possibly of Aragonese origin, are still visible among the modern houses that line the main street of Mamoiada. In 1770 the town was mentioned by the Savoyard viceroy, Des Hayes, as a place of some interest with numerous vineyards and an exceptional number of sheep. Flocks are still taken every summer to the slopes of Barbagia di Ollolai to graze.

TRADITIONAL FESTIVALS IN THE BARBAGIA

S'Incontru, the procession held in the streets of Oliena on Easter day, commemorates the resurrection of Christ and his subsequent encounter with the Virgin Mary. On this occasion, and during the festivities in honour of San Lussorio on 21 August, you can admire the colourful traditional costumes and watch the impressive procession of horsemen through the streets of the town.

The *S'Incontru* procession

At Mamoiada the lively celebrations on the night of Sant'Antonio Abate (17 January), Shrove Tuesday and the last night of Carnival, all revolve around the figures of the *Mamuthones* and *Issohadores*. The former wear tragic masks and shepherds' garb, with a set of cow bells tied on their backs. The bells jangle in time with their rhythmical steps as they go through the village to the main square, where there is music and dancing all evening. The *Issohadores*, with their red waistcoats, are more colourful: they "capture" spectators and drag them inside the circles of the traditional round dance.

The carnival *Mamuthones* at Mamoiada

A typical street in the town of Oliena

Mamoiada is best known for the dark, forbidding masks of the *Mamuthones,* who appear in the village streets on the feast days of Sant'Antonio Abate (17 January), the Sunday of Carnival and in particular on Shrove Tuesday, during the Barbagia's most famous Carnival celebrations *(see p29).*

Environs: About 5 km (3 miles) southwest of Mamoiada, along a secondary road towards Gavoi, is the **Santuario di San Cosimo**. This typical rural church has a central structure surrounded by *cumbessias,* lodgings for pilgrims to the sanctuary. The present-day church dates from the 17th century and its main feature is the single nave. At the end of the nave, recent restoration has brought to light an Aragonese niche with columns and an architrave made of volcanic rock.

A further 6 km (4 miles) to the south is the **Santuario della Madonna d'Itria**, an imposing church with *cumbessias.* Here, on the last Sunday of July, there is a horse race around the church, known as *Sa Carrela.*

Oliena **9**

Road map D3. 🏚 *8,000.* ⬛ *Town Hall (0784 28 02 00).* ⬛ *Easter am: S'Incontru; 21 Aug: San Lussorio.*

The approach to Oliena towards evening, along the northern road from Nuoro, is an unforgettable sight. The lights of the town shine at the foot of the steep white mass of Supramonte, which rises

eastwards towards the Golfo di Orosei. The countryside is covered in vineyards, which yield the famous Sardinian wine Cannonau.

Some original houses, built around courtyards with external stairways and pergolas and brightly coloured rooms, are still visible along the narrow streets and alleyways. There are also several religious buildings, such as the church of **Santa Croce**, said to be the oldest in the town. Rebuilt in the 17th century, it has a bell tower decorated with an unusual trident motif.

The **Jesuit College** on Corso Vittorio Emanuele II is a reminder of the arrival of this religious order in Oliena. From the beginning of the 17th century onwards, the Jesuits encouraged the town's economy by promoting wine-making and the breeding of silkworms. Next door to the Jesuit college, the church of **Sant'Ignazio di Loyola** has wooden statues of Sant'Ignazio and San Francesco Saverio, as

well as an altarpiece depicting San Cristoforo.

Oliena, known for its good wine, is also famous for its jewellery, cakes and the traditional costumes worn by the women: a black shawl, interwoven with silk and gold, and a light blue blouse.

There are two important festivals at Oliena that end with impressive processions: *San Lussorio* in August and *S'Incontru* on Easter morning.

Environs: South of Oliena, it is possible to take various hiking tours on the rugged and spectacular rocks of the **Supramonte di Oliena**. Starting from the Monte Maccione refuge, you can cross the chain and descend into the Lanaittu valley floor.

The **Su Gologone** natural springs are 8 km (5 miles) east of Oliena. The waters, which have cut channels through the mountain rock, are refreshingly cool in summer and turn into an extremely cold, rushing torrent in winter. Su Gologone is the largest spring in Sardinia, with an average production of 300 litres (66 gallons) per second. It lies in a pleasant wooded area ideal for picnics in the shade.

For many years speleologists have been exploring the depths of the underground cave of **Grotta Sa Oche**, in the Supramonte mountains. Every year divers penetrate further underground into the Supramonte mountains to study the various aspects of this natural phenomenon.

The Su Gologone natural spring at the foot of Supramonte

Tiscali ⑩

A little over a century ago some woodcutters, travelling over the mountain range that dominates the Lanaittu valley, discovered a nuraghic settlement hidden in the depths of an enormous chasm in Monte Tiscali. The village of Tiscali, which had been inhabited up to the time of the Roman invasion, consists of a number of round dwellings with juniper wood architraves around the doors and roofs. Years of neglect have led to the partial deterioration of the site, but it is still one of the most exciting nuraghic finds in Sardinia, in particular because of its unique position. The climb to Tiscali can be hazardous and tiring, and is over rocky ground.

The Path to the Village
Red arrows on the rocks indicate the way to the village.

The chasm had no natural springs, so the inhabitants collected water that dripped down the walls of the rock.

Dwellings
Round nuraghic dwellings are still visible among the crumbling rocks and ruins.

Bronze Model
Cagliari's Museo Archeologico (see p58) has a model of the dwellings.

View of Monte di Tiscali
Hidden inside this 518-m (1,700-ft) high mountain, the nuraghic village of Tiscali was discovered in the 19th century. Archaeological excavations did not begin until many years later.

VISITORS' CHECKLIST

Road map D3. ◯ *9am–7pm (Oct–May: 5pm).* 🅿 📷 ℹ *Town Hall, Dorgali (0764 961 13) or Pro Loco, Dorgali (0784 933 05). The following organize tours and hikes:* **Cooperativa Enis** *Tel 0784 28 83 63* **www. coopehis.it;** **Gennargentu Escursioni** *Tel 0784 943 85* **www**.gennargentu.com; **Cooperativa Ghivine** *Tel 0784 967 21* **www**.ghivine.com

Entrance to the Chasm
The difficult terrain and steep walls were the best defence for the inhabitants of Tiscali.

TIPS FOR TRAVELLERS

From Oliena take the road east towards Dorgali. After about 5 km (3 miles), take the right-hand turn for Su Gologone. Just after the hotel of the same name (see p175), take the dirt road to the right that goes to the Lanaittu plain. Proceed along the floor of the valley (keeping to the left) until the road becomes too difficult for vehicles. Clear red arrows on the rocks and trees indicate the footpath to the chasm of Tiscali. The walk will take you about 3–4 hours and can be extremely difficult. It is highly advisable to go with a tour guide.

It is possible to make other trips in this area, and again it is recommended you go with a guide. Places to head for include the Gole di Su Gorroppu ravines, parts of the caves of Su Bentu, Sa Oche or S'Elicas Artas, or the climb down to the Codula di Luna valley (see p85).

The roofs were made of juniper wood.

The walls of the dwellings were made of limestone blocks.

THE NURAGHIC VILLAGE OF TISCALI

This reconstruction of the nuraghic village shows how the settlement would have looked. A crater opening allows natural light in and steps from the entrance made the descent easy.

MURALS IN SARDINIA

Sardinian murals began to appear on walls at Orgòsolo in the 1960s and soon became a feature of many of the island's villages and towns. The most famous of these is San Sperate *(see p62)*, the home town of the artist Pinuccio Sciola. The themes of this particular artistic genre are satirical, political or social. The styles vary greatly but are always characterized by bright colours. Even in the open

Mural at Orgòsolo

country you may come across faces, shapes, hands and penetrating stares painted onto the boulders, rocks or cliffs. The *Associazione Italiana Paesi Dipinti* (Italian Association of Painted Towns) was founded to preserve and publicize the towns with these murals and also to encourage creativity and cultural exchange between different regions.

Mural on a wall at San Sperate

A mural painted on rock near Orgòsolo

Orgòsolo ⓫

Road map D3. 🚶 *4,800.*
🛈 *Town Hall (0784 40 09 01).*
🎎 *first Sun of Jun: Sant'Anania;*
15 Aug: Festa dell'Assunta.
www.comune.orgosolo.it

This characteristic village in the interior of the island has been compared to an eagle's nest and a fortress, perched precariously on the mountainside. The villagers are known as rugged and hardy shepherds, proud of their lifestyle and traditions. Rampant banditry in the 1960s was documented in Vittorio De Seta's film *Bandits at Orgòsolo,* in which the hard life of the shepherds and their mistrust of the government is narrated with cool detachment. The passion of the locals for social and political issues is also visible in the hundreds of murals painted on the walls of houses and on the rocks around Orgòsolo. The images describe the harsh life of the shepherds, their struggles to keep their land and Sardinian traditions, as well as injustices committed in other parts of the world.

Simple low stone houses line the steep and narrow streets of the town and some original features are still visible on a few isolated houses. On Corso Repubblica, the church of

San Pietro retains its 15th-century bell tower. Traditional dress, a brightly coloured apron embroidered with geometric patterns and a saffron-yellow headscarf, is still worn by some local women.

In summer two popular local festivals draw large crowds: the Assumption Day Festival on 15 August and Sant'Anania's feast day on the first Sunday of June.

Environs: Just outside Orgòsolo is the 17th-century church of **Sant'Anania**. The church was built where the saint's relics are said to have been found. Orgòsolo is an ideal starting point for excursions up to the surrounding Supramonte mountains, where open pastures are interspersed with dense forests of oak.

Sculpted detail on San Gavino, Gavoi

A road leads to the **Funtana Bona**, 18 km (11 miles) south of Orgòsolo. These natural springs emerge at an altitude of 1,082 m (3,550 ft), at the foot of the limestone peak of **Monte Novo San Giovanni**, 1,316 m (4,316 ft) high. From here it is also possible to reach the shady **Foresta di Montes**, a forest of holm oak that stretches out to the south.

Gavoi ⓬

Road map C3. 🚶 *3,100.* 🛈 *Town Hall (0784 52 90 80).* 🎎 *last Sun of Jul: rural festival at Sanctuary of the Madonna d'Itria; second Sun after Easter: Sant'Antioco's feast day.*

For many centuries this village was famous in Sardinia for the production of harnesses and bridles. Today its most characteristic product is cheese, including *fiore sardo* pecorino, made from sheep's milk *(see p181).* The centre of town is dominated by the pink façade of the 14th-century church of **San Gavino**, which overlooks the square of the same name. Some of Gavoi's oldest and most characteristic streets begin here. A stroll down these narrow alleys will reveal historic buildings with dark stone façades and balconies overflowing with flowers, such as the two-storey building on Via San Gavino.

In the little church of **Sant' Antioco**, in the upper part of town, dozens of ex votos in gold and silver filigree are pinned to the wall. There is also a fine statue of the saint, whose feast day is celebrated the second Sunday after Easter.

View of the Lago di Gusana seen from Gavoi

Fonni ⑬

Road map D3. 🏘 *4,600.* ℹ *Town Hall (0784 572 85).* 📅 *first Sun & Mon in Jun: Madonna dei Martiri.* **www**.comune-fonni.it

Fonni is one of the highest towns in Sardinia, lying at an altitude of 1,000 m (3,280 ft). Its economy relies on tradition and tourism, offering locally made produce, such as traditional sweets, as well as fabrics and rugs known for their fine workmanship. Although recent new building has slightly diminished its charm, at first sight the town gives the impression of sprouting from the mountainside.

On the edge of town is the Franciscan **Madonna dei Martiri** complex, which dates from the 17th century. Inside is a curious statue of the Virgin Mary made from pieces of ancient Roman sculptures.

The town's major festival is held in mid-June to celebrate the return of the shepherds and their flocks from the winter pastures.

On the road towards Gavoi, 4 km (2 miles) west of Fonni, is the **Lago di Gusana**, a large artificial lake. Its tranquil shores, surrounded by holm oaks, make it a popular spot.

Teti ⑭

Road map C4. 🏘 *900.* ℹ *Town Hall (0784 680 23).* 📅 *third Sun in Sep: San Sebastiano.* **www**.comune.telti.ss.it

Perched on the rocky mountains that dominate Lago di Cucchinadorza, the village of Teti distinguishes itself by its small museum, the **Museo Archeologico Comprensoriale**. Run by a team of enterprising young local people, the museum illustrates the history of the area's ancient nuraghic settlements (in particular the village of S'Urbale and the sacred precinct of Abini). The display cases contain pieces found during excavations, including everyday objects used by the nuraghic people. One hall has a reconstruction of a round dwelling dating from about 1000 BC.

Bronze statuettes found at Teti, Cagliari Museo Archeologico

Inside are spinning tools, pots, small axes and granite mills. In the middle of the house is the area used as a fireplace.

The halls of the lower floor are used for temporary exhibitions on local culture and traditions, such as traditional costumes and handicrafts.

Environs: About one kilometre (half a mile) southwest of Teti is the entrance to the nuraghic archaeological site of **S'Urbale**. The village was inhabited from 1200 to 900 BC, and the ruins of many prehistoric dwellings are still visible. The ancient nuraghic village of **Abini** is found 10 km (6 miles) to the north of Teti.

🏛 **Museo Archeologico Comprensoriale**
Tel *0784 681 20.* 🕐 *9am–12:30pm, 3–8pm (Oct–May: 3–5:30pm).*
📷 📷 ♿

FORESTA DI MONTES

At the foot of the rocky bluffs of Monte Novo San Giovanni and Monte Fumai is the largest holm oak forest in Europe. Although many trees were destroyed in the past by fires – often started by shepherds in order to acquire more grazing land – the vast forest is once again increasing in size thanks to replanting, and today it attracts visitors

Monte Novo San Giovanni

from all over the island. Even in the heat of the summer, a walk through this area and the plateau around the River Olai is very enjoyable, as the dense forest offers shade from the sun and there is a chance to see sheep and pigs, as well as asphodels in bloom. The many footpaths around the Funtana Bona forest headquarters offer opportunities for hiking and mountain-biking.

The rural Sanctuary of San Mauro, near Sòrgono

Sòrgono ⓰

Road map C4. 🏛 2,100. 🛈 Town Hall (0784 62 25 20). 📅 26 May: San Mauro feast day.

The Pisan fountain at Sòrgono

Set in a densely cultivated area of orchards and vineyards, famous for producing Cannonau wine (see p182), Sòrgono has been an important town since Roman times. Today it is the administrative centre of the Mandrolisai area.

Two rather dilapidated sites in the town are worth a visit; the 17th-century **Casa Carta**, featuring a typical Aragonese window, and a medieval fountain of Pisan origin.

Just west of town is one of the most interesting and oldest rural sanctuaries in Sardinia, the **Santuario di San Mauro**. This imposing church is surrounded by the traditional *cumbessias*, the houses used by the pilgrims during their stay at the sanctuary. The building is a mixture of local architectural features and the characteristic Gothic-Aragonese style.

A fine stairway flanked by two stone lions leads to the grey trachyte façade, which boasts a beautiful carved Gothic rose window. Numerous inscriptions are recorded on the stones of the church, some many centuries old and others more recent, carved by pilgrims to commemorate their visits to the sanctuary.

The interior of San Mauro has a single vault and is interrupted only by an arch that leads into the presbytery. Here there are a Baroque altar and some statues.

Various buildings were added to the original church to accommodate pilgrims and offer them adequate dining facilities, in particular during the San Mauro feast day. One of Sardinia's most important livestock and horse fairs used to be held on this day in the grounds of the sanctuary.

Not far from the church are two further sites worth visiting: the **Tomba di Giganti di Funtana Morta** (Tomb of the Giants) and, on a hilltop overlooking the church, the **Talei Nuraghe**, built with large granite stones and partly into the surrounding rock.

Làconi ⓰

Road map C4. 🏛 2,500. 🛈 Town Hall (0782 86 62 00).

The town of Làconi is built around a rocky spur of the Sarcidano mountain range and boasts beautiful panoramic views. Làconi also features the ruins of **Castello Aymerich** in the park above the town. Only a single tower from the original fortress, built in 1053, remains. The rest of the castle includes later additions such as the 15th-century hall and the 17th-century portico. The magnificent park around the castle includes a botanical garden and waterfall, and today it is a popular destination for walks and picnics.

Once the seat of the local noble overlords, Làconi has preserved the Neo-Classical **Palazzo Aymerich**, built in the first half of the 1800s by architect Gaetano Cima from Cagliari. Near the 16th-century parish church is the birthplace and small museum of **Sant' Ignazio da Làconi**, a miracle worker who lived here in the second half of the 18th century. There is also a monument in his honour in the square. The **Museo Archeologico**, on Via Amiscora, as a collection of 40 pre-nuraghic menhir statues.

Environs: The area around Làconi has many prehistoric remains. Among these are the anthropomorphic menhirs, single stones on which ancient sculptors carved human features. These can be seen at Perda Iddocca and Genna 'e Aidu, but it is advisable to be accompanied by a local guide.

The ruins of Castello Aymerich at Làconi

The Cagliari–Sòrgono Railway ⑰

The train ride between Cagliari and Sòrgono is a slow approach to the foothills of the Gennargentu mountain range (the journey takes four-and-a-half hours, while you can cover the same distance by car in two hours). The narrow-gauge railway nevertheless offers a scenic route through spectacular mountains and an insight into travel from another age. DH Lawrence described the trip in his book *Sea and Sardinia* (1921). In the first stretch, up to Mandas, the train goes over the rolling hills of Trexenta. It then climbs up to the road house at Ortuabis, an area of thick vegetation with a backdrop of mountain peaks, and on beyond Belvì through a wood of dense tree heathers.

Lush scenery *and waterfalls characterize the stretch between Làconi and Meana.*

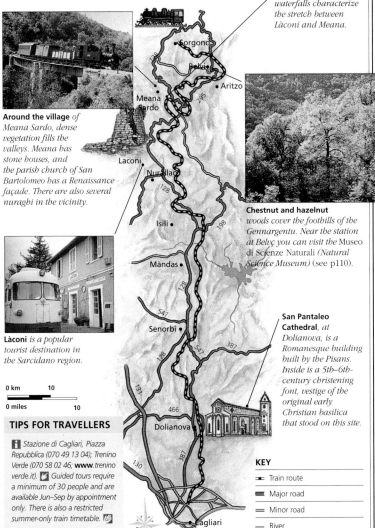

Around the village *of Meana Sardo, dense vegetation fills the valleys. Meana has stone houses, and the parish church of San Bartolomeo has a Renaissance façade. There are also several nuraghi in the vicinity.*

Chestnut and hazelnut *woods cover the foothills of the Gennargentu. Near the station at Belvì you can visit the* Museo di Scienze Naturali *(Natural Science Museum) (see p110).*

Làconi *is a popular tourist destination in the Sarcidano region.*

San Pantaleo Cathedral, *at Dolianova, is a Romanesque building built by the Pisans. Inside is a 5th–6th-century christening font, vestige of the original early Christian basilica that stood on this site.*

0 km   10
0 miles   10

TIPS FOR TRAVELLERS

🏠 *Stazione di Cagliari, Piazza Repubblica (070 49 13 04); Trenino Verde (070 58 02 46;* **www.***trenino verde.it).* 📷 *Guided tours require a minimum of 30 people and are available Jun–Sep by appointment only. There is also a restricted summer-only train timetable.* 🚂

KEY

▬ Train route
▬ Major road
▬ Minor road
— River

Map labels: Sòrgono, Belvì, Aritzo, Meana Sardo, Laconi, Nurallao, Isili, Mandas, Senorbì, Dolianova, Cagliari

Canoeing on the Flumendosa river near Aritzo

Aritzo ⑱

Road map C4. 🏔 *1,700.* 🛈 *Town Hall (0784 62 72 23).* 🎉 *second Sun in Aug: Sant'Isidoro; first weekend Nov: chestnut festival.*

The small town of Aritzo was once famous for selling snow, at a very high price, packed in straw-lined boxes and transported throughout the island during the hot summer months. Under Aragonese rule, the town had the privilege of being governed by its own inhabitants, locally elected.

There are still many traces of the old town. Some houses retain typical stone façades and long, wooden balconies. Among the most important buildings are the **Casa degli Arangino** (in Neo-Gothic style) and the impressive 17th-century stone **Aritzo prison** on Via Maggiore.

The market for snow no longer exists, but the town has continued its tradition of making wooden furniture, such as hand-carved wedding chests. These are sold from the craftsmen's workshops.

The good climate, the high altitude and panoramic views make Aritzo a pleasant tourist destination in the summer. Rodeos are a popular attraction outside town and interesting walking tours and horseback rides take place

towards the Gennargentu massif and the upper Flumendosa river valley. Here canoeing on the river is a popular activity.

Environs:
Just north of Aritzo is the **Tacco di Texile**, a vertical limestone pinnacle, 975 m (3,200 ft) high, in the shape of a mushroom. From here there are spectacular views of the mountains of the Barbagia region.

Wedding chest made by Aritzo craftsmen

During the Middle Ages, the humble saint Efisio lived in this area. For many years he preached to the local inhabitants and eventually converted them to Christianity.

The rodeo held near Aritzo

Belvì ⑲

Road Map C4. 🏔 *810.* 🛈 *Town Hall (0784 62 92 16).* 🎉 *28 Aug: Sant'Agostino feast day.*

The village of Belvì lies in a dominating position overlooking the Iscra river valley, which is full of fields of hazelnut trees and orchards.

In the past it must have been an important economic and trading centre, as the surrounding mountain region, Barbagia di Belvì, has also adopted the name.

The narrow-gauge railway which connects Cagliari and Sòrgono runs along the stretch of road near the village. The route goes through magnificent scenery as well as tackling a thousand tortuous bends and high viaducts *(see p109)*.

In the village, several old houses are still visible. One of these, on the main street, Via Roma, houses the private **Museo di Scienze Naturali** (Natural Science Museum). Founded in 1980 by a group of enthusiasts (including a German naturalist who lived in Belvì for almost ten years), the museum has interesting palaeontology and mineralogy departments, as well as occasional exhibitions of its collection of typical Sardinian fauna and insects.

🏛 **Museo di Scienze Naturali**
Via San Sebastiano. *Tel 0784 62 92 63.* ⏱ *by appt only.* 📷 📹

Overlooking Dèsulo

Dèsulo ⑳

Road map C4. 🏘 *3,200.* 🛈 *Town Hall (0784 61 92 11).* 🎉 *second Sun of Pentecost, Corpus Domini.* **www**.comune.desulo.nu.it

Perched at an altitude of 895 m (2,900 ft) on the slopes of Gennargentu, the village of Dèsulo was not converted to Christianity or ruled by outsiders until the 7th century. Unfortunately, unregulated building development has had a devastating impact on the village and has almost eliminated the traditional schist houses. It is still quite common, however, to see villagers in traditional dress.

The local economy is based on sheep-raising and the ancient tradition of cultivating the chestnut groves and mountain pastures. Until quite recently, the inhabitants, skilled in wood-carving, used to travel to the various markets and fairs throughout Sardinia to sell their hand-made spoons, cutting boards and other wooden objects, as well as locally grown chestnuts.

The parish church of **Sant'Antonio Abate**, and other churches such as the **Madonna del Carmelo** and **San Sebastiano**, are worth a visit for a series of colourful wooden statues sculpted in the mid-1600s. But the main reason to visit this village is its natural scenery and the splendid views of the highest

peak on the island. There are plans to give the area National Park status, incorporating it into the Gennargentu National Park. Dèsulo is a favourite destination for hikers keen to climb up Gennargentu and Punta La Marmora *(see p82).* As groups of walkers become more common, a number of hotels and hostels catering for this new form of tourism have been built.

Tonara ㉑

Road map C4. 🏘 *2,600.* 🛈 *Town Hall (0784 63 799).* 🎉 *second Sun in Aug: Sagra del Torrone.*

In the past the economy of Tonara was based largely on the chestnut and hazelnut groves that surround the town, and on other products typical of a mountain environment. Since tourism discovered this side of the mountain, the local production of cow bells, *torrone* (nougat) and hand-woven rugs has become famous. During the local festivals in the town square, blacksmiths forge the celebrated Tonara bells by hammering

Chestnuts

the metal on specially shaped stone moulds. The inhabitants will be more than willing to tell you how to arrange to see craftsmen at work and purchase traditional rugs. The atmosphere of a typical mountain village can still be seen in the shepherds' houses, which have not changed in over a century.

Tonara is another popular starting point for excursions to the Gennargentu massif. One of the most interesting is the tour to **Punta Mungianeddu** (1,467 m, 4,800 ft). A road climbs through holm oak and chestnut woods to reach the summit, from which there are magnificent views.

Stone used as a mould for making cow bells at Tonara

SARDINIAN NOUGAT

Nougat *(torrone* in Italian) is one of the most common sweets in the culture and tradition of central Sardinia. Every local fair or festival will have stalls selling the delicious, hard nougat made in Tonara, Dèsulo or one of the other mountain villages. The main ingredients are almonds, walnuts, hazelnuts, various qualities of honey and egg whites (in some cases the yolk is also used). Cooking – during which the mixture has to be stirred continuously – takes more than five hours. The different styles of nougat are created by variations in the type of honey, the flavour of the nuts or number of eggs used. There are many nougat confectioners and, no matter how big or small the premises, visitors are always welcome to watch the preparation and choose a favourite flavour. Blocks of nougat are cut for you while you wait. One excellent outlet is Signora Anna Peddes in Tonara, at No. 6 Via Roma; she makes particularly delicious and fragrant nougat.

The Nougat Festival at Tonara

THE WESTERN COAST

*E*ach year thousands of flamingoes choose the marshes and wetlands of western Sardinia as their favoured place for overwintering, creating clouds of pink against the vegetation of the maquis. The coastline is vulnerable to the cool mistral, and years of strong winds have sculpted massive dunes along the shore.

The natural harbours and fertile land in this part of Sardinia have attracted foreign ships for centuries. The Phoenicians discovered the safe harbours of Sulki and Tharros as well as the great commercial potential of the obsidian from the slopes of Monte Arci. The Romans and Spaniards also left their mark at Bosa, the latter transforming Alghero into a Catalonian town.

The area around Oristano is one of the largest wetland areas in Europe. As well as freshwater pools and marshy lakes, there are saltwater lagoons, sandbanks and sand dunes. A combination of the waters of the Tirso river and the mistral is responsible for this particular ecosystem. Over the course of centuries massive dunes have formed at the river mouth, whipped up by the violent winds from the west, effectively blocking the flow of water out to sea. At the beginning of the 20th century, this marshland was infested with malaria-transmitting mosquitoes but, thanks to land reclamation in the 1930s and the Rockefeller-funded anti-malaria campaign, the soil can now be cultivated without risk. Today this is one of the most fertile areas in Sardinia, producing spring vegetables for sale to mainland Italy, as well as olives and citrus fruits. Vineyards cover the land around Oristano and near the beaches in the Sinis region, yielding quantities of white Vernaccia wine. The coastline is lovely – small beaches and seaside resorts nestle against sand dunes shaded by thick pine forests. Some beaches are made of grains of translucent quartz, which suits wild lilies. Some stretches of cliff, wild and rocky, can only be reached by boat or after a lengthy trek.

The historic town of Bosa seen from the Temo river

◁ **A lateen-sail dinghy off the coast near Stintino**

Exploring the Western Coast

The western coast of Sardinia offers a wide variety of activities – whether you prefer to explore the towns and countryside, or relax on a beach at places like Is Arenas, Is Arutas or Bosa Marina. There are extensive nature reserves teeming with wildlife, and fortified cities with Romanesque cathedrals. One of Sardinia's best-known wines, Vernaccia, is made in this region, from the vineyards north of Oristano. At Tharros you can explore the ruins of a Phoenician coastal town, founded in the 8th century BC. The relatively short distances between sights and the flattish terrain, especially in the Sinis and Campidano di Oristano regions, make this area ideal for cycling tours. Walkers may prefer the hiking trails and riders can choose from the bridle paths that converge at the riding school in Ala Birdi. At the headland of Capo Caccia you can explore caves and grottoes, some of which extend for kilometres under the cliff.

Limestone rocks at Capo Caccia and the island of Foradada

SEE ALSO

- *Where to Stay* p176
- *Where to Eat* p186

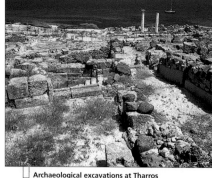

Archaeological excavations at Tharros

View from Capo Falcone towards the island of Asinara

SIGHTS AT A GLANCE

Traditional fisherman's house, San Giovanni di Sinis

0 km   10

0 miles   10

KEY

—— Major road

—— Secondary road

—— Minor road

—— Scenic route

---- Main railway

—— Minor railway

△ Summit

GETTING AROUND

The coastal road is quite good but not especially fast; the same is true of the roads connecting the villages and those used for mountain tours. The SS131, known as the Carlo Felice road, goes from Oristano to Sassari. There are good railway connections from Oristano to Cagliari, Olbia and Porto Torres, the main ports for ferry connections.

Street-by-Street: Alghero ❶

42

Old street
number

In the early 12th century, the aristocratic
Doria family from Genoa decided to
establish two strongholds in Sardinia, which
became Castelgenovese (now Castelsardo) and
Alghero. Because of the abundant
quantities of algae off the coast, the latter
city was named Alquerium – *s'Alighera* in
Sardinian dialect and *l'Alquer* in Catalan.
After a very short period of Pisan rule, Alghero was
conquered by the Aragonese in 1353, and has always
been the most Spanish city on the island. The old centre
lies within the ancient fortified quarter and the local
economy is based on tourism and handicrafts –
particularly jewellery and other items made of coral.

★ San Francesco
*Parts of this jewel of Catalan
architecture date back to the fi
half of the 14th century. The
lovely cloister becomes an open
air concert venue in summer.*

Sign in Catalan
*The street signs in Alghero
are still written in Catalan.*

Porta Terra tower

The Maddalena tower
and ramparts

PIAZZA
CIVICA

MAGELLANO

VIA ROMA

BASTIONI

Alghero Marina
*Via Garibaldi starts at the marina and
runs alongside Alghero's long, sandy
beach towards the lido and Fertilia.*

BASTIONI

Torre di
Sant'Erasmo

Torre della
Polveriera

★ Duomo Doors
*Built in the mid-
1500s, the carved
doorway, together
with the bell tower, is
the oldest part of
Alghero's cathedral.*

KEY

– – – Suggested route

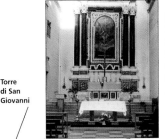

Torre
di San
Giovanni

San Michele
This Baroque church contains two stucco altars dating from the second half of the 17th century.

VISITORS' CHECKLIST

Road map B2. 41,148.
Alghero Fertilia, 24 km
(15 miles) N. 079 97 90 54.

Torre dello Sperone
This is one of the towers in the walls surrounding Alghero. It overlooks Piazza Sulis, the heart of city life.

Chiesa della Misericordia

VIA DELLA MISERICORDIA
VIA C. ALBERTO
COLOMBO
BASTIONI
VIA CAVOUR
POLO

Torre San Giacomo

Via Carlo Alberto is the central shopping street in the city. In the summer months craftsmen set out their coral jewellery to tempt visitors to buy.

Chiesa del Carmelo

The Al Tuguri Restaurant
This small restaurant in the historic centre of Alghero offers some of the best food in Sardinia. Al Tuguri specializes in fresh fish cooked according to old Catalan recipes.

| 0 metres | 50 |
| 0 yards | 50 |

★ Ramparts
Positioned between the old city and the sea, the ramparts are now popular places for strolling, especially on warm evenings.

STAR SIGHTS

★ Duomo Doors

★ San Francesco

★ Ramparts

Exploring Alghero

Despite the considerable damage wrought by Allied bombardments in World War II, the heart of the old city is, for the most part, intact and can easily be explored on foot. The main roads from Bosa (to the south) and Sassari (to the northwest) lead to the city walls, and the best way to explore is to leave your car outside and walk around the narrow, high-sided streets of the old city. Strongly influenced by Spanish culture, Alghero remains the most Spanish city in Sardinia. The Alghero dialect is closely related to that of Catalonia, so much so that since 1970, street signs have been printed in Italian and Catalan, and you are likely to hear as much Catalan spoken on the streets as Italian.

🏯 Porta a Terra
Piazza Porta a Terra.
This 14th-century city gate now has a rather stranded air, as most of the associated fortifications were demolished to make room for present-day Via Sassari. The gate was once known as Torre degli Ebrei (dels Hebreus in Cata-lan), or Tower of the Jews, because of the contribution made by the Jewish community to Catalan king Pietro III's conquest of the city. The tower was originally one of two gates. A drawbridge linked Porta a Terra and the large Gothic arch which is now a war memorial. The ground floor, covered by a stone vault, is now used as a small exhibition centre.

A window at Palazzo d'Albis

🏯 Torre di San Giacomo
Situated in front of the 17th-century church of Carmen, on the waterfront, is the restored Torre di

San Giacomo. It differs from the other towers in Alghero with its unique octagonal form. It is also known as the Torre dei Cani (the Dogs' Tower) reflecting its earlier use as an enclosure for the stray dogs of the town.

🏯 Bastione and Forte de la Magdalena
Around sunset locals and tourists alike enjoy the pleasant stroll along the seafront. Starting from the south, Lungomare Dante is followed by Lungomare Cristoforo Colombo and Lungomare Marco Polo, which has a series of ram-parts with towers (the Torre di San Giacomo, the Mirador rampart, the Torre de la Polvorera, the Torre de Castilla), leading to the port. Not far from the steps which run from the seafront to the old Porta a Mare city gate, is Forte de la Magdalena, the city's most important

The 15th-century Torre di San Giacomo

Spanish fortification. On its walls a plaque commemorates Giuseppe Garibaldi's landing here on 14 August 1855.

🏯 Palazzo d'Albis
Piazza Civica (*Plaça de la Dressana*).
This 16th-century palace with twin lancet windows is also known as Palazzo de Ferrera. It is a rare example of Catalan civic architecture, and is famous for having hosted Charles V in October 1541. The emperor stopped at

The old town, Alghero

Alghero with his fleet on the way to Algiers, and was very flattering in his reactions to the city. According to tradition, the emperor spoke to the populace from the balcony of Palazzo d'Albis, and had the following to say about the city: "Bonita, por mi fé, y bien assentada". ("Beautiful, by my faith, and quite solid") and told the inhabitants "Estade todos caballeros" ("You are all gentlemen"). The monarch's sojourn ended with a massive requisition of cattle, which he needed for the Spanish troops. The animals were then slaughtered after an impromptu bullfight, held by the palazzo in Piazza Civica.

🏛 Cattedrale di Santa Maria
Piazza Duomo. **Tel** *079 97 92 22.*
⭕ *6:30am–noon, 5–8pm.*
The doorway of Alghero's Neoclassical Cathedral opens out onto the small Piazzetta Duomo. The cathedral, dedicated to Santa Maria, was first built in the 14th century. In the mid-1500s the building was restructured in the Catalan-inspired late Gothic

View of the harbour and broad seafront in Alghero

style. The unusual octagonal bell tower dates from the same period.

In the interior there is a striking difference between the layout of the central part, which is late Renaissance, and that of the 16th-century Gothic presbytery. Items of Catalan jewellery are on display in the sacristy.

Displays of coral jewellery

🏛 Via Principe Umberto

This narrow street, which begins at the Cathedral, was one of the main arteries in the old walled city. Of interest are the Casa Doria (16th century), Palazzo della Curia and, in Piazza Vittorio Emanuele II, the 19th-century Savoyard Teatro Civico.

🏛 San Francesco and Cloister

Via Carlo Alberto. *Tel 079 97 92 58.*
☐ *7:30am–noon, 4:30–8pm.*
San Francesco may very well be the most important Catalan monument in the whole of Sardinia. Built at the end of the 1300s and then partially rebuilt when some of the structure collapsed, the church

displays different stylistic influences. The bell tower is Gothic, with a hexagonal body set on a square base. The cupola, dressed with multi-coloured tiles, has become the symbol of Alghero.

The two-aisle, white sandstone interior still has Baroque altars made of carved wood and, under the star-spangled Gothic vault of the presbytery, there is an 18th-century altar. The sculptures include a *Dead Christ* and *Christ at the Column*.

The cloister, accessible from the sacristy, is well worth a visit. It is an eclectic sandstone construction, built in different periods. The lower part dates from the 14th century, while the upper part was added in the 1700s. The 22 columns are in two sections, with round or polygonal bases and sculpted capitals. During the summer music season, the Estate Musicale Internazionale di Alghero, concerts and other cultural events are held in these lovely surroundings. In other seasons of the year events and art exhibitions are held in the old refectory.

The Beaches

The port of Alghero has never been an important trading place, partly because of its position and the low-lying coast. There is no heavy industry here and, as a result, the sea is not polluted. A series of resorts can be found just outside the old town. The best-known beach is the Bombarde, a strip of pure white sand bordered by crystal-clear sea, 8 km (5 miles) northwest

of the city. Another good beach nearby is the Lazzaretto, which owes its name to the hospital for the poor which was there during the period of the black plague. When the weather is clear, the impressive vertical profile of Capo Caccia stands out on the horizon.

Environs: To the north is the coastal town of **Fertilia**, a small yacht harbour built during the Fascist era as the centre of the land reclamation programme. Nearby you can still see the 13 arches of the Roman bridge at the ancient city of Carbia. At one time the bridge connected Carbia to Portus Nympharum, now Porto Conte bay. A few minutes away stands the site of **Palmavera Nuraghe**. This prehistoric complex contains two towers and a courtyard surrounded by a barbican.

East of Alghero are the **Necropolis Anghelu Ruju**, the largest pre-nuraghic burial place of its kind in Sardinia, and the Sella & Mosca vineyard and museum (*see p189*).

Entranceway to the prehistoric site of Palmavera Nuraghe

Porto Torres ❷

Road map B2. 👥 22,000.
ℹ️ 079 51 50 00.

The chief port in northern
Sardinia lies in the Golfo
dell'Asinara. Porto Torres was
known to the Romans as
Turris Libisonis, and was once
a prosperous colony. Trade
with the city of Kàralis
(today's Cagliari) was carried
out along the main road on
the island. Relations with
Rome were very close, as can
be seen from the ancient
mosaics at the Foro delle
Corporazioni in Ostia Antica.

After a lengthy period of
decline that began in the
Middle Ages, Porto Torres
began to recover in the 19th
century, when it became the
port for Sassari, and again in
the 20th century with the development of local industries.

The basilica of **San Gavino**
is one of the most important
Romanesque churches
in Sardinia, built in
the Pisan style
in 1111.
Noteworthy
elements are
the portal in
the northern
façade, with
its 15th-century
bas relief, and
the other Gothic
doorway, which
shows Catalan
influences.

Inside there is a crypt, with
access to an area of late
Roman-Early Christian ruins,
as well as the 18th-century
statues of the martyrs Gavino,
Proto and Gianuario, and a
medieval inscription celebrating emperor Constantine.

The **Terme Centrali**
archaeological area presents a
reasonably faithful picture of
an ancient Roman quarter,
and the **Antiquarium
Turritano** contains finds
from the excavations here.
Not far away, the 135-m
(440-ft), seven-arched **Ponte
Romano** (Roman bridge)
crosses the Mannu river.

Environs: A short distance
from here lies one of the
most interesting sites in
ancient Sardinia, the pre-

San Gavino, in Porto Torres

nuraghic **Santuario di Monte
d'Accoddi**. From Porto Torres,
head towards Sassari along the
SS131; a short distance after
the Sorso junction (at kilometre
marker 222.3) a signposted
road leads to the archaeological site. The sanctuary
dates from the Copper Age
(2450–1850 BC) and provides
the only example of a megalithic altar in the entire western
Mediterranean. The
shape is that of a
truncated pyramid
with a trapezoid
base, supported
by walls of
stone blocks.
On the
southern side,
a ramp leads to
the top, about 10
m (33 ft) high,
while the base is
about 30 m by 38 m
(98 ft by 124 ft).

Around the altar you can
see foundations for houses,
some sacrificial stone slabs
and fallen menhirs. A group
of *domus de janas* (rock-cut
tombs) was once part of this
complex. The material found

**Gold bracelet from the
Porto Torres excavations**

at this site, including ceramics,
is on display at the Museo
Nazionale in Sassari (*see p163*).

🏛 **Antiquarium Turritano**
Tel *079 51 44 33 or 333 254 13 14.*
⏰ *9am–7:30pm Tue–Sun.* 🈵 🎫 ♿
⛪ **Santuario di
Monte d'Accoddi**
⏰ *9am–4:30pm (Apr–Oct: to 8:30pm).*
Tel *328 483 99 95.* 🈵 🎫 📷

Stintino ❸

Road map B2. 👥 1,200. ℹ️ *Town
Hall (079 52 30 53).* 📅 *end Aug: Vela
Latina; 8 Sep: Santissima Maria Imma-
colata* **www**.comune.stintino.ss.it

The road to Capo Falcone,
the northwestern tip of
Sardinia, passes by the large
wind turbines at the Alta
Nurra ecological energy plant.
Beyond this is the pleasant
fishing village of Stintino
(named from the Sardinian
word *s'isthintinu*, or narrow
passageway, the traditional
name for the inlet where the
village lies). Now a holiday
town, Stintino was once
important for its tuna fishing
grounds, off the island of
Asinara. In the summer the
two ports, Portu Mannu and
Portu Minori, have facilities
for aquatic sports of all kinds.
The long, sandy beach is the
most accessible in the area
and very popular.

North of Stintino, the road
skirts the coastline as far as
Capo Falcone. The place is
still "defended" by a tower on
its highest point and by the
two Spanish fortifications at
Pelosa and Isola Piana, in the
inlet of Fornelli, opposite
the island of Asinara.

Portu Mannu, one of the two harbours in Stintino

The barren cliffs on the island of Asinara

Parco Nazionale dell'Asinara ❹

Road map B1. 📋 *079 50 33 88 or 800 561 166.* 🖼️ 🎫 *compulsory.* **www**.parcoasinara.it

This rugged island, once home to the Fornelli maximum-security prison, became a National Park in 1997. Asinara is less than 18 km (11 miles) long and 7 km (4 miles) wide and ends at the headland of Scomunica. The island's ecosystem is unique in the entire western Mediterranean and includes rare and endangered animal species.

In fact, the pristine coastline and lack of traffic on its 51 sq km (19 sq miles) make Asinara an ideal refuge for raptors, various species of sea birds, moufflons and wild boar. There is also a rare species of small endemic albino donkey, after which the island must have been named (*asino* meaning donkey). The rocky, volcanic terrain supports a holm oak forest, and the typical low-level maquis brush shields numbers of rare plants.

As a protected area, the island cannot be visited unaccompanied. Day boat trips start at Stintino and Porto Torres. Tours are by bus, on foot or, for the most comprehensive, by offroad vehicle.

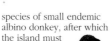

Albino donkey from Asinara

Argentiera ❺

Road map B2.

Many places in Sardinia still carry reminders of the island's former mining industries. At Argentiera, not far from the modern town of Palmadula, the ancient Romans, and the Pisans in the Middle Ages, dedicated themselves to mining the precious metal that gave its name to the area (*argento* means silver).

In the 19th century, mining complexes, with wooden and masonry buildings, were constructed along the coast, so that the mined silver could then be transported by sea to other destinations, where it could be processed and eventually sold. In recent years ambitious restoration and restructuring projects, many of which are yet to be completed, have changed the face of the town, but it still remains one of the most fascinating examples of industrial archaeology in Sardinia.

In the summer, the tranquil bay at Argentiera, with its crystal-clear water, is a great favourite with visitors.

The old mine buildings at Argentiera

Capo Caccia ❻

Towering above the sea, the Capo Caccia promontory, with a lighthouse perched on the outermost point, offers wonderful views of Alghero. Wild pigeons, swifts, peregrine falcons and herring gulls nest in the crevices and gullies of the precipitous cliffs. On the western side of the headland – opposite the barren profile of the island of Foradada – 656 steep steps (known as the Escala del Cabirol, or Roe-deer's Staircase) take you down the cliff to the fascinating caves of the Grotta di Nettuno (Neptune's Grotto). The cave can also be reached in about three hours by boat from Alghero.

Griffon vulture
Only a few of these rare creatures survive in Sardinia.

Herring gulls
These birds nest in cliff crevices and ravines.

Torre del Tramariglio

Torre Pegna

Cala d'inferno

Peregrine falcons
These raptors prefer calm, open spaces with rocky cliffs – Capo Caccia is a favoured ground.

Capo Caccia
In the past this promontory was frequented by travellers and prominent naturalists such as Alberto La Marmora. The name Capo Caccia derives from the caccia, or wild pigeon hunting, that was once popular here.

VISITORS' CHECKLIST

Grotta di Nettuno ⓘ *Alghero
(079 94 65 40).* ⓐ *Apr–Sep:
9am–6pm daily; Oct: 10am–5pm
daily; Nov–Mar: 9am–2pm daily.*
🚫 🖼 ⓒ *compulsory. In bad
weather, boat trips from Alghero do
not stop at the Grotta di Nettuno.*

Grotta Verde
*The name of this large cave, Green Grotto, derives
from the colour of the moss and other plants that
cover the stalagmites and stalactites. On the shores
of a small lake at the far end of the gallery,
ancient graffiti have been discovered.*

Escala del Cabirol
*From the ridge of land
separating the headland from
the lighthouse point, the
Escala del Cabirol steps wind
down to the entrance of the
Grotta di Nettuno.*

Punta del Quadro

Punta del bollo

Lago La Marmora

Isola Foradada

Grotta di Nettuno
*Neptune's Grotto, one of the most
picturesque caves in Sardinia, was first
explored in the 1700s. The grotto
extends for 2,500 m (8,200 ft), while
the guided tour covers 200 m (650 ft).*

Romanesque Santo Stefano, at Monteleone Rocca Doria

Monteleone Rocca Doria ❼

Road map B3. 👥 140.
ℹ️ 079 92 51 17.

Situated on the top of the Su Monte cliff (420 m, 1,380 ft), the little village of Monteleone Rocca Doria has a sweeping view of Lake Temo and the Nurra plain. Today it is tranquil, although inhabitants look back proudly on a noble, warlike past. In the 13th century the Doria family from Genoa built a fortress here which was totally destroyed in 1436 after a three-year siege by troops from Aragon, Sassari, Bosa and Alghero.

Many inhabitants departed to found the town of Villanova Monteleone, but a few people remained behind. Monteleone was not included in development programmes and, at one point, locals tried to improve their lot by putting the village up for sale. In the centre of Monteleone is the 13th-century Romanesque parish church, **Santo Stefano**.

Bosa ❽

See pp126–7.

Macomer ❾

Road map C3. 👥 12,000.
ℹ️ Town Hall (0785 79 08 51).
🎭 17 Jan: Sant'Antonio Abate.

Built on a platform of volcanic rock, Macomer is one of the most important commercial centres in the interior of Sardinia. Macomer developed around key communication routes – the Carlo Felice road (the N131 that runs through most of the island) and the railway – and owes its prosperity to agriculture, livestock raising, dairy products and light industry, while retaining traces of its past. The parish church of **San Pantaleo** is an example of 17th-century Spanish Gothic. On the evening of 17 January the traditional *Sa Tuva* celebration is held in honour of Sant'Antonio Abate. The event takes place in the large square in front of Santa Croce, and a huge bonfire lights up the entire quarter.

San Pantaleo, in Macomer

Environs: Not far from the town centre, near the Carlo Felice road, a short walk will take you to the impressive **Santa Barbara Nuraghe**. Its sheer size means that it dominates a series of smaller towers and ramparts.

Sedilo ❿

Road map C3. 👥 2,700.
ℹ️ 0785 56 00 01. 🎭 5–8 Jul: S'Ardia at Santu Antine sanctuary.

The rocky terrain in the Abbasanta plateau gave the people of Sedilo the raw material to build their houses. There are still a few originals remaining, representing a style that has virtually disappeared. The main sight of interest is the church of **San Giovanni Battista** in the centre of town. However, Sedilo's most notable claim to fame is the **Sanctuary of Santu Antine**, otherwise known as San Costantino, or Constantine, after the early champion of Christianity who is much revered in Sardinia. The church, with the typical *cumbessias* houses for pilgrims, stands on a cliff overlooking Lake Omodeo. Within the precinct there are numerous nuraghic sculptures on display, including the so-called *Perda Fitta*, a monolith which, according to legend, is actually the body of a woman who was turned into stone because she was disrespectful towards the patron saint.

The open space opposite the sanctuary is the setting for the annual *S'Ardia*. This horse race ends the July festivities commemorating Constantine the Great's victory over Maxentius in the battle of the Milvian Bridge in AD 312. The inside walls of Santu Antine are covered with quantities of ex votos.

The S'Ardia horse race run around the Santu Antine sanctuary, Sedilo

The Losa nuraghe near Abbasanta

Ghilarza ⓫

Road map C3. 🏛 *4,700.*
ℹ️ *Town Hall (0785 540 38).*

An unfinished Aragonese
tower stands in the centre
of Ghilarza, but the place is
known principally as the
town in which the famous
Italian political thinker and
writer Antonio Gramsci spent
his childhood years. A small
door on Corso Umberto leads
to the **Casa di Gramsci**, now
occupied by a research and
study centre. There is also an
exhibition of historical
material relating to the
Communist leader, who died
in prison during the Fascist
era. On the second floor is
the small bedroom that was
Gramsci's from 1898 to 1908.

Environs: A short distance
from Ghilarza, on the road to
Nuoro, is the beautiful church
of **San Pietro di Zuri**, which
was relocated, along with the
village of the same name,
after the artificial lake
Omodeo was created in 1923.
The original church dates
from 1291. The building was
commissioned by Mariano
d'Arborea, and carried out by
architect Anselmo da Como.
The architecture is prevalently
Romanesque, with some
interesting details which
anticipate the transition
towards the Gothic style.

🏛 **Casa di Gramsci**
Corso Umberto 57. **Tel** 0785 541 64.
🕐 10am–1pm, 4–7pm daily (Nov–Mar:
10am–1pm, 3:30–6:30pm Fri–Sun). 🏛

Abbasanta ⓬

Road map C3. 🏛 *2,700.*
ℹ️ *Town Hall (0785 542 29).*

This village, the centre of
which still has some old
traditional houses made of
dark local basalt stone,
revolves around the parish
church of Santa Cristina, with
its impressive Renaissance-
inspired architecture. Situated
in the middle of a highly
developed agricultural region,
Abbasanta owes its impor-
tance to its strategic position
near main artery routes, both
ancient and modern.
In the vicinity are two of
the most important archaeological sites in the whole of
Sardinia: the **Losa Nuraghe**
and the **Santa Cristina**
nuraghic complex near
Paulilàtino *(see p137)*. In
order to reach the Losa

Nuraghe, take the Carlo Felice
road towards Cagliari until
you reach kilometre marker
123 (indicated on a road
sign). Here, a turning to the
right leads to the entrance to
the archaeological site, which
is fenced off. Together with
the monuments at Barùmini
(see pp64–5) and Torralba
(see pp22–3), this nuraghic
complex is one of the most
important remaining from the
immediate pre-Punic period.
In the middle of this vast
structure is a keep thousands
of years old, dating from the
second millennium BC, while
the ramparts were built some
centuries later. The outer
defensive walls were the last
to be built, and date from the
7th century BC.
Inside the nuraghe you can
visit three roofed chambers
with a great many niches,
which were probably used
for storage. A spiral staircase
leads to the upper floor,
which has a terrace above.
All around the main
structure are the foundations
of a series of later buildings,
dating from the Bronze Age
to the Middle Ages.
A small **Antiquarium**
stands about 100 m (328 ft)
from the nuraghi themselves. It
houses an interesting exhibition of plans and illustrations of
a number of nuraghic monuments in this part of Sardinia.

🏛 **Losa Nuraghe**
SS Carlo Felice 123.5 km.
Tel 0785 52 302. 🕐 9am–5pm daily
(to 8pm summer). 🏛 🏛 🏛 🏛

ANTONIO GRAMSCI

Antonio Gramsci was born at Àles
at Àles in 1891 of humble family. After
completing his studies at Turin, he
entered politics full-time. He was
one of the co-founders of the
radical weekly *L'Ordine Nuovo*
and in 1921 helped to found the
Italian Communist Party, later
becoming its Secretary-General.
He was elected to parliament but
was arrested by the Fascists in
1926 and given a 20-year prison

The young Gramsci

sentence. He did not see freedom again, dying in prison in
1937. The complete edition of his writings, *Quaderni del
Carcere* (Prison Notebooks) was not published until 1976.
Lettere dal Carcere (Letters from Prison) are a moving
statement of his sufferings as a prisoner.

Bosa

Dominated by the Castello dei Malaspina, the pastel-coloured houses of Bosa lie on the right bank of the Temo river, the only navigable river in Sardinia. The town was originally founded by the Phoenicians on the opposite bank of the river. In the Middle Ages, under threat from constant pirate raids, the townspeople sought the protection of the Malaspina family on the slopes of the hill of Serravalle. Bosa was granted the status of royal city under Spanish rule and always maintained a close relationship with the Iberian peninsula. This fascinating town is famous for its artisan traditions of gold-filigree jewellery and lace-making. In the Sa Costa medieval quarter, a labyrinth of cobblestone alleys and steps, you can still see women sitting outside their homes making lace. Environmentalists say the nearby seaside is the cleanest in Italy.

Locally made jewellery

Interior of the Cathedral in Bosa, with Baroque ornamentation

🏠 Cathedral

Piazza Duomo. **Tel** *0785 37 32 86.* ◯ *10am–noon, 4–6:30pm daily.*
Dedicated to the Virgin Mary, the Cathedral was rebuilt in the 19th century in the majestic late Baroque Piedmontese style. In the interior is a statue of the *Madonna and Child*, of the Catalan school, sculpted in the 16th century. On either side of the main altar are two marble lions killing dragons. The side altars are made of multicoloured marble.

🏛 Corso Vittorio Emanuele II

The main street in Bosa, paved with stone, runs parallel to the river. It is lined with aristocratic buildings and goldsmiths' workshops where filigree and coral jewellery are made.

🏛 Pinacoteca Civica

Casa Deriu, Corso Vittorio Emanuele II 59.
Tel *0785 37 70 43.* ◯ *10am–1pm, 5–7pm daily (Jul–Sep: 11:30am–1pm, 7:30–11pm).*
Casa Deriu is a typical 19th-century Bosa building which has been transformed into an exhibition centre. The first floor features traditional locally made products such as cakes, wine and bread, as well as a display of old black-and-white photographs. On the second floor is a fine reconstruction of the elegant Deriu apartment, with its olive wood parquet, frescoed vaulted ceiling, majolica tiles from Ravenna and locally made lace curtains.

Detail of the architrave of San Pietro

The top floor houses the Pinacoteca Civica (municipal art gallery), featuring the collection of Melkiorre Melis, a local artist and one of the leading promoters of 20th-century applied arts in Sardinia.

The works on display span a 70-year period of graphic art, oil painting, ceramics and posters. Also shown here are the Arab-influenced works of Melis, executed while he headed the Muslim School of Arts and Crafts in Tripoli.

🏛 Castello Malaspina

Via Ultima Costa 14. **Tel** *333 544 56 75.* ◯ *10am–12:30pm, 4–6:30pm.*
Built in 1112 by the Malaspina dello Spino Secco family, this castle is still impressive, even though only its towers and outer walls have survived. It was enlarged in the 1300s and covers a large area. Very little remains of the castle itself: only parts of the wall on the northeast corner, at the foot of the main tower. The tower was built of light ochre trachyte in the early 1300s and is being restored. Inside the walls the only

View of Bosa from the Temo river, with fishing boats

For hotels and restaurants in this region see p176 and p186

Aerial view of Bosa Marina with its Aragonese tower

building left standing is the church of **Nostra Signora di Regnos Altos**, built in the 14th century. Restoration carried out in 1974–5 brought to light a cycle of Catalan school frescoes, one of the few left in Sardinia. From the ramparts there are splendid views of the church of San Pietro, the lower Temo river valley and the red roofs of the Sa Costa quarter. You can walk down to the centre of town by following the steps skirting the walls that once defended Bosa to the east.

Sas Conzas

The buildings on the left bank of the Temo river were once used as tanneries. Abandoned years ago after a crisis in the leather goods market, the buildings are still waiting to be restored. In the meanwhile a small restaurant is housed here. The Sas Conzas quarter can best be admired from the palm-lined street on the other side of the river, Lungotemo De Gasperi, where the fishermen of Bosa moor their boats.

San Pietro
ask custodian at cathedral for key.

About 1 km (half a mile) east of the left bank of the Temo stands the church of San Pietro, built in red trachyte stone, one of the most interesting of Sardinia's Romanesque churches. It was built in different periods, beginning in the second half of the 11th century, while the bell tower, apse and side walls were added the following century. The façade combines some elements of Romanesque with touches of

Bosa coat of arms

French Gothic, imported by the Cistercian monks. On the architrave of the doorway is a singular *Madonna and Child with Saints Peter, Paul and Constantine*. It is unfortunately difficult to arrange a visit to the interior.

Environs: Bosa Marina, just over 2 km (1 mile) from the centre of town, has a lovely secluded beach with dark sand. Isola Rossa is linked to the mainland by a long jetty. The Aragonese tower is open in July and August and hosts temporary exhibitions.

The coastline between Bosa and Alghero is spectacular. Part of the Trenino Verde route *(see pp92–3)* goes from Bosa Marina to Macomer, skirting the Pedras Nieddas (black stones) beach before going up the Rio Abba Mala valley to Modolo, Tresnuraghes and Sindia.

VISITORS' CHECKLIST

Road map *B3.* 7,786.
Pro Loco (0785 37 61 07).
Easter Week: Settimana Santa Bosana; 29 Jun: boat procession on river; first Sun of Aug: Santa Stella Maris; second Sun of Sep: Sagra di Nostra Signora di Regnos Altos.
www.comune.bosa.nu.it

The Castello Malaspina in Bosa

The paired horse race held during Carnevale at Santu Lussurgiu

Santu Lussurgiu ⑬

Road map B3. 🏇 *2,900.* 🚉 🔢
Town Hall (0783 55 191). 🎭 *Carnevale: horse race in town centre; 2–3 Jun: Horse Fair; 21 Aug: San Lussorio.*
www.*comunesantulussurgiu.it*

Santu Lussurgiu lies at 500 m (1,640 ft) above sea level on the eastern slope of Mount Montiferru, laid out like an amphitheatre on the edge of a volcanic crater, and surrounded by olive groves.

The historic centre is fascinating, with its steep, narrow streets and tiny squares surrounded by beautiful tall stone houses painted in bright colours. Some have decorated architraves and wrought-iron balconies. In Via Roma, an elegant 11-room 18th-century building houses the **Museo della Tecnologia Contadina**, (Museum of Rural Culture), founded by the local Centro di Cultura Popolare. The "Su Mastru Salis" collection is the work of Maestro Salis, the museum curator, who in over 20 years has collected more than 2,000 objects related to the culture and traditions of Santu Lussurgiu.

A guided visit to this interesting museum is like making a trip backwards in time. Room after room contains fascinating displays of everyday objects used by the farmers, shepherds and coal merchants who worked at the foot of Mount Montiferru. Some of the most interesting exhibits are in the sections given over to spinning and weaving, cooking and crafts. The room devoted to wine-making is also interesting. Equipment includes a fulling-mill, the implement used to soften and felt fabric. Over 40 of them were once in use in the Santu Lussurgiu area.

In the upper part of town is the 15th-century church of **Santa Maria degli Angeli**, which has a fine 18th-century carved wooden altar.

There are still craftsmen in Santu Lussurgiu who specialize in making knives and fittings for horse-riding (bridles, bits, saddles and leather riding boots).

At Carnevale the street in front of the museum is turned into a track for a breakneck horse race between pairs of riders dressed as knights.

The Museum of Rural Culture

FLAMINGOES IN THE SALE PORCUS RESERVE

The Sale Porcus marsh is one of the largest reserves on the Sinis peninsula, its many white sand dunes covered with maquis vegetation. In winter and spring over 10,000 flamingoes and thousands of cranes, wild geese, cormorants and mallards make their home here, making the area look like a colourful East African lake. In summer, drought reduces the water level, transforming the lake into a white area with a thick, hard salty crust that you can walk across. One of the least intrusive ways to explore this natural oasis is by horse. For more details on environmentally friendly visits to the reserve, contact Engea Sardegna, the regional chapter of an association of horse-back guides.

🐎 **Oasi Sale Porcus**
🕐 *daily.* **Tel** *0783 52 81 00.*
www.*engeasardegna.it*
www.*sitogea.net*

Flamingoes in the Sale Porcus reserve

One of the seven springs at San Leonardo de Siete Fuentes

Environs: A few kilometres from Santu Lussurgiu there is a forest of pine, holm oak and oak near the village of **San Leonardo de Siete Fuentes**, which is famous for its seven springs of radio-active, diuretic water that flow out of seven fountains at a constant temperature of 11°C (52°F). The streams pass through a wood popular for family outings. In the centre of town is the small church of San Leonardo, which once belonged to the Knights of Malta. It was constructed with dark trachyte stone in the 12th century, and acquired its present Romanesque-Gothic appearance the following century. The single-nave interior bears the insignias of the Knights of Malta. Opposite the church stands a small public library.

In early June, San Leonardo plays host to an important saddle-horse fair.

🏛 **Museo della Tecnologia Contadina**
Via T Meloni 1. **Tel** 0783 55 06 17.
🕐 by appt only. 💳 📷

Cuglieri ⑭

Road map B3. 🏙 3,400. ⓘ Viale Regina Margherita (0785 36 82 00).
🎭 Good Friday: procession and 'Iscravamentu; 5 Aug: Madonna della Neve. **www**.comune.cuglieri.or.it

The agricultural town of Cuglieri lies 500 m (1,640 ft) above sea level on the western slopes of Mount Montiferru, with a panoramic view of the sea. It is dominated by the striking church of **Santa Maria della Neve**, which has an 18th-century façade and twin bell towers. The walk up to the church is lovely, winding through alleyways and stepped streets lined with tall stone houses.

The square in front of Santa Maria offers a fine view of the town and the coast between Santa Caterina di Pittinuri and Porto Alabe.

Santa Maria della Neve, in Cuglieri

Environs: The coast is 15 km (9 miles) away on main road 292. **Santa Caterina di Pittinuri** is a seaside town set around a white-stone inlet enclosed by a limestone cliff, where the Spanish Torre del Pozzo tower stands. This stretch of coast is scenic, with rocky headlands and white sand and pebble beaches. The most famous sight is **S'Archittu**, a large natural bridge created by coastal erosion. A dirt road off main road 292, between Santa Caterina di Pittinuri and S'Archittu, goes to the ruins of the Punic-Roman city of **Cornus**, the setting for the last battle between the Romans and Sardinian-Carthaginians headed by Amsicora (215 BC).

In the 9th century the city was abandoned because of repeated Saracen raids and the inhabitants founded a new city, Curulis Nova, present-day Cuglieri, on the nearby mountain-side. The dirt road peters out just before the Early Christian town of Columbaris, while the acropolis of Cornus is visible on the hill to the southwest. Although the archaeological site may seem abandoned, it still has some sarcophagi and the remains of a three-nave basilica. It seems likely that all of these date back to the 6th century.

The cliff with the famous S'Archittu di Santa Caterina natural bridge at Pittinuri, near Cuglieri

Aerial view of the Cabras marsh area

Cabras ⑮

Road map B4. 🏘 *10,000.* 🚆 ℹ
*Pro Loco (0783 29 68 28); Town Hall
(0783 3971).* 🎪 *first Sun in Sep:
Festa di San Salvatore.*
www.comune.cabras.or.it

The town of Cabras, a short
distance from Oristano, is
characterized by its old, one-
storey houses. It stands on
the edge of the largest
freshwater lake and marsh in
Sardinia (2,000 hectares, 5,000
acres), and is connected to
the sea via a series of canals.

The presence of both fresh
and salt water attracts coots,
marsh harriers, peregrine
falcons and purple gallinules.
The water itself is rich in
mullet and eels.

In the past, local fishermen
used long, pointed boats,
called is *fassonis*, which were
made of dried rushes and
other marsh plants, using
a technique similar to that
known to the Phoenicians.
Another Phoenician survival
is the marinading technique
called *sa merca*, in which
fresh fish is wrapped in plant
leaves from the lake and left
to soak in salt water.

Environs: At the northern end
of the Golfo di Oristano is the
Laguna di Mistras. Separated
from the sea by two sandbars,
in wetlands of international

scientific importance, this
lagoon makes an ideal habitat
for flamingoes, cormorants,
grey heron and ospreys. The
nearby Mar 'e Pontis marshland
is also rich in ornithological
interest. At the Peschiera
Pontis, once a fish farm, you
can still see the old sluices
and gratings.

San Salvatore ⑯

Road map B4. ℹ *Cabras.* 🎪 *end
of Aug–first Sun in Sep: Corsa degli
Scalzi di San Salvatore.*

Typical white houses for
pilgrims, or *cumbessias*,
surround the country church
of San Salvatore. They are
occupied for nine days each
year in late August and early
September, for the novena of

the saint's feast day. In the
1960s the church's central
square was used as a location
for "spaghetti westerns". San
Salvatore was built in the 17th
century on the site of a
nuraghic sanctuary for the
worship of sacred waters. In
the 6th century the site was
transformed into an underground church. In the left-
hand nave stairs lead to the
hypogeum, which has six
chambers: two rectangular
ones flanking a corridor
leading to a circular atrium
with a well, around which
three further chambers lie.
The hypogeum was partly
hewn out of the rock; the
vaulted ceilings are made of
sandstone and brick. On the
walls are graffiti of animals
(elephants, panthers and
peacocks) and heroes and

The annual Corsa degli Scalzi (barefoot race) at San Salvatore

Marsh samphire, a typical plant growing in the Cabras marshes

gods (Hercules fighting the Nemean lion, Mars and Venus with a small winged cupid). There are even Arabic writings about Allah and Mohammed, and numerous depictions of ships, which experts believe are ex votos.

The Latin letters RVF, interlaced as in a monogram and repeated several times, seem to derive from the Phoenician language and are said to stand for "cure, save, give health".

On the first Saturday in September, the feast day of San Salvatore is celebrated. The event is marked with a barefoot *(scalzi)* race in memory of local youths, who, in the Middle Ages, left the village to escape from the Saracens but returned to save the statue of the saint.

Just east of the sanctuary are the ruins of the Domu 'e Cubas Roman baths.

San Giovanni di Sinis ⑰

Road map B4. 🏃 40. ℹ️ *Cabras.*

At the edge of the Sinis peninsula there is a bathing resort that was once famous for its fishermen's huts made of wood and reeds *(see p115)*. Today only a few have survived; the largest group lies east of the motorway, not far from the famous archaeological site of Tharros *(see pp132–3)*.

As visitors enter the small village of San Giovanni di Sinis they will see the early Christian church of **San Giovanni** which, together with San Saturnino in Cagliari, is the oldest in Sardinia. It was built in the 5th century, though much of the present-day church was the result of 9th- and 10th-century rebuilding. The three-nave interior is barrel-vaulted.

Environs: Near San Giovanni di Sinis is the WWF **Torre 'e Seu** reserve, where some of the last dwarf palms in the area survive. A dirt road at the northern end of San Giovanni di Sinis leads to the reserve. At the gate there is a path to the sea and the Torre 'e Seu Spanish tower.

THE VERNACCIA WINE OF SARDINIA

The countryside north of Oristano is one of the most fertile areas in Sardinia, carpeted with olive trees and grapevines. The Vernaccia made in Oristano is perhaps Sardinia's most famous white wine and is produced in the towns of San Vero Milis, Cabras, Zeddiani, Narbolia,

Vernaccia grapes

Riola and Baratili. The wine is full-bodied and strong, with 15 degrees of alcohol, and is aged for at least three years in large oak barrels. You can tour the wine-producing area, and pause for a wine-tasting at the Cantina Sociale della Vernaccia, where the entrance is framed by an impressive 18th-century gate.

🏛 **Cantina Sociale della Vernaccia**
Località Il Rimedio 149. **Tel** *0783 33 155.*
🕐 *10am–noon Mon–Fri.* 📷 📹 book in advance.
www.vinidocsardegna.it/cantine_vernaccia.htm

The 18th-century gate, Cantina Sociale

Wine barrels in the Cantina Sociale della Vernaccia

Rows of Vernaccia vines

Tharros ⑱

1st-century AD oil lamp

The city of Tharros was founded by the Phoenicians around the end of the 8th century BC, on a spit of land called Capo San Marco, which offered safe anchorage for cargo-laden ships. By the 6th and 5th centuries BC, Tharros had become a flourishing port and this prosperity continued under the Romans, from 238 BC on. With sea on two sides, this is one of the most intriguing ancient sites in the Mediterranean. Only a third of the area has been unearthed so far. Most of the visible remains date back to the Punic-Roman era, but there is also evidence of previous civilizations: the nuraghic village (late Bronze Age) and the Tophet (Phoenician) located on the hill, Su Murru Mannu.

7th–6th century BC necklace
Made of gold and cornelian, this necklace was found in the southern necropolis.

Deep tombs were installed by the fortifications north of the city during Roman

San Giovanni Spanish tower

Capo San Marco
At the southern tip of the Sinis peninsula, Capo San Marco still has the remains of nuraghe Baboe Cabitza, dating back to the late Bronze Age. During this time, the whole peninsula was likely subject to intense settlement.

Remains of the Fortifications
At the foot of San Giovanni is a quadrangular base of squared sandstone blocks thought to date back to the 3rd century BC.

Distinctive Residence
The presence of a courtyard of basalt millstones in this house has led archaeologists to believe that this was an area dedicated to working wheat, or possibly even a bakery.

STAR SIGHTS

★ Corinthian Columns

★ Cistern

Drainage System
A drain ran along the middle of the paved road. The system was linked to the rows of houses on either side of the street.

VISITORS' CHECKLIST

Road map B4. *San Giovanni di Sinis.* ⚑ *Cooperativa Penisola Sinis (0783 37 00 19).* ⭘ *9am–9pm summer, 9am–5pm winter.*
📷 ✏

Sanctuary of Demeter

Tophet

The Castellum Acquae
is an imposing rectangular building, the function of which is still in doubt. The archaeologist G Pesce thought that this was the cistern feeding the city's water system.

Head of Goddess
Found in the Punic necropolis, this 5th-century BC head is now in Cagliari's archaeological museum (see p58).

Baths

★ Corinthian Columns
These reconstructed columns are part of the process of re-erecting monuments that occupied Tharros between the 1st and 3rd centuries AD. One of the columns has an original Corinthian capital.

Baths

★ Cistern
This quadrangular cistern (3rd–4th centuries AD) on the southern side of the temple is made of large blocks of sandstone and adorned with Doric half-columns.

Oristano ⓳

Interior of Cathedral dome

Placed at the northern border of the Campidano region, between the mouth of the Tirso river and the Santa Giusta marshlands, Oristano is the largest town in western Sardinia. It was founded in 1070, after the powerful and prosperous city of Tharros was abandoned, the inhabitants defeated by constant pirate raids. The period between 1100 and 1400 saw the rise of the city under enlightened rulers such as Mariano IV and his daughter Eleonora, who controlled most of Sardinia. Oristano became the provincial capital only in 1974. The town stands in the middle of a fertile plain with a network of pools, well-stocked with fish. The historic centre, once protected by the city walls, is small and mostly a pedestrian-only zone.

The Cathedral of Oristano with its octagonal campanile

🛈 Cattedrale

Piazza Mannu. **Tel** 0783 786 84.
7am–noon, 4–6:30pm daily.

Dedicated to the Blessed Virgin Mary, the Cathedral was built in 1228 by Lombard architects and masons for Mariano di Torres. It was totally rebuilt in the 17th century in the Baroque style and now displays a mixture of influences. The remaining original elements are the octagonal bell tower with its onion dome and brightly coloured majolica tiles, the bronze doors and the Cappella del Rimedio, which has a fine marble balustrade decorated with Pisan bas relief sculpture depicting Daniel in the lions' den. The Renaissance choir behind the main altar is another important work. The rich and varied Tesoro del Duomo, the cathedral treasury, is housed in the chapterhouse, and silverwork, vestments and illuminated manuscripts can be seen upon request. On Piazza del Duomo are the Palazzo Arcivescovile (arch-bishop's palace) and the Seminario Tridentino.

🏰 Torre di Mariano II

Piazza Roma.
Also called Torre di San Cristoforo or Porta Manna, this sandstone tower at the northern end of the former city walls was built in 1291 by the ruler of the Arborea principality, Mariano II. This and the Portixedda tower, just opposite, are the sole surviving remains of the old city walls. At the top of the tower is a large bell made in 1430. The Torre di Mariano is open on its inner façades and looks over Piazza Roma, the heart of city life, with its fashionable shops and outdoor cafés.

🏰 Corso Umberto

This pedestrian street, also known as Via Dritta, is the most elegant in Oristano with impressive buildings such as Palazzo Siviera, once the residence of the Marquise

---

THE KNIGHTS OF THE STAR

The Sa Sartiglia procession and tournament is centuries-old and is held on the last Sunday of Carnival and on Shrove Tuesday. It was probably introduced in 1350 by Mariano II to celebrate his wedding. On 2 February the procession leader, *su Componidori*, is chosen. On the day of the event he is dressed by a group of girls. A white shirt is sewn on him, his face is wrapped in fasciae and covered with a woman's mask, and a bride's veil and black hat are placed on his head. He then leads a procession of knights, trumpeters and drummers through the city to the tournament grounds by the Arcivescovado and the Cathedral. At a given signal the tournament begins. The leader has to run his sword into the hole in the middle of a star hanging from a string, and pick it up. If he succeeds, this signals a prosperous year.

The Sa Sartiglia tournament at Oristano

d'Acrisia, which has a dome on top, and Palazzo Falchi, built in the 1920s. Oristano's smartest shops are found here and it is the most popular street for the traditional evening stroll.

🏛 Piazza Eleonora D'Arborea

This long, irregular, tree-lined square is named after the ruler who established the famous Carta de Logu body of laws in 1392. A 19th-century statue of Eleonora stands in the middle of the square. This piazza

Eleonora d'Arborea

also boasts noble buildings such as Palazzo Corrias and the Palazzo Comunale, the town hall, once the Scolopi monastery. The octagonal church of San Vincenzo was part of the monastery.

🏛 San Francesco

Piazza Mannu. **Tel** 0783 782 75. 7:30–11:30am, 4–7pm daily. This Neo-Classical church was built over the remains of a Gothic church which was completely destroyed in the early 19th century. The façade has six columns with Ionic capitals. In the interior is one

of the most interesting statues in Sardinia: a crucifix executed by an unknown late 14th-century Catalan artist. Another important work, by Pietro Cavaro, depicts *The Stigmata of San Francesco*.

🏛 Santa Chiara

Via Garibaldi. **Tel** 0783 780 93. 5–6pm daily.
The Gothic church of Santa Chiara was built in the 14th century. The façade displays sandstone ashlars, a severe rose window and small bell gable. The interior has wooden Gothic corbels with carved animal figures.

🏛 Antiquarium Arborense

Palazzo Parpaglia, Via Parpaglia 37. **Tel** 0783 79 12 62. 9am–2pm, 3–8pm daily.
Housed in the Neo-Classical Palazzo Parpaglia, this museum features archaeological finds from Tharros, an art gallery and a section given over to medieval Oristano. The gallery has interesting altarpieces in Catalan style: the San Martino *retablo* (15th century)

VISITORS' CHECKLIST

Road map B4. 🏛 *32,000.* 🚉
🚌 🛈 *EPT, Piazza Eleonora 19,
(0783 368 31).* **Antiquarium
Arborense** *ticket also valid for
guided tour of the historic centre.*
www.comune.oristano.it

attributed to the workshop of the Catalan artist Ramon de Mur; the *Retablo di Cristo* (1533), by followers of Pietro Cavaro, of which only nine panels remain; and the *Retablo della Madonna dei Consiglieri* (1565) by the Cagliari artist Antioco Mainas, representing the councillors of Oristano kneeling before the Virgin Mary.

The archaeological collection contains over 2,000 Neolithic obsidian scrapers, bone hair slides, small amphoras from Greece and Etruria, and Roman glass objects and oil lamps. These all belong to the Collezione Archeologica Efisio Pischedda.

Among the most notable objects in the collection are a terracotta mask used to ward off evil spirits, scarabs made out of green jasper, and carved gemstones from the Roman period.

ORISTANO

Antiquarium Arborense ⑦
Cattedrale ①
Corso Umberto ③
Piazza Eleonora ④
San Francesco ⑤
Santa Chiara ⑥
Torre di Mariano II ②

0 metres 300
0 yards 300

Key to Symbols *see back flap*

Fishermen using *fassonis*, traditional sedge boats, on the Santa Giusta lake

Santa Giusta ⑳

Road map B4. 🚶 *4,700.*
ℹ️ *Via Amsicora 17 (0783 35 45 00).*
🎉 *14 May: Sagra di Santa Giusta.*

This agricultural town, built
on the banks of the Santa
Giusta lake and marsh, was
built over the ruins of the
Roman city of Ottona. The
cathedral of **Santa Giusta**, a
jewel of Pisan Romanesque
architecture blended with
Arab and Lombard elements,
stands on the rise as you
enter the town.
The cathedral
was built in the
first half of the
12th century
and has a
narrow
façade,
with a
triple-
lancet
window.
The

columns in the interior are in
various styles, and originally
came from the nearby Roman
cities of Neapolis, Tharros
and Othoca. From the sacristy
there is a lovely view of the
lake, one of the best fishing
areas in Sardinia, where you
can still see the long *is
fassonis* sedge boats
of Phoenician
derivation. On
the feast day
of Santa Giusta in
May, a lively
regatta is held
here. The local
gastronomic speciality is
bottarga (salted mullet roe).

Soapstone scarab found in
Santa Giusta digs

⌂ Santa Giusta
Via Manzoni. **Tel** 0783 35 92 05.
◯ 9am–noon, 3–7pm (2–6pm winter).

Arborea ㉑

Road map B4. 🚶 *3,900.* ℹ️ *Town
Hall (0783 80 331).* 🎉 *Good Friday:
living representation of the Passion of
Christ.* **www**.comune.arborea.or.it

Arborea was
founded in
1930 during the
Fascist period
and was
initially

named Mussolinia. The town
was built on a regular grid
plan typical of modern cities.
All the civic buildings (school,
parish church, hotel and town
hall) are found in Piazza
Maria Ausiliatrice, from which
the main streets radiate.
The avenues are
lined with trees
and the two-
storey Neo-
Gothic houses
are surrounded
by gardens. In
the **Palazzo del
Comune** (town
hall) there is a small collection of archaeological finds
from excavations in the area,
including the Roman necropolis of S'Ungroni, north of
Arborea, discovered during
work on land reclamation.
About 9 km (6 miles) to the
southwest is the pretty fishing
village of Marceddi, on the
edge of the marsh of the same
name, dominated by the 16th-
century Torrevecchia.

🏛 Palazzo del Comune
Piazza Maria Ausiliatrice. **Tel** 0783
803 31. ◯ 10am–1pm Mon–Fri,
3–6pm Mon–Tue. ⬛ ♿

Fordongianus ㉒

Road map C4. 🚶 *1,200.* ℹ️ *Via
Traiano 7 (0783 601 23).* 🎉 *21 Apr
& 21 Aug: Festa di San Lussorio.*

Ancient Forum Traiani was
once the largest Roman city in
the interior. Located in the
Tirso river valley, it was fortified against the local Barbagia
people. Today the centre
consists of houses in red and

Cathedral of Santa Giusta, a masterpiece of Romanesque architecture grey stone. One of the best preserved is Casa Madeddu, a typical old "Aragonese house" of the early 1600s with Catalan-style doorways and windows. On the same street is the 16th-century parish church of San Pietro Apostolo, in red trachyte, which has been almost entirely rebuilt. The **Roman Baths**, currently being restored, lie on the banks of the river. The rectangular pool still contains warm water from the hot springs and the local women use it to do their washing. The portico and the rooms with mosaic pavements are closed to the public at present.

A short distance south of Fordongianus stands the little rural church of San Lussorio, built by Victorine monks around AD 1100, over an early Christian crypt.

Earrings found at the Forum Traiani

Paulilàtino 🉃

Road map C4. 🏘 2,500. 🚹 Viale della Libertà 33 (0785 556 23). 🎉 second Sun in May: Sagra di Santa Cristina.

This rural village at the edge of the Abbasanta basalt plateau is surrounded by olive groves and cork oak woods. The houses are built of dark stone and have Aragonese doorways and small wrought-iron balconies. The same stone was used to build the church of San Teodoro in the 17th century. This Aragonese Gothic church has a stained-glass rose window and a bell tower with an onion dome. **Palazzo Atzori** houses a museum of folk culture with domestic tools and objects on display.

🏛 Palazzo Atzori
Via Nazionale 127. **Tel** 0785 554 38. 🕐 9am–1pm all year; 3–5:30pm (Oct–Mar); 3:30–6:30pm (Apr–June) 4:30–7:30pm (Jul–Sept). 🚫 Mon. 🈂 🔊 ♿

Environs: About 4 km (3 miles) from town, a turning off state road 131 takes you to the nuraghic village of **Santa Cristina**. A stone wall encloses the archaeological area, where

there is a well temple dedicated to the local mother-goddess dating from the 1st millennium BC. The well is in a good state of preservation, and a broad stone stairway leads to its vaulted underground chamber. Nearby is an enclosure that was probably used for general assemblies. The sacred nature of this site has been maintained over the centuries with the construction of a church dedicated to Santa Cristina. Worshippers continue to flock to the church, which is surrounded by *muristenes*, houses intended for those who come here for novena on the saint's feast day.

To the right of the church, among the olive trees, another archaeological zone includes a well-preserved nuraghe and two rectangular nuraghic-age stone dwellings. The best preserved of these is 14 m (46 ft) long and 2 m (6 ft) high.

🎵 Santa Cristina
Km 114,300, SS131 Cagliari-Sassari. 🚹 Cooperativa Archeotour (0785 554 38). 🕐 9am–dusk.

Panoramic view of Àles at the foot of Monte Arci

Steps leading to the temple of Santa Cristina at Paulilàtino

Àles 🉄

Road map C4. 🏘 1,700. 🚹 Town Hall (0783 91 131). 🎉 first Sun in Aug: Santa Madonna della Neve. **www**.comune.ales.or.it

Àles, the main village in the Marmilla area, lies on the eastern slope of Monte Arci. In the upper part stands the cathedral of San Pietro, built in 1686 by Genoan architect Domenico Spotorno, who used the ruins of the 12th-century church on this site as material for his construction.

Twin bell towers with ceramic domes rise above the elegant façade, while in the Baroque interior, the sacristy has lovely carved furniture and a rare 14th-century crucifix. The Archivio Capitolare contains elegant gold jewellery.

In the same square stand the Palazzo Vescovile and the seminary and oratory of the Madonna del Rosario.

Àles is also the birthplace of Antonio Gramsci (1891–1937) *(see p125)*. The house is marked with a plaque.

Environs: Àles is a good starting point for a hike to the top of Trebina Longa and Trebina Lada, the highest peaks on **Monte Arci**, the remnants of an ancient crater. Along the way you are likely to spot pieces of obsidian, the hard black volcanic glass which was cut into thin slices and used to make arrowheads, spears and scrapers. The obsidian of Monte Arci was in great demand, and not only supplied the whole of Sardinia, but was also sold throughout the Mediterranean in the 4th–3rd millennium BC.

THE NORTH AND THE COSTA SMERALDA

ortheastern Sardinia's beauty is familiar from the classic images of a rugged coastline, beautiful inlets, sparkling turquoise sea and beaches of brilliant white sand. To the north, the islands crowded in the Straits of Bonifacio, a stone's throw from Corsica, have great appeal for those in search of unspoilt calm.

The most well-known development in the northeast is the famous Costa Smeralda, founded by a consortium of financiers including the Aga Khan in 1962. In the space of 40 years, few areas in Sardinia have undergone such profound changes as the northeastern coastline. Villas and residential hotels have sprung up almost everywhere, and small harbours have been equipped as marinas. The surroundings are undeniably beautiful, with spectacular scenery at headlands such as Capo d'Orso and Capo Testa. The perfume of the Mediterranean maquis still manages to reach the beaches of pure white sand, and there are still unspoilt areas that have resisted the encroachment of holiday homes. Tourism brings its own problems however, and there is increasing recognition of the need for stricter controls on building, if the growing influx of visitors is not to damage the island's unique environment.

In the interior, the Gallura region displays quite a different character, with extensive forests of cork oak trees and rough, rocky terrain. Granite outcrops create enchanting landscapes like the Valle della Luna near Aggius *(see p152)*. This part of Sardinia is characterized by its wholesome cooking, the continuing practice of traditional handicrafts and frequent reminders of its long history. As well as prehistoric nuraghe, an exceptional series of Romanesque churches survives in the Loguoro area *(see pp156–7)*, culminating in the black and white striped stone church of Santissima Trinità di Saccargia *(see pp158–9)*.

The island of Caprera, ideal for bathing and sunbathing

◁ Two coves on the island of Mortorio, separated by a thin strip of land

Exploring the North and the Costa Smeralda

The port and airport in Olbia handle most of the visitors headed not only for the Costa Smeralda holiday villages, but the rest of Sardinia as well. The appeal of the northern part of Sardinia is the beautiful long coastline, with magnificent beaches and wind-eroded cliffs. From Olbia the road winds northwards to Santa Teresa di Gallura, then turns westwards, beyond the Castelsardo headland, until it reaches Porto Torres. In the interior, Tempio Pausania, capital of the Gallura region, makes an excellent starting point for local tours.

The bear-like cliff at Capo d'Orso

SIGHTS AT A GLANCE

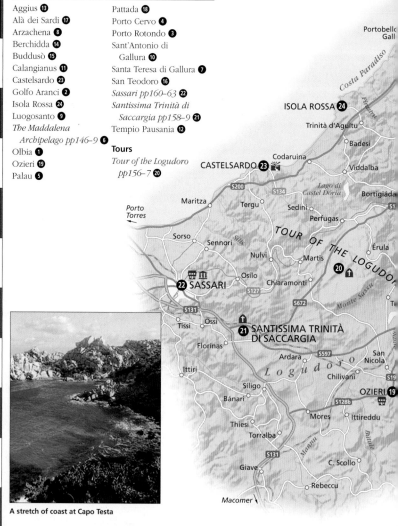

A stretch of coast at Capo Testa

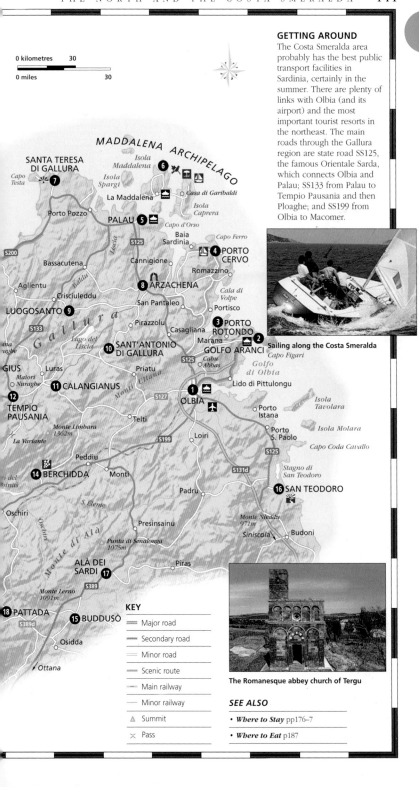

0 kilometres 30

0 miles 30

GETTING AROUND

The Costa Smeralda area probably has the best public transport facilities in Sardinia, certainly in the summer. There are plenty of links with Olbia (and its airport) and the most important tourist resorts in the northeast. The main roads through the Gallura region are state road SS125, the famous Orientale Sarda, which connects Olbia and Palau; SS133 from Palau to Tempio Pausania and then Ploaghe; and SS199 from Olbia to Macomer.

MADDALENA ARCHIPELAGO

SANTA TERESA DI GALLURA **7**

Capo Testa

Isola Maddalena **6**

Isola Spargi

La Maddalena

Casa di Garibaldi

Porto Pozzo

PALAU **5**

Capo d'Orso

Isola Caprera

S200

Bassacutena

Baia Sardinia

Cannigione

Capo Ferro

PORTO CERVO **4**

Romazzino

Aglientu

Crisciuleddu

ARZACHENA **8**

San Pantaleo

Cala di Volpe

Portisco

LUOGOSANTO **9**

Pirazzolu

Casagliana

PORTO ROTONDO **3**

Marana

GOLFO ARANCI **2**

S133

Lago del Liscia

SANT'ANTONIO DI GALLURA **10**

Priatu

Cabu Abbas

Capo Figari

GIUS

Maiori Nuraghe

Luras

CALANGIANUS **11**

S125

Golfo di Olbia

Isola Tavolara

OLBIA **1**

Lido di Pittulongu

TEMPIO PAUSANIA **12**

La Variante

Monte Limbara 1362m

Telti

S127

Porto Istana

Porto S. Paolo

Isola Molara

Capo Coda Cavallo

Peddiu

S199

Loiri

BERCHIDDA **14**

Monti

S131d

Stagno di San Teodoro

Oschiri

Padru

SAN TEODORO **16**

Presinsainu

Monte Nieddu 971m

Siniscola

Budoni

S. Elene

Punta di Senalonga 1075m

ALÀ DEI SARDI **17**

Piras

Monte Lerno 1091m

S389

KEY

PATTADA **18**

S389d

BUDDUSÒ **15**

Osidda

Ottana

Major road	
Secondary road	
Minor road	
Scenic route	
Main railway	
Minor railway	
△ Summit	
✕ Pass	

Sailing along the Costa Smeralda

The Romanesque abbey church of Tergu

SEE ALSO

The ruins at Cabu Abbas

Olbia ❶

Road map D1 & 2. 🏛 *43,000.*
🛬 🏠 🚌 ⛴ 🛈 *0789 21 453.*
🎭 *15–20 May: San Simplicio.*
www.comune.olbia.ss.it

Olbia is only 200 km (125 miles) from the port of Civitavecchia on the mainland of Italy, and has always been the main arrival point on the island, rather than the capital Cagliari. The building of the airport just outside Olbia, to serve the Costa Smeralda, has confirmed this role.

Olbia is a modern city and usually considered as a stop-off on the way to the coast. Of interest in the town are a Roman cistern in Piazza Margherita, proof of ancient Roman occupation, and the Romanesque **San Simplicio.** This church was built from the 11th century onwards and enlarged in the 13th century.

Environs: There are two interesting prehistoric sites near Olbia: the **Cabu Abbas** nuraghic complex (4 km, 2 miles to the northeast) and the **Sa Testa** holy well.

To reach Cabu Abbas from the old port of Olbia, go along Corso Umberto and then Via d'Annunzio. Once past the railway you will see the country church of Santa Maria Cabu Abbas. From here a dirt path winds up towards the top of the mountain, another 15 minutes on foot. The site offers a magnificent view of the island of Tavolara. There is a central well with a tower where remains of sacrifices – burnt bones and pieces of pottery – were found in 1937. This large megalithic zone extends for about 200 m (656 ft).

To reach the Sa Testa holy well, take road SP82 to Golfo Aranci as far as the Pozzo Sacro hotel. This site consists of a wide paved courtyard, from which 17 covered steps lead down to a well chamber.

Golfo Aranci ❷

Road map D1. 🏛 *2,100.* 🚌 ⛴
🛈 *0789 21 453.* 🎭 *15 Aug: Assunta.* **www**.golfoaranci.com

The name "Aranci" means oranges, but you will not see orange groves here. Golfo Aranci owes its name to a mistaken interpretation of the local place-name *di li ranci,* meaning "some crabs". Formerly a part of Olbia, the village of Golfo Aranci became an independent town in 1979. Since 1882 increasing numbers of ferries from the mainland have used Golfo Aranci as a stopping place. It is also the official port of call for the Ferrovie dello Stato (Italian State Railway) ferries.

The Porto Rotondo Yacht Club

Porto Rotondo ❸

Road map D1. 🛈 *0789 21 453.*

Porto Rotondo is not so much a town as a large, well-planned tourist village which grew from nothing during the Costa Smeralda boom. The buildings, placed around the inevitable yacht marina, were designed to fit in as much as possible with the natural surroundings. The result is certainly pleasant, and Porto Rotondo has been a great success as a tourist resort, despite its perhaps slightly artificial air.

The Porto Rotondo quay and Piazzetta San Marco are

Mussel beds at sunset in the Bay of Olbia

Aerial view of Porto Rotondo

lined with famous designer shops, and throughout the summer the cafés and restaurants are crowded with visitors, lunching, dining, meeting friends, listening to music and just watching the world go by. Out of season Porto Rotondo is quiet and even deserted.

The church of San Lorenzo, designed by Andrea Cascella, holds pretty wooden statues by Mario Ceroli depicting Biblical figures.

Just outside Porto Rotondo is the attractive headland called Punta della Volpe, which separates the Golfo di Marinella from the Golfo di Cugnana.

Architecture on the Costa Smeralda

Nearly 40 years have passed since a stretch of coastline in northeastern Sardinia was transformed into the most exclusive tourist resort in the Mediterranean, the Costa Smeralda or Emerald Cast. Back in 1962 the beaches were the preserve of grazing cattle, then taken to overwinter on the islands of Mortorio, Soffi and Li Milani. The Consorzio Costa Smeralda was formed to transform the area. The group initially consisted of the landowners, but expanded to include property owners. Building regulations were established and an architectural committee was founded to supervise any new building in the area. The prominent architects Luigi Vietti, Jacques Couelle, Giancarlo and Michele Busiri Vici, Antonio Simon, Raimond Martin and Leopoldo Mastrella were appointed to design the resorts. The area has since changed beyond recognition. Luxury hotels, sumptuous villas and huge holiday villages have gone up, together with sporting facilities: the famous Yacht Club and one of the most attractive golf courses in the Mediterranean, as well as small villages such as Porto Cervo.

The Neo-Mediterranean style *is a combination of the various elements frequently seen in Mediterranean architecture.*

In planning Porto Rotondo, *the architects decided that only native plants should be used, so trees such as pine, poplar and eucalyptus are banned because they would not blend in with the local strawberry trees, myrtle, lentiscus, oleanders and mimosa.*

The materials *used must be traditional – local stone, pebbles, curved tiles and brick.*

An aerial view of Porto Cervo

Porto Cervo ❹

Road map D1. ⓘ *0789 89 20 19.*

The heart of the Costa Smeralda and a paradise for European VIPs, Porto Cervo is centred around two yacht harbours with some of the most spectacular private craft in the world. In summer there is a series of top sporting events, including regattas and golf tournaments (*see p198 and p201*). The traditional evening stroll along the quay is almost obligatory, with fashionable designer shops on one side, and luxury yachts on the other. The church of Stella Maris has a canvas attributed to the painter El Greco.

Environs: There are plenty of good beaches around Porto Cervo, such as Liscia Ruja to the south, framed by the sheltered Cala di Volpe.

Palau ❺

Road map D1. ⚄ *3,300.* ⓘ *0789 70 85 56 or 0789 70 95 70.*

The logical departure point for a trip to the Maddalena archipelago, Palau also owes its success to the appeal of the narrow-gauge Sassari-Tempio-Palau railway, part of the Trenino Verde (*see pp92–3*). Life here is rather frenetic in the summer and revolves around the ferry boat wharf and the yacht harbour. From Palau you can travel to some of the most fascinating and famous places on the coast, such as the jagged

Capo d'Orso (Bear Cape) promontory, which ends in a large, bear-shaped rock, sculpted by the wind.

To get to Punta Sardegna, take the road that goes up to Monte Altura and then go on foot to the beach of Cala Trana, on the tip of the headland. There is an extraordinary view of the coast and the islands, which is particularly lovely in the early morning and at

Sunset at Palau, departure point for the Maddalena Archipelago

sunset, despite the fact that 21st-century construction work is slowly but surely spoiling the unique beauty of this part of Sardinia.

The Maddalena Archipelago ❻

See pp146–9.

Santa Teresa di Gallura ❼

Road map C1. ⚄ *4,200.* ⓘ *0789 75 41 27.* ⚄ *15–18 Oct: Festival.* **www**.comunesantateresagallura.it

The area around Santa Teresa was inhabited in Roman times and was also important to the Pisans, who used the local granite for building. The present-day town was built from scratch during the Savoyard period. It has a regular grid plan with streets intersecting at right angles, in

THE AGA KHAN AND THE COSTA SMERALDA

The Consorzio Costa Smeralda group of foreign investors was founded in 1962 with Prince Karim Aga Khan IV at its head. The Harvard-educated prince, rich and charismatic, was then in his mid-twenties. He is reputed to have spent more than 1,000 million dollars in creating an opulent jet-set playground, complete with yachting marinas, luxury hotels, villas and elegant restaurants along the Gallura coastline, all designed to harmonize with the rugged Sardinian landscape. The project has proved very successful: Porto Cervo and the nearby villages quickly became popular holiday spots, especially for the wealthy and famous of the international jet set, who can be seen on the quays of Porto Cervo in the summer.

Aga Khan IV

Overlooking Santa Teresa di Gallura

the middle of which is a small square and the church of San Vittorio. The local economy is based on fishing (including coral fishing) and tourism.

On the rocky headland stands the Torre Longosardo, a tower built in the 16th century during the Aragonese period; it affords a magnificent view of Porto Longone bay and, in the distance, the white cliffs circling the city of Bonifacio in Corsica, which is only 12 km (7.5 miles) away.

To the left the coast falls away to the beach of Rena Bianca, which ends not far from the Isola Monica, a tiny island which has the remains of an abandoned quarry.

The Capo Testa lighthouse

Environs: About 5 km (3 miles) away is **Capo Testa**, a rocky promontory connected to the mainland by a thin sandbar. The headland can be reached via a very pretty route around the bays of Colba and Santa Reparata. A walk through the ancient and modern quarries – which supplied the Romans with the granite for the columns in the Pantheon – accompanied by the sweet fragrance of the maquis will take you to the Capo Testa lighthouse.

Arzachena ❽

Road map D1. 🏘 *12,000.* ℹ *0789 89 20 19.*

Around 40 years ago, this was a peaceful shepherds' village. Today it is the centre of one of the most famous tourist resorts in the world, the Costa Smeralda, and has undergone considerable change. Towering above the houses is a curious rock formed by wind erosion, called the Fungo (mushroom), and there are many traces of prehistoric settlements in the vicinity. Must-see sites include the **Albucciu Nuraghe**, the **Tomba di Giganti Coddu Vecchju** and the **Li Muri Necropolis**.

🏛 Albucciu Nuraghe
Cooperativo Lithos **Tel** *335 127 68 49.* ⬜ *Easter–15 Oct: 9am–7pm daily (no guided tours between 1 & 3pm); Oct 16–Easter: by appt only.* 📷♿🏛 *lithos@portocervo.net*
From Arzachena, take the road to Olbia and after about 600 m (650 yds), at the end of town, follow the turn-off and then

take the footpath on the right. Once at the nuraghe, go up the ladder to the upper level, to visit the side section.

The stone brackets that once supported the original wooden structure are still intact.

🏛 Tomba di Giganti Coddu Vecchju
For contact details & opening hours see Albucciu Nuraghe. 📷♿🏛
To get to the Giants' Tomb, take state road SS427 towards Calangianus and, after about 3 km (2 miles), take the turning to the right signposted Luogosanto. After about 1,800 m (1 mile) you join the Capichera road, and another 500 m (550 yds) on there is a path leading to the tomb, which lies to the right. In the middle of the funerary monument there is a stele 4 m (13 ft) high, surrounded by a semicircular wall of stone slabs set into the earth.

🏛 Li Muri Necropolis
For contact details & opening hours see Albucciu Nuraghe. 📷 *(book ahead for a trek combining archaeology and nature).*
Once outside Arzachena, follow signs for Calangianus (SS427) and then the right-hand turning for Luogosanto. Continue for 4.5 km (3 miles) and take another turning to the right (a dirt road), which goes to the necropolis of Li Muri.

This site includes a number of ancient tombs: burial chambers surrounded by concentric circles of stones. These funerary circles constitute the most important monumental complex left from the era archaeologists now refer to as the Arzachena Culture.

The mistral whipping up the surf off Capo Testa

The Maddalena Archipelago ❻

Subalpine warblers

Seven islands (Maddalena, Caprera and Santo Stefano to the south-east, Spargi, Budelli, Razzoli and Santa Maria to the northwest) make up the Arcipelago della Maddalena. Beyond lie the Straits of Bonifacio, which became a marine reserve of international status at the beginning of 1997. Rugged, jagged coasts, rocks hewn by wind and water erosion, and tenacious maquis vegetation characterize this group of islands, known during the Roman period as *Cuniculariae*, or "rabbit islands". In the 18th century Maddalena was used as a military base – it is a convenient landing place and lay in a strategically important position. A tour of the island would be incomplete without a visit to Caprera, to see the places where the Italian hero Giuseppe Garibaldi lived and is buried.

Budelli
Cactus grows on the shores of this island, popular with divers.

Spargi
Uninhabited, like Budelli, Razzoli and Santa Maria, this island has marvellously clear water and secluded beaches, making it an ideal site for swimmers, snorkellers and scuba divers.

A scenic route of just over 20 km (12 miles) runs around the island, providing magnificent views of the archipelago, Corsica and the four Corsican islands of Lavezzi.

Bird Life
The many rock formations in this archipelago are frequently visited by sea birds such as cormorants, to the delight of bird-watchers.

★ **La Maddalena**
This is the most important town in the archipelago. Town life centres around Piazza Umberto I and Piazza Garibaldi. There is a wide choice of boat trips to the nearby islands from the harbour.

Regattas
The west wind, an almost constant presence in the Maddalena archipelago, makes this a popular place for yachting competitions.

VISITORS' CHECKLIST

Road map D1.
🚢 *from Palau, departures every 20 mins in the summer (once an hour after midnight) and winter.*
🛈 *0789 73 63 21.*
Caprera *can be reached from Maddalena via a 600-m (2,000-ft) bridge over the Passo della Moneta.*
www.lamaddalena.com

Guardia Vecchia is the highest mountain on the island. The Savoy rulers chose it as the site for the fort of San Vittorio, which is now occupied by a lighthouse.

Monte Teialone is the highest point on Caprera.

The Bridge over Passo della Moneta
Constructed in 1891, this bridge links the islands of Maddalena and Caprera.

SANTO STEFANO

CAPRERA

Caprera
The island of Caprera extends over nearly 1,600 hectares (3,950 acres).

★ Tomb of Garibaldi
The "hero of two worlds" was buried here on 2 June 1882.

STAR SIGHTS

★ La Maddalena

★ Tomb of Garibaldi

Exploring the Maddalena Archipelago

The small Maddalena Archipelago is a favourite with sailing fanatics, fans of underwater fishing and with people who appreciate tranquillity and unspoilt surroundings. Except for the two largest islands, the archipelago is uninhabited and, together with the many other small islands, make perfect summer destinations for boat trips, sunbathing and swimming in solitude.

The Sardinia Regional Naval headquarters at La Maddalena

La Maddalena
Road map D1. 🏛 12,000.
🚹 0789 73 63 21. 🚢 from
Palau. 🎭 20–22 Jul: Santa
Maria Maddalena.

The town that is now the capital of the island was founded in 1770 and replaced a small village built on the shores of the Cala Gavetta bay. After the unsuccessful invasion on the part of the French in 1793, British admiral Horatio Nelson stopped at La Maddalena in 1804 and in 1887 the entire Maddalena Archipelago was turned into a naval base by the Savoy rulers. On Via Amendola, which runs along the seafront, a series of 19th-century buildings bears witness to the rapid development of the town in this period. In Piazza Garibaldi, the Municipio (town hall) has on display a French bomb dating from France's attempt to conquer Sardinia in 1793.

In the evening, particularly in summer, the residents of the island can be found taking a leisurely stroll around Via Garibaldi. Not far away is the church of Santa Maria Maddalena, which has two candelabra and a silver cross given by Admiral Nelson to

the island's inhabitants. La Maddalena is still the head-quarters of the Sardinia Regional Navy.

🧭 The Scenic Route
The road around the island is about 20 km (12 miles) long and goes through the Cala Spalmatore, Stagno Torto and Baia Trínita bays.

On your way from La Maddalena, you will see the church of the Trinità, then the turn-off for Monte Guardia Vecchia, on the summit of which is the Savoyard fort of San Vittorio, and lastly the island of Giardinelli, which is connected to La Maddalena by

a narrow strip of land. Further north are Porto Massimo, the inlets of Abbatoggia and Cala d'Inferno, and the other large fortification on the island, Forte dei Colmi. In the first stretch of this tour is the **Museo Archeologico Navale "Nino Lamboglia"**, the maritime museum with finds from the "ship of Spargi", an ancient Roman cargo vessel discovered in the 1950s.

> 🏛 **Museo Archeologico Navale "Nino Lamboglia"**
> Località Mongiardino. 🕘 9:30am–12:30pm. 🌞 Sun (Apr–Sep). **Tel** 0789 79 06 60/33. 📷

Caprera
Road map D1. 🚹 0789 73 63 21.
This small island has 34 km (21 miles) of coastline, and is connected to the island of Maddalena by the 600 m (1,968 ft) Passo della Moneta bridge. Walkers will enjoy the climb up the steps to the top of Monte Teialone (212 m, 695 ft).

The island of Caprera became the property of Giuseppe Garibaldi in 1856 (see pp40–41). His estate is now part of the **Compendio Garibaldino** museum area. A visit here includes a fascinating tour of the stables, moorings and the Casa Bianca (white house) where Garibaldi lived. The stable still has a period steamengine used for threshing, while the Casa Bianca contains mementos of Garibaldi's adventurous life, including weapons, flags, portraits, the hero's clothes (including his famous red shirt) and a model of the Battle of Solferino.

GARIBALDI AND CAPRERA

The legendary Italian hero and revolutionary Giuseppe Garibaldi escaped to the island of Caprera in 1849, after the fall of the Roman Republic. He returned in 1855 after the death of his wife Anita and decided to buy most of the island. The rest of the land was then given to him by some English friends. Garibaldi, who went on to play a key role in the unification of Italy, settled on Caprera permanently in 1857, and died here in 1882.

Giuseppe Garibaldi wearing the famous red shirt

The famous pink sand beach at Budelli

Garibaldi's favourite room was the salon, and he asked to be taken there before he died. The calendar and clocks in the room have not been changed since that day, and still show the exact time of his death: 6:20pm on 2 June 1882.

Caprera also has a famous sailing school, the Centro Velico Caprera *(see p199).*

🏛 Compendio Garibaldino
Tel *0789 72 71 62.* ⏲ *9am–1:30pm Tue–Sun (Jun–Sep: to 6:30pm).* 🚫 *1 Jan, 25 Dec.* 🚫 📷 ♿
www.compendiogaribaldino.it

Santo Stefano
Road map D1.
🛈 *0789 73 63 21.*
The small island of Santo Stefano lies halfway between Palau and *the* island of Maddalena and can be reached via the boats that depart at regular intervals from La Maddalena harbour. Dominating the scene is the Santo Stefano (or San Giorgio) fortress, also known as Napoleon's fort, built at the end of the 18th century.

There is a tourist village on the beach of Pesce, on the western coast.

Spargi
Road map D1. 🚢 *from La Maddalena.* 🛈 *0789 73 63 21.*
Spargi is little more than 2 km (1 mile) in diameter and is completely uninhabited. The terrain is fairly barren and the coast steep and inaccessible, but there is a lovely beach for bathing, although keep in mind that it has no facilities. An ancient Roman ship was found opposite the Cala Corsara cove on the southern coast; its cargo is now in the Museo Archeologico Navale "Nino Lamboglia" at La Maddalena. Tourist boats make regular stops at Cala Corsara.

Budelli
Road map D1.
🛈 *0789 73 63 21.*
This beautiful uninhabited island is remarkable for its unique beach of rose-coloured sand. Even though there are no facilities, Budelli is popular with visitors because of its beautifully unspoiled natural setting. It was also used in a film by the director Michelangelo Antonioni.

The clear, unpolluted water is also ideal for scuba diving, either to observe marine life or for underwater fishing.

SAILING IN NORTHERN SARDINIA

The Straits of Bonifacio are dotted with small islands and rocks with lighthouses which create natural buoys, making the area ideal for yacht and dinghy racing. The wind is pretty constant, and in summer the west wind blows steadily at 40 km per hour (24 mph).

The Costa Smeralda Yacht Club at Porto Cervo, founded by the Aga Khan, is the main sailing facility in this area. This world-famous club organizes several major sailing races and other competitions. The most well-known are the Sardinia Cup, an international deep-sea championship held in even-numbered years, and the Settimana delle Bocche, a summer race for speed-boats from all over Italy.

In the odd-numbered years the old harbour at Porto Cervo provides space for 50 or so vintage boats: from the *gozzo* with its characteristic lateen sail to 30-m (98-ft) schooners. This popular event, which has been held since 1982, is usually followed by the world yacht championship for boats in the Maxi class. Other important races, such as the European and world championships of various yacht categories, also take place here. The Costa Smeralda Yacht Club represented Italy in the 1983 America's Cup with the yacht *Azzurra* and in 1987 the club organized regattas to select the Italian representative in the America's Cup in Perth, Australia.

Yachts racing in the Straits of Bonifacio

San Trano, a 12th-century hermitage near Luogosanto

Luogosanto **9**

Road map C1. 🏘 *1,900.* ℹ *Town Hall (079 65 790).* 🎭 *first Sun in Aug: San Quirico's feast day.*

The village of Luogosanto is surrounded by maquis, and is well known for the production of bitter honey, often served with *seadas (see p181).* The village is typical of the Gallura region, backed by greenery and wind-eroded pinkish-grey rocks. Every seven years a colourful and solemn ceremony celebrates the opening of the Porta Santa (holy door) of the church of Nostra Signora di Luogosanto.

San Quirico's feast day ends with a dinner for all the villagers. The traditional dish *carr'e cogghju*, made with pork and cabbage, is served.

About 1 km (half a mile) to the east of Luogosanto is the **San Trano hermitage**, perched at 410 m (1,345 ft), dominating the landscape towards the north of the town. This small church was built in the 12th century in memory of the hermit saints San Nicola and San Trano, who, according to the legend, lived in the small cave to the rear of the altar.

Nearby is the Filetta spring, whose waters are famous throughout the island. In recent years, squares, steps and street lamps have been set around the spring.

Sant'Antonio di Gallura **10**

Road map D1. 🏘 *1,700.* 🚌 ℹ *Town Hall (079 66 90 13).* 🎭 *last weekend in Sep: Sant'Antonio.*

This village has always been an important farming and sheep-raising centre. In the heart of town, situated on a rocky spur, is a small, recently founded archaeological park, known for its intricate landscape of wind-sculpted rocks. This same site was inhabited in prehistoric times. During the first week of September, the feast days of Sant'Antonio, San Michele and Sant'Isidoro are celebrated with a procession. Decorated oxen and tractors follow the statues of the saints through the streets.

Environs: 2 km (1 mile) away is the artificial lake of Liscia, capable of holding 150,000,000 cubic m (5 billion cubic ft) of water.

Calangianus **11**

Road map C2. 🏘 *4,800.* 🚌 ℹ *Town Hall (079 66 00 00).* 🎭 *third Sun in Sep: Sant'Isidoro's feast day.*

In the forests around the town of Calangianus you can see evidence of cork harvesting everywhere: the barked cork oaks have that characteristic reddish colour that will remain until the bark grows again, while the cork strips themselves are heaped up in large piles to dry.

Calangianus is the cork production centre of the Gallura region and there are numbers of workshops and factories for processing the material. There is also an important trade school whose curriculum focuses on the cultivation of cork oaks and

The artificial lake of Liscia near Calangianus

making the maximum use of cork bark. In September every year Calangianus hosts an exhibition and trade fair of cork oaks and their many by-products, both on an industrial and domestic scale.

In the centre of the old town, in a small, isolated square, is the small parish church of Santa Giusta, which was built in the 17th century.

Cork items produced in the Gallura region

Environs: Near the village of **Luras** (northwest of Calangianus), a series of prehistoric dolmens is open to visitors. To reach the site, go through the village in the direction of Luogosanto and then turn right just before the end of town. At the point where the paved road ends, take the dirt road on the right, which takes you to the **Ladas Dolmen**, the most impressive of them all. It has a rectangular plan, is roofed with two granite slabs, and is 6 m (19 ft) long and 2.20 m (7 ft) wide.

Tempio Pausania ⑫

Road map C2. 🚶 14,000. 🚉
ℹ️ *Pro Loco (079 639 00 80).*
🎭 *Shrove Tuesday: Carnival.*

The capital of Gallura, Tempio Pausania consists of a large number of modern buildings which tend to obscure the charming old town. Investigate further and discover two- and three-storey buildings with dark granite stone walls and characteristic balconies. A short walk from the central Piazza Gallura, site of the town hall and other public buildings, is the **Cathedral** – founded in the 15th century but rebuilt in the 1800s. Also nearby are the Oratorio del Rosario and the small **Santa Croce** church.

Not far from town are the **Rinaggiu springs**, whose mineral water is famous for its beneficial qualities. As well as the traditional festivals, an international folklore festival is held here in July *(see p27).*

Environs: A short distance away, on state road SS133, is the turning for the **Maiori Nuraghe**, one of the best preserved megalithic structures in the area.

Detail of Santa Croce

By heading south from the town on state road 392 for 17 km (10 miles) you will pass close to the summit of **Monte Limbara** (1,359 m, 4,459 ft), which can be reached in a few minutes on foot from the paved road.

Along the way you will see the Curadoreddu road house (about 6 km, 4 miles, from Tempio Pausania); here, a turning to the left will take you to an abandoned fish farm, from which you can admire an impressive view of mountain rock pools and waterfalls. Water flows from one great mass of rocks to the other, creating cascades and hollows. The spectacle is at its most striking during the winter months.

The bed of the mountain stream near Curadoreddu

CORK AND THE HANDICRAFTS OF GALLURA

Cork is obtained from the stripped bark of cork oak trees (Quercus suber) and has always been a fundamental part of the Gallura regional economy. The material is used for everyday purposes as well as local handicrafts. Among kitchen utensils in use are cork spoons and ladles (such as the s'uppu, a small ladle used to collect water), buckets and different containers for water and wine, and large serving dishes – called agiones in dialect – for roasts and other dishes. Today the Tempio Pausania region produces 90 per cent of the bottle stoppers used in Italy, although the cork is also used as a building and insulating material. Cork is very versatile, thanks to its lightness, resistance to air and water, its insulating properties and long life.

Strips of cork bark ready for processing

Cork cannot be stripped from the tree before it is at least 25–30 years old. The first layer stripped is porous and elastic and of scant commercial use. Only nine to ten years after this first barking process is the true – and profitable – new layer of cork obtained. The trees are then stripped every nine to ten years, and the layers thoroughly seasoned before use.

A barked cork oak tree

The Valle della Luna (Valley of the Moon) near Aggius

Aggius ⑬

Road map C1. 👥 *1,200.*
ℹ️ *Town Hall (079 62 03 39).*
🎉 *first Sun in Oct: feast days of
Santa Vittoria and Madonna del
Rosario.* **www**.*aggius.net*

Natural features have
shaped this village and
its surroundings. A granite
outcrop dominates the landscape of Aggius, both in the
high ground of the Parco
Capitza, which towers over
the town, and in the amazing
labyrinth of rock formations
in the nearby Valle della Luna.
    Once the dominion of the
Doria family from Genoa, and
then ruled by the Aragonese,
Aggius owes its present prosperity to the quarrying and
processing of granite. Local
handicrafts are also important
to the economy – especially
rug-making, every stage of
which is carried out using
traditional techniques.
    The centre of Aggius is a
pleasant place to walk; the
old stone houses have been
lovingly preserved and they
are among the most attractive

in the Gallura region. On the
first Sunday in October
traditional festivities are held,
including the *di li 'agghiani*,
for unmarried men, at which
the Gàllura *suppa cuata* (bread
and cheese soup) is served.
    The road to Isola Rossa
quickly brings you to the
Valle della Luna, with its
weird rock formations, the
result of glaciation.
    On a left-hand curve
a dirt road veers right.
Follow this almost up to
the bridge, then continue
along the small road on
the right, which leads to
the **Izzana Nuraghe** in the
middle of the valley.

Rock formations above Aggius

Berchidda ⑭

Road map C2. 👥 *3,400.* 🚌
ℹ️ *Town Hall (079 70 39 01).*

Built on the southern
slopes of Monte Limbara,
in a hilly landscape which
stretches as far as Monte
Azzarina, Berchidda is a large
village whose economy is
based on sheep raising, dairy
products, cork processing and
viticulture. The leading local
wine is Vermentino (one of
the best known of Sardinian
white wines), and the local
pecorino cheese is also of
excellent quality.
    About 4 km (2 miles) from
the centre of Berchidda, a
steep climb will take you to
the ruins of the **Castello di
Montacuto**, which was the
fortress of Adelasia di Torres
and her husband Ubaldo
Visconti before becoming the
domain of the Doria and
Malaspina families from the
mainland. Monte
Limbara, the
geographical
heart of the
Gallura
region,
towers in
the back-
ground.

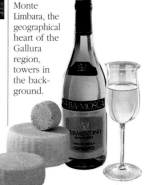

**Cheese and white
Vermentino wine, locally made
produce from Sardinia**

Buddusò ⑮

Road map C2 & D2. 👥 *6,500.*
ℹ️ *Town Hall (079 715 90 00).*

The town of Buddusò is
fairly prosperous thanks
to sheep farming, granite
quarrying and the processing
and sale of cork.
    The stone-paved streets in
the old part of town wind
around buildings made of
dark stone. In the Roman era
the main road from Kàralis

(Cagliari) to Olbia crossed the town, then known as Caput Thirsi. The church of **Santa Anastasia** and the paintings in the sacristy are worth a visit. A tour through the **Monti di Alà** is another worthwhile excursion.

Environs: Nearby are the **Iselle Nuraghe** (towards Pattada) and **Loelle Nuraghe**, on the road to Mamone.

A *Cuile*, or shepherd's hut

San Teodoro ⑯

Road map D2. 🏛 *2,900.* ℹ
0784 86 57 67.
www.santeodoroturismo.com

To the south of the Capo Coda Cavallo headland, just opposite the rocky island of Tavolara, the village of San Teodoro has grown rapidly in recent years due to increasing numbers of tourists.

The village also makes an excellent starting point for excursions to the Cinta beach, a long strip of sandy terrain that separates the **Stagno di San Teodoro** from the sea. Fairly close to the Orientale

THE ISLAND OF TAVOLARA

This island is a mountain of limestone rising from the sea to a height of 500 m (1,640 ft). The eastern side is an inaccessible military zone, but the low sandy area called Spalmatore di Terra has beaches, a small harbour, a couple of restaurants and a few houses. Together with the neighbouring islands of Molara and Molarotto, home to over 150 moufflons, Tavolara is a marine reserve. The granite cliffs are pierced by caves and crevices. Sea lilies grow in the Spalmatore di Terra area and the rock is covered with juniper, helichrysum, rosemary and lentiscus. According to tradition, Carlo Alberto, the king of Piedmont and Sardinia, landed on the island to find the legendary "goats with golden teeth" (a phenomenon caused by a grass they eat), and was so fascinated by the island that he officially dubbed its only inhabitant, Paolo Bertolini, "king of Tavolara". In the summer there is a regular boat service to the island from Olbia *(see p142)* and Porto San Paolo. Visit **www**.tavolara.it

The unmistakable profile of the island of Tavolara

Sarda road, this 200-hectare (494-acre) lake and marsh is one of the few remaining coastal marshes that once lay south of the Bay of Olbia. Mallards and coots are easily sighted on the water. When the birds glimpse a bird of prey or other danger, they gather in large groups and make a loud noise to defend themselves.

Grey and red heron as well as Kentish plovers can be seen in search of food. Another common sight is the hovering kestrel, one of Italy's smallest raptors.

Granite outcrops are used as a resting place by ducks.

The clear, still water is rich in food for birds.

Grey heron

Kestrel

The shores are ideal for mud-dwelling creatures.

Lapwing

The Stagno di San Teodoro

The village of Alà dei Sardi

Alà dei Sardi ⓐ

Road map D2. 👥 *2,000.*
ℹ️ *Buddusò Town Hall
(079 715 90 00).* 📅 *4 Oct: countryside feast day of San Francesco.*

Rocks and maquis, and
forests of enormous cork
oaks with the characteristic
marks of recent stripping,
make up the landscape of Alà
dei Sardi and its plateau, the
last tract of the rocky interior
overlooking the Bay of Olbia.
  The main street of the
village is lined with the
small granite stone houses
characteristic of this region.

Environs: Not far from Alà
dei Sardi, off the road which
leads to Buddusò, is the **Ruju
nuraghe**, with the remains of
a prehistoric village almost
buried in the scrub.

Following signs to the town
of Monti, the route crosses a
sizeable plateau studded with
astonishingly varied rock
formations. At a fork, the
road deviates for the
sanctuary of San Pietro
l'Eremita, and passes
through some stunning
scenery, with gaps
allowing occasional
views of the sea and
the unmistakable
profile of the island of
Tavolara *(see p153)* in
the distance. The
Romanesque church of
San Pietro l'Eremita
has been relatively
recently restored.
Every year in August
at Ferragosto
(Assumption Day), the
church is crowded
with pilgrims from the
surrounding villages.

Pattada ⓑ

Road map C2. 👥 *3,800.*
ℹ️ *Town Hall (079 75 51 14).*
📅 *29 Aug: Santa Sabina.*

Situated in the middle of a
territory rich in prehistoric
nuraghi and other vestiges
of the past, Pattada is world-
famous for the production
of steel knives, which began
here because of a rich vein
of iron ore which has been
worked for centuries. The
village blacksmiths still carry
on the tradition of making
steel blades, and handles
from animal horn, and dozens

The Sa Fraigada forest near Pattada

THE KNIVES OF PATTADA

The best-known style of shepherd's knife
made in Pattada is the *resolza* (the word
derives from the Latin *rasoria*, or razor). The
resolza is a jack-knife with a steel blade
that may be as much as 14 cm (5 inches)
long. The blacksmiths of Pattada only use
traditional materials. Steel is hammered into shape in
a forge and on an anvil; the handle is made from wood, or
from moufflon, sheep or deer horn. The production of
Pattada knives dates from the mid-19th century, and the best
knives are still
hand-made by
skilled
craftsmen.

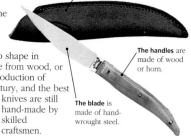

Sheath

The handles are
made of wood
or horn.

The blade is
made of hand-
wrought steel.

Among the masters at work today some, like
Salvatore Giagu and Maria Rosaria Deroma,
draw inspiration from the oldest types of
Pattada knives, such as the fixed-blade *corrina*,
which dates back to the 18th century. It is not
easy to find real Pattada knives on sale, and you
should avoid imitations. Production is a slow
and complicated affair, but it is possible to
order a Pattada knife to be made for you,
although this procedure will take about a year.

An assortment of Pattada knives

The artificial lake created by the Rio Mannu at Pattada

of imitations of these Sardinian knives can now be found on the Italian mainland.

Environs: In the vicinity of Pattada is the **Fiorentini** – an area of greenery resulting from reforestation – and the ruins of the medieval castle of Olomene.

Earthenware found in the Grotta di San Michele

Ozieri ⑲

Road map C2. 🏛 12,000. 🖪 🖪
Town Hall (079 78 12 00); Pro Loco (079 78 61 94); Comunità Montana del Monte Acuto (079 781 06 00).
🎏 second Sun in May: Sant'Antioco di Bisarcio **www**.comune.ozieri.ss.it

Ozieri lies in a natural hollow and its situation is one of the most attractive sights in northeast Sardinia. Both the traditions and architecture here are interesting, and the town has a fascinating history that goes back millennia and has added to the knowledge of the remote pre-nuraghic cultures which developed here.

The fabric and layout of the town are quite varied and blend in well with the slopes of the hills. Among the tall houses the occasional covered roof terrace filled with flowers can be glimpsed.

The major sights in the old town are **Piazza Carlo Alberto** and **Piazza Fonte Grixoni**, centred around an ancient fountain. On the edge of the historic quarter is the Neo-Classical **Cathedral**, which contains a splendid 16th-century Sardinian polyptych by the artist known as the

Maestro di Ozieri. The painting depicts the famous miracle of the Sanctuary of the Madonna of Loreto, and reveals Spanish influences as well as traces of Flemish mannerism. The 17th-century San Francesco monastery houses the **Museo Archeologico**, with finds from the archaeological digs in the area. Most of this material belongs to the era of the Ozieri civilization, the predominant culture here from 3500 to 2700 BC. It is also known as

San Michele, from the name of the cave in which major finds were discovered.

The territory surrounding Ozieri is also rich in historic and archaeological sites and ruins, such as the *domus de janas* at Butule, the San Pantaleo necropolis and the dolmen at Montiju Coronas.

The **Grotta di San Michele** is a cave that lies behind the Ozieri hospital, near the track and field stadium (in fact, during the construction of the latter, part of the cave was destroyed). Large quantities of decorated ceramics were found here, as well as human bones, a mother-goddess statuette and pieces of obsidian from Monte Arci. All these finds support the theory that there was some continuity from the earlier Bonu Ighinu culture to the time of the Ozieri.

🏛 **Museo Archeologico di Ozieri**
Piazza Canonico Spano. **Tel** 079 785 10 52. ⏲ 9am–1pm, 4–7pm Tue– Sat; 9:30am–12:30pm Sun. 🚻 🚹

🏛 **Grotta di San Michele,**
Ozieri Hospital. ⏲ Apr–Sep. 🚻 combined ticket for both sites.

Terraces of houses climbing the slopes of the town of Ozieri

Tour of the Logudoro ⑳

Detail, Sant'Antioco di Bisarcio

After the fall of the Roman Empire, Sardinia did not return to a central role in the Mediterranean until after the year 1000, when Pisan and Genoese merchants, soldiers and preachers came into contact with the different regional cultures of the island. The Romanesque churches in the north of Sardinia are the result of these encounters. It is difficult to assess how much of each single monument was created by local artists and artisans and how much by those from Pisa and Genoa. Whatever the facts, east of Sassari there is a series of Romanesque churches that has few equals in the rest of mainland Italy.

Nostra Signora di Tergu ⑦
This church was built over the remains of a monastery founded by monks from Montecassino in Tuscany.

Santissima Trinità di Saccargia ①
The Santissima Trinità, built in striped layers of black and white stone, is the most significant example of Romanesque architecture in northern Sardinia. The apse is decorated with frescoes of Christ and the saints. The church was restored in the early 1900s *(see pp158-9)*.

Castelsardo

Valledoria

Sassari ←

Nuraghe di Camarzu

San Michele di Salvènero (Ploaghe) ②
In the 12th century the monks of Vallombrosa built this church near the village of Salvènero, which has since disappeared. The church now stands abandoned in the middle of a series of road interchanges. Restored in the 13th century and again in 1912, this splendid monument needs to attract greater care and respect to safeguard its future.

Ploaghe

Santa Maria del Regno (Ardara) ③
Consecrated in 1107, this Pisan-Romanesque church is famous for the *Retablo Maggiore di Ardara*, one of the best on the island. The paintings on the altar-step are by the Sardinian Giovanni Muru (1515).

San Pietro di Simbranos (or delle Immagini) ⑥

The traditional name of this church derives from the bas-relief on the façade depicting an abbot and two monks (the *immagini* or "images"). San Pietro, in the Bulzi area, was first built in 1113 and rebuilt in its present form a century later. This isolated and tranquil monument has a particular fascination because of its desert setting among canyons and rocks.

VISITORS' CHECKLIST

Road map C2.
Santissima Trinità di Saccargia and **Sant'Antioco di Bisarcio**
◯ *normal opening hours;* **San Michele di Salvènero** ◉ **Nostra Signora di Castro** ◯ *variable, the cumbessias precinct can be visited;* **Santa Maria del Regno di Ardara**, *enquire at priest's house;* **Nostra Signora di Tergu** ◉ *can usually only be seen from outside;* **San Pietro di Simbranos** ◯ *normal opening hours, or ask Bulzi parish priest.*

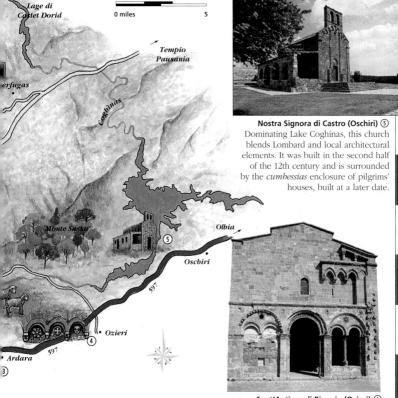

Nostra Signora di Castro (Oschiri) ⑤

Dominating Lake Coghínas, this church blends Lombard and local architectural elements. It was built in the second half of the 12th century and is surrounded by the *cumbessias* enclosure of pilgrims' houses, built at a later date.

KEY

▬ Major road

= Other roads

— River

Sant'Antioco di Bisarcio (Ozieri) ④

Sant'Antioco is a combination of Pisan Romanesque and French influences. Sant'Antioco was built from the second half of the 11th century to the late 12th century and was initially the cathedral of the Bisarcio diocese. It differs from the other churches on this tour in its architectural complexity, shown in the unusual two-storey porch, small windows and the decorative detail on the façade.

Santissima Trinità di Saccargia ㉑

Portico frieze

Both simple and impressive, Sardinia's most famous Romanesque church stands in the middle of a windswept valley. Its name probably derives from *sa acca argia*, "the dappled cow". According to legend, this animal used to kneel in prayer on the site, which is why there are carvings of the cow on four sides of one of the capitals in the portico. Another account relates how, around the year 1112, the ruler of the region, Constantine, donated the small church to the Camaldolesi monks, who then decided to enlarge it with the help of Tuscan architects, craftsmen and labourers. Initially they added the apse and the bell tower with its alternating layers of black trachyte and white limestone. At a later stage they built the porch, the only one on a Sardinian church. The austere interior, with a tall, narrow nave lit by small openings or slots in the side walls, is very atmospheric.

Animal frieze
The severity of the exterior of the church is lightened with sculptures of animals.

★ Façade
Two rows of blind arches adorn the façade, each level decorated with rose windows and multi-coloured diamonds. The central arch has an opening in the form of a cross.

The campanile is 41 m (134 ft) tall and each side is 8 m (26 ft) wide.

★ Carved Cows
It may be that the church was named after the carved cows on this capital, even though the portico was built after the main church.

VISITORS' CHECKLIST

Road map C2. **Tel** *079 43 53 75.*
☐ *8am–8pm daily (Oct–Mar:*
to 1pm). From Sassari, follow the
SS131 for 10 km (6 miles), then
turn off on the SS597 to Olbia.

Double-lancet Windows
These date from the late
12th century.

**The black and white
stripes** reveal Pisan
influence.

Monastery Ruins
Only a few black and white
stone archways are left
of the first and most
important
Camaldolese
monastery in
Sardinia.

Fresco
of Christ
Christ is depicted holding a
book in the act of benediction.

The aisleless nave
was built after the
apse, which dates
from 1116.

★ The Apse Frescoes
Romanesque frescoes are rare
in Sardinia – these are
attributed to Pisan artists.

Portico Capitals
The portico is supported by
columns with carved
capitals. They carry the
classic Romanesque motifs
of plants and animals.

STAR FEATURES

★ Carved Cows

★ Façade

★ Apse Frescoes

Sassari ㉒

Coat of arms of Sassari

Sardinia's second most important city commercially, politically and culturally, Sassari lies on a tableland that slopes down to the sea among olive groves and fertile and well cultivated valleys. The city has a long history of invasions, conquests and raids, but also boasts a tradition of stubborn rebellion and uprisings. Pisans, Genoese and Aragonese have all attempted to subdue the city, but the indomitable spirit of the Sassari citizens has always succeeded in asserting independence. The city's hero is a rebel named Carlo Maria Angioj, who headed a revolt in 1796 against the Savoyard government, which had sought to impose a feudal system. Two presidents of the Italian Republic, Antonio Segni and Francesco Cossiga, were born in Sassari, as was the prominent Italian Communist Party leader Enrico Berlinguer *(see pp44–5)*.

The *Li Candareri* festival in Sassari

Exploring Sassari

The old town, with its winding alleyways branching off from the main streets, was once surrounded by walls that ran along present-day Corso Vico, Corso Trinità, Via Brigata Sassari and Corso Margherita. Only a few parts of the city walls (such as the section at the beginning of Corso Trinità) have survived the effects of time, but the old centre has preserved its original layout, even though it is now somewhat dilapidated.

A morning should be enough time for a walk around the old town. The main sights are the Duomo (cathedral), the Fontana del Rosello fountain, the churches of Sant'Antonio, Santa Maria di Betlem and San Pietro in Silki, and the Sanna museum.

🔒 Duomo

Piazza Duomo. **Tel** *079 23 20 67.*
🕐 *4–7pm daily.* 📷 ♿
www.diocesi.sassari.it

Sassari cathedral is dedicated to San Nicola (St Nicholas). Its impressive Baroque façade is in rather striking contrast to its size and to the small, simple and elegant 18th-century Piazza Duomo with its characteristic semicircular shape. The end result of successive enlargements and changes carried out over the centuries, the Duomo was originally built on the site of a Romanesque church. The base of the façade and bell tower are still intact.

At the end of the 15th century the original structure underwent radical transformation that not only changed its shape but created today's unusual proportions. The side walls were propped up by buttresses decorated with gargoyles of mythical and monstrous animals, while the interior was rebuilt in the Gothic style.

In the late 18th century the upper portion of the façade was radically changed with the addition of rather grand decoration: volutes, flowers, cherubs and fantastic figures. In the middle, the statue of San Nicola is surmounted by the figures of the three martyr saints, Gavino, Proto and Gianuario, set in three niches. At a later stage, an octagonal section decorated with multi-coloured majolica tiles was superimposed on the original Lombard-style lower part of the campanile. The interior, which has been totally restored, has retained its simple Gothic lines despite the presence of lavishly decorated Baroque altars. The choir, the work of 18th-century Sardinian artists, is particularly striking.

The Museo del Duomo, reached through the Cappella Aragonese (Aragonese chapel) on the right, houses

Detail of the façade of Sassari Cathedral

The Fontana del Rosello, dating from the Renaissance

VISITORS' CHECKLIST

Road map B2. 🏘 120,000.
🚌 🚉 🛈 079 29 95 44 or
29 95 46; 079 23 17 77.
🎉 last Sun of month:
Antiques Show in Piazza
Santa Caterina; Easter
Week: Maggio Sassarese;
penultimate Sun in
May: Cavalcata Sarda;
14 Aug: Faradda de li Candareri.

the processional standard, a panel painting by an anonymous 15th-century artist. There is also a silver statue of San Gavino, embossed using a Mexican technique that was in fashion in the late 17th century.

🪆 Fontana del Rosello
Via Col di Lana.
On the right-hand side of the church of Santissima Trinità, in Piazza Mercato, a small stone stairway known as the Col di Lana will take you to the Fontana del Rosello, the fountain at the lower end of the Valverde gorge.

Unfortunately, very little remains of the steep valley and woods that were once the natural backdrop for this little jewel of late Renaissance art. However, this has not diminished the locals' love for their fountain, which has become one of the city's symbols.

This was once the haunt of the enlightened bourgeoisie and the place where the local water-carriers drew water from the eight lions' mouths sculpted at the base of the fountain.

The fountain was executed in the early 1600s by Genoese artists, who still had a preference for the classical styles of the Renaissance. The base consists of two superimposed white and green marble boxes. The lions' mouths are surrounded by statues symbolizing the four seasons. The original statues were destroyed in the 1795–6 uprisings (see p160).

In the middle, a bearded divinity, known as Giogli, is surrounded by small towers symbolizing the city. On the top of the fountain are two arches which protect the figure of San Gavino.

SASSARI

Corso Vittorio Emanuele ②
Duomo ①
Fontana del Rosello ③
Mostra Permanente dell'Artigianato ⑥
Museo Archeologico Nazionale ⑨
Piazza d'Italia ⑧
Sant'Antonio Abate ④
Santa Caterina ⑦
Santa Maria di Betlem ⑤

0 metres   300
0 yards   300

Key to Symbols see back flap

🔒 Sant'Antonio Abate
Piazza Sant'Antonio.
◻ 7–10am daily, 4:30–7:30pm Sat.
Dating from the early 1700s, the stately Baroque façade of this church, with its simple elegance and harmonious proportions, dominates the tree-lined square at the end of Corso Trinità.

The upper part of the portal still bears the emblem of the brotherhood responsible for building the church. The Latin cross interior boasts one of the most elegant high altars in Sassari, which bears a carved and gilded wooden altarpiece. The panels were executed in the late 1700s by the Genoese painter Bartolomeo Augusto.

The church stands in Piazza Sant'Antonio, once the site of the old northern gate of the same name, and formerly the hub of the city's commercial and political life. The only vestiges of the past are a part of the medieval city walls, and a battlemented tower to the left of the church.

🔒 Santa Maria di Betlem
Piazza Santa Maria. **Tel** 079 23 57 40. ◻ 7:30am–noon, 5–7pm daily.
The church of Santa Maria di Betlem is situated in the square of the same name, at the northwestern entrance to the city. Built by Benedictine monks in 1106, it was later donated to the Franciscans. Unfortunately, the elegant original structure was the subject of frequent rebuilding in the 18th and 19th centuries, and the church has lost its early qualities of lightness and purity of form. The only intact part of the earlier church is the 13th-century

The Romanesque church of San Pietro in Silki, Sassari

façade, decorated with small columns and capitals and pierced by a lovely 15th-century rose window. The Gothic interior, once austere, has been spoiled by the heavy-handed Baroque decoration and altars; yet the original side chapels are intact, each dedicated to a craftsmen's guild as a reminder of the social role the church played in the community. To this day, on 14 August, the date of the *De li Candareri* festivities, the votive candles donated by the various guilds are carried here in procession from the Chiesa del Rosario.

The cloister is partly walled in but can still be visited. It contains the 14th-century granite stone Brigliadore fountain, once the source of most of Sassari's water supply.

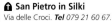

Detail of an Art Nouveau-style house

🔒 San Pietro in Silki
Via delle Croci. **Tel** 079 21 60 67.
◻ 6am–noon, 3:30–6pm daily.
The Romanesque church of San Pietro in Silki faces a lovely tree-lined square and was most probably

named after the medieval quarter built here in the 1100s. Its simple 17th-century façade has a large atrium leading to the Gothic nave with four side chapels. The first of these was dedicated to the Madonna delle Grazie in the second half of the 15th century. It is named for a statue of the Virgin Mary, found inside a column from the square in front of the church. The statue is one of the best examples of Catalan Gothic sculpture in Sardinia.

On the other side of the square, opposite San Pietro, is the Frati Minori monastery, which houses one of the island's richest libraries. The collections consist of over 14,000 volumes, removed from Franciscan monasteries after their closure.

🚏 Corso Vittorio Emanuele
The city's main street crosses the heart of the old town and connects Piazza Sant'Antonio and Piazza Cavallino. The Corso is lined with 19th-century houses and 16th-century Aragonese buildings, and you can often catch a glimpse of courtyards and interiors that testify to their former splendour. This is Sassari's main shopping street, with shops of all kinds, from clothing to ironmongery.

🏛 Mostra Permanente dell'Artigianato
Viale Tavolara. **Tel** 079 23 01 01.
◻ 9:30am–1pm, 5–8pm Mon–Sat.
📷 ♿
Facing the Emiciclo Garibaldi public gardens, a shop in a modern building houses the Permanent Exhibition of

The church of Santa Maria di Betlem in Sassari

Sardinian Handicrafts, a collection of the best work from the island's crafts cooperatives. The large rooms overlook an inner garden which allows light into the display cases housing the most precious objects. These include filigree necklaces and earrings, coral jewellery designed according to old drawings, and pottery and ceramics created using traditional techniques.

Hanging on the walls are traditional Sardinian rugs, which resemble abstract paintings with their geometric patterns. There is also fine bobbin lacework and – still interesting though not so valuable – baskets of dwarf palm wood, terracotta pots and other everyday objects whose design and techniques have been handed down over centuries of tradition. Items on display are for sale.

🏛 Museo Archeologico Nazionale "GA Sanna"

Via Roma. **Tel** 079 27 22 03.
⏱ 9am–8pm Tue–Sun.

The Sassari archaeological museum was donated to the Italian state by the Sanna family, who built these premises in 1931 to house finds collected by Giovanni Antonio Sanna, an important figure in the island's history and director of the local mine.

Two entire storeys are given over to various periods of Sardinian civilizations, from the Neolithic to the Middle Ages. Arrowheads, nuraghic bronze statuettes, amphoras, furnishings, weapons, tools,

Entrance to the Museo Nazionale "GA Sanna" in Sassari

ceramics and jewels are on display in chronological order. On the ground floor, panels illustrate the evolution of Sardinia, and every room has time charts on display.

There are also architectural reconstructions of prehistoric buildings such as dwellings, *domus de janas* (rock-cut tombs) and giants' tombs. In the last hall, among floor plans, sarcophagi and statues there is a reconstructed mosaic floor from a patrician Roman villa in nearby Turris Libisonis (present-day Porto Torres). The mosaic shows lobsters, sea horses, and seals chasing one another in an eternal circle. The next room contains a small art gallery with works by Sardinian artists from the 14th to the 20th centuries.

There is also a traditional crafts section divided into four rooms with jewels, costumes, musical instruments and craftsmen's tools, almost all of which are still used in central-northern Sardinia.

🏛 Piazza d'Italia
🛠 for restoration.

This large square is laid out at the edge of the 19th-century quarter of Sassari. It is a well-proportioned public space, surrounded by elegant Neo-Classical buildings and with tall palm trees and well-kept flower beds, guarded by a statue of Vittorio Emanuele II.

One of the finest buildings is the Palazzo della Provincia (provincial government building), built in pure Neo-Classical style. The council chamber on the first floor is open to the public. On the walls are 19th-century paintings depicting important events in the city's political history, such as *The Procla-mation of the Sassari Statutes* and *Carlo Maria Angioj Entering Sassari (see p160)*. You can also see the adjacent royal apartments, built in 1884 on the occasion of the King of Sardinia's visit. In summer the courtyard is the venue for concerts and plays.

The lovely 19th-century Bargone and Crispi arcades on the northwestern side of Piazza d'Italia shelter the city's oldest bars and pastry shops and lead to Piazza Castello.

🔒 Santa Caterina
Via Santa Caterina. **Tel** 079 23 16 92.
⏱ pm for mass.

This church was built at the end of the 16th century for the Jesuits and combines Sardinian Gothic style with Renaissance elements.

In the interior there are paintings by the artist Giovanni Bilevelt.

Sassari's Piazza d'Italia, framed by the Neo-Classical Palazzo della Provincia

The harbour at Castelsardo

Castelsardo ㉓

Road map C2. 5,500. Pro Loco (079 47 15 06). Easter Monday: Lunissanti procession. **www**.comunedicastelsardo.it

Perched on a volcanic headland, Castelsardo has known a number of name changes in its history. The town was founded in 1102 by the aristocratic Doria family from Genoa, and was originally known as Castelgenovese, a name it kept until 1448, when it became Castellaragonese, after the town's new conquerors. The present name dates from 1776.

The town is dominated by the castle (**Castello**), which now houses a museum with exhibits of traditional basketweaving. Overlooking the sea is the cathedral of Sant'Antonio Abate.

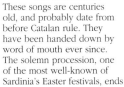

Local basketwork

The alleyways of the centre of town are lined with small shops selling all kinds of local handicrafts. Fish-lovers will do well here, as the local cuisine is based on freshly caught fish and lobsters.

On Easter Monday, the traditional **Lunissanti** procession is held in Castelsardo. The streets are lit by flaming torches, and traditional hooded figures form a slow procession, to the sound of three songs, *Lu Stabat, Lu Jesu* and *Lu Miserere*. These songs are centuries old, and probably date from before Catalan rule. They have been handed down by word of mouth ever since. The solemn procession, one of the most well-known of Sardinia's Easter festivals, ends at the church of **Santa Maria**.

Castello and Museo dell'Intreccio

Via Marconi. **Tel** 079 47 13 80. 9:30am–1pm, 3–5:30pm (Jul & Aug: 9am–midnight) daily.

Built in the 13th and 14th centuries, this fortress is now occupied by the **Museo dell'Intreccio** (museum of wickerwork). Local baskets are made from traditional materials such as palm, asphodel and cane. From the castle terraces there are lovely views of the Golfo dell'Asinara; on clear days you can even see Corsica.

Sant'Antonio Abate in Castelsardo

Cattedrale di Sant'Antonio Abate

Via Seminario. 8am–6pm daily.
Constructed in the 17th century on the site of an existing Romanesque church, the cathedral has a bell tower roofed with majolica tiles. From the tower there is a splendid view of the water below. The cathedral contains fine 16th-century, carved wooden furnishings.

The town of Castelsardo and the castle above

The Roccia dell'Elefante (Elephant Rock) near Castelsardo

🔒 Santa Maria

Via Vittorio Emanuele. ☐ *ask priest for keys.*

In the heart of the old town, the upper part of Castelsardo, stands the church of Santa Maria. The building does not have a façade, and entry is gained through the side door. In the interior is a 14th-century crucifix known as the *Cristo Nero* (Black Christ). The church is the focus of the Lunissanti Easter procession, which starts and ends here.

🏞 La Roccia dell'Elefante

To one side of the road near Multeddu, not far from Castelsardo, stands the impressive Roccia dell'Elefante (Elephant Rock). This massive block of dark trachyte rock has been gradually sculpted by the wind into the shape of an elephant with its trunk raised. In ancient times the rock was used as a burial place. At the base you can still see small carved openings for several *domus de janas* (rock-cut tombs).

Isola Rossa ㉔

Road map C1.

The hills of Gallura slope down towards the sea, forming a landscape characterized by rose-coloured crags, sculpted into strange shapes by wind erosion. The small fishing village of Isola Rossa lies on a headland, at the foot of an impressive 16th-century sentinel tower.

The village is not an island (*isola*), but was given its name ("red island") after the small, reddish-coloured rock island out in the bay. Fishing boats are drawn up on the beach below the village after each day's catch is brought in.

The coastline either side of Isola Rossa is worth visiting, especially towards the east, where Monte Tinnari overlooks the sea. To the west, the coast gently slopes to meet the mouth of the Rio Coghina, a short distance from Castelsardo.

Environs: A short distance from Isola Rossa is the small agricultural town of **Trinità d'Agultu**, which developed in the late 19th century around the church of the same name. As is so often the case in Sardinia, the simple country church became a sanctuary and pilgrimage site. As a result, it is also an important trade and commercial centre during the associated religious festivities and pilgrimages.

The fishing fleet at Isola Rossa

THE FISHING INDUSTRY

The Sardinians are historically a nation of shepherds. Despite this, fishing is still an important activity, even though for centuries it has been carried out almost exclusively by non-Sardinian immigrants: people from the island of Ponza at Castelsardo, and Neapolitans, who founded the village of Isola Rossa in the early 20th century. Nowadays a major source of income in these two places is the cultivation of mussels and shellfish. Tuna fishing, once widespread off the northwest coast, no longer survives in Sardinia, the small trawlers having been unable to compete with deep-sea fishing, now practised on an industrial scale.

Craftsman at work making a lobster pot

TRAVELLERS' NEEDS

WHERE TO STAY

The legendary allure of the beaches in Sardinia has resulted in a boom in tourist facilities, especially along the coast, and visitors can now choose from a wide range of hotels and holiday villages. The exclusive and world-famous hotels built on the Costa Smeralda in the early 1960s cater for the wealthy, but it is not difficult to find less expensive accommodation. You can find luxury hotels and resorts in the south, while the western coast offers plenty of

Logo of ESIT, the Sardinian Tourist Board

reliable family-run lodgings. On the eastern coast, comfortable and well-equipped tourist villages are easily found, many offering self-catering as an option. There are some excellent hotels in the interior, especially in the Gennargentu and Barbagia areas, where you can also take advantage of organized tours and hikes. For further information, listings and descriptions of hotels, farm holidays and tourist villages, turn to page 171 and pages 174–7.

The Hotel Torre Moresca at Cala Ginepro, Orosei *(see p175)*

GRADES OF HOTEL

As in the rest of Italy, hotels in Sardinia are graded on a star-rating system, from one star for minimum comfort and service, to five stars for luxury accommodation. The four-star category offers first-class service without the very high prices of five-star hotels. Three-star lodgings, especially family-run establishments, sometimes offer better value for your money, but here this is generally the exception rather than the rule.

Most Sardinian hotels also have a restaurant which is usually open to non-residents as well. The majority of hotels, whatever their category, provide a range of facilities. Along the coast, for example, hotels are likely to offer beach equipment such as umbrellas and deckchairs.

HOLIDAY VILLAGES

The holiday villages of Sardinia, mostly situated on or near the coast, offer a variety of types of accommodation. The choice varies from vast establishments with hundreds of rooms and good facilities and service, to smaller sites, which may be upmarket and expensive. The larger holiday villages offer more than one type of lodging within a single site. At Forte Village, for example, there are seven different hotels, each in a different style, ranging from the 43-room Le Dune to the 175-room Castello. At some places you can choose between serviced apartments *(residence)* or a normal three- or four-star hotel, with a range of charges. Some tourist villages offer all-inclusive packages that even include drinks at the bar. Sardinian tourist villages often require guests to take half or full board, as do many hotels.

Logo of the Hotel Sporting at Porto Rotondo

In some resorts guests may choose to rent a self-catering apartment or bungalow and then decide whether or not to have the other services and facilities included in the package. These services usually include the use of sports facilities and entertainment, such as a disco or night club, babysitters for those travelling with small children, beach facilities, the swimming pool and use of the various bars and restaurants. Many villages offer an excellent range of equipment for water sports.

Renting an apartment in a tourist resort is a worthwhile alternative to renting a villa, especially if you plan to be on holiday for less than a month. It allows you to be independent while at the same time giving you access to a range of useful services and facilities.

For a listing of these resorts see page 171.

A café in the small square at Porto Cervo

◁ The warm, turquoise waters along the Sardinian shore

The Hotel Victoria at Tortolì, near Arbatax *(see p175)*

PRICES

Italian law requires every hotel to place the National Tourist Board price list, with the maximum prices for the current year, on the door of each room. The prices quoted should never be exceeded. Room prices shown on this list, or quoted by the hotel staff when you book, normally include taxes and service. However, it is advisable to check whether or not breakfast is included, to avoid any misunderstandings.

Hotels on the coast often require guests to take half or full board. In low season you could try asking for a bed and breakfast rate, but this is unlikely to be possible in the high season. Winter rates are quite different from summer rates: in the summer prices can easily be as much as double. Hotel prices reach their peak in the two middle weeks of August. This is also true of the tourist villages (except that rates here are calculated on a weekly basis).

The location of your hotel will also affect the price. All types of accommodation on the coast are always more expensive than lodgings in the interior.

You may be able to negotiate special rates for groups or for longer stays.

EXTRAS

Generally speaking, you will pay separately for drinks consumed with your meal, anything taken from the mini-bar in your room, room service and telephone calls.

In some cases air conditioning may be charged as an extra. Glimpses of Sardinia's coast may also be regarded as chargeable and you may pay extra for rooms with a sea view. It is always a good idea to check on extras like this when booking or choosing your room. Tipping in hotels is at the visitor's discretion.

LOW SEASON

If you plan to go to Sardinia in any season other than summer, it is a good idea to check beforehand on the availability of accommodation. Some hotels are run on a seasonal basis; and tend to open around Easter and close in the autumn. The end of the season may very well depend on unpredictable circumstances such as a sudden turn of bad weather.

BOOKING AND PAYING

If you decide to travel during the summer, especially in the Italian holiday months of July and August, and if you want to stay on the coast, you must book well in advance, since the island is overflowing with visitors in this period. If you are booking your hotel separately from your travel arrangements, you will almost certainly be asked to send some money as a deposit. This can be done by credit card or international money order. When you arrive at your hotel or village, the receptionist will ask for your passport; this is to register travellers with the police, a legal requirement. You will be given a receipt on checking out, another legal formality.

CAMPING

Together with *agriturismo*, or farm holidays, camping is the most inexpensive way of staying on the island. Sardinia has a number of good camp sites, some of which are located in quiet areas with lovely views. Most of them are situated along the coast, often in eucalyptus or pine woods. There are far fewer sites in the interior.

Camp sites, like hotels, get extremely crowded in the summer. If you are travelling around and have not booked in advance, you need to start looking for a place to stay early in the day.

Some camp sites also have a small number of bungalows or chalets with a bathroom and kitchen area. These are often very attractive but the prices can be steep.

Most Sardinian camp sites are open from Easter to October. Some may be open for the Christmas period, offering bungalows or camper vans with heating.

Camping outside official sites is strictly forbidden, and camping on the beach is particularly frowned on. You need permission to camp on private property (from the owner), and in state forests.

The Hotel Hieracon, on the island of San Pietro *(see p174)*

The L'Agnata holiday farm at Tempio Pausania

FARM HOLIDAYS

A farm holiday *(agriturismo)* is an excellent way of coming into direct contact with Sardinian customs and traditions. Accommodation is often basic, but rooms are usually comfortable and homely. Farmhouses in Sardinia tend not to be placed in isolated countryside: true to tradition, at least half the farms are in villages. Local farmers and shepherds often live in villages and travel some distance to work the fields or take their sheep to pasture.

The highest concentration of *agriturismo* is found in the provinces of Sassari and Oristano, while there are very few in the Cagliari area. The only drawback – depending on your point of view – might be a certain lack of privacy: everybody eats at the same table, guests and host family alike. You will probably find yourself becoming almost a part of the family before you leave. Meals consist of produce grown on the farm – cheese, meat, vegetables and even honey – cooked according to local tradition. It is an excellent way of getting to

know the specialities of the region. In general, farms offer accommodation by the week on a half- or full-board basis. Many of them also organize hikes, horseback riding and mountain bike and canoe excursions.

It is sometimes possible to eat at an *agriturismo* without being a guest there. *AgriSardinia*, available at many tourist offices, is a good source of information.

A typical holiday house for rent in the Sulcis region of Sardinia

VILLA RENTAL

Renting a house for two weeks or a month is an economical solution for a family or a group of friends who want to spend their entire holiday by the sea. This option is especially good for families with small children

and babies. Note however that the charge for cleaning tends to be the same for a week as for a longer stay.

If you are looking for a house to rent you should contact the local tourist offices; they sometimes supply lists of private homes available in the vicinity and their prices. Travel agents and holiday companies can also arrange this type of accommodation.

Prices for rental are usually quoted on a weekly basis, and a deposit will be requested. When renting it is advisable to ascertain the exact number of bedrooms as in some houses the living room also functions as a bedroom. Before signing any contract, also check if gas, water, electricity and telephone expenses are part of the rent or are considered "extras". Make a note of the readings on the meters on arrival if these items are extra.

SARDINIA IN THE SADDLE

The great climate and varied scenery of Sardinia make it an ideal location for a holiday in the saddle. Organized off-road tours, following the paths and tracks of the island, particularly of the inland areas, are becoming very common in Sardinia, while road-based holidays are more suitable for the independent traveller. You can rent vehicles in most holiday towns, but it is inadvisable to attempt cross-country on your own, unless you are certain of your route, and know that motor vehicles are allowed. Location Sardinia (www.locationsardinia.com) offers useful information for planning such a trip.

Luxury holiday villas in Porto Cervo, Costa Smeralda

DIRECTORY

HOLIDAY VILLAGES

Club Méditerranée
Caprera,
Isola La Maddalena.
Road map D1.
Tel 0789 72 70 78.
Tel 0700 258 29 32 (UK).
Fax 0789 72 74 14.
www.clubmed.co.uk

Hotel Relais Monte Turri
Località Bellavista, Arbatax.
Road map D4.
Tel 0782 66 75 00.
www.hotel
philosophy.net

Villaggio Cala Moresca
Località Bellavista,
Arbatax. Road map D4.
Tel 0782 66 73 66 or
02 58 30 58 10.
Fax 0782 66 73 71.
www.wsvillage.it

Villaggio Cugnana Verde
Cugnana Verde (Olbia).
Road map D1 & 2.
Tel 0789 331 94.
www.cugnanaverde.net

Villaggio Valtur Baia di Conte
Fertillia (Alghero).
Road map B2.
Tel 079 94 90 00.
www.valtur.it

Villaggio Valtur di Colonna Beach
Località Sos Aranzos
(Golfo Aranci).
Road map C1.
Tel 0789 63 066.
www.valtur.it

Villaggio Valtur di Santo Stefano
Isola Santo Stefano
(La Maddalena).
Road map D1.
Tel 0789 70 60 39.
www.valtur.it

CAMPING

Arcobaleno
Località Porto Pozzo,
Santa Teresa di Gallura.
Road map C1.
Tel 0789 75 20 40.
www.camping
arcobaleno.com

Baia Blu La Tortuga
Località Vignola Mare,
Aglientu (Sassari).
Road map C1.
Tel 079 60 20 60 or
079 60 22 00.
www.baiaholiday.com

Cala Fiorita
Località Agrustos,
Budoni (Nuoro).
Road map D2.
Tel 0784 84 62 90 or
0784 84 70 00.

Cala Gonone
Cala Gonone, Dorgali
(Nuoro). Road map D3.
Tel 0784 931 65.
www.camping
calagonone.it

Camping Torre Chia
Località Chia (Cagliari).
Road map C6.
Tel 339 165 379.
www.campeggio
torrechia.it

Europa
Località Torre del Pozzo,
Cuglieri (Oristano).
Road map B3.
Tel 0785 380 58.
www.europacamping
village.it

International Camping
Località Valledoria.
Road map D6.
Tel 079 58 40 70.
www.camping
valledoria.com

Isola dei Gabbiani
Località Porto Pollo, Palau
(Olbia). Road map D2.
Tel 0789 70 40 19
or 0789 70 40 24.
www.isoladeigabbiani.it

La Caletta
Carloforte, Località La
Caletta. Road map B6.
Tel 0781 85 21 12 or
348 699 08 78.

Limoni Beach Camping
Cala Sinzias (Castidas).
Tel 070 99 50 06.
www.limonibeach.it

Nurapolis
Narbolia (Oristano).
Road map B4.
Tel 0783 522 83.
www.nurapolis.it

Porto Pirastu
Località Capo Ferrato,
Muravera (Cagliari).
Road map D5.
Tel 070 99 14 37/8.
www.portopirastu.net

Sos Flores
Tortolì, Arbatax (Nuoro).
Road map D4.
Tel 0782 66 74 85.

Telis
Località Porto Frailis,
Tortolì (Nuoro).
Road map D4.
Tel 0782 66 71 40.
www.campingtelis.com

Villaggio Camping Golfo di Arzachena
Località Cannigione,
Arzachena.
Road map D1.
Tel 0789 881 01.
www.camping
arzachena.com

Villaggio Camping La Mandragola
Santa Lucia di Siniscola
(Siniscola). Road map D2.
Tel 0784 81 91 19.
www.mandragola
villaggio.com

FARM HOLIDAY ASSOCIATIONS

Agriturist
Via Bottego 7, Cagliari.
Road map C6.
Tel 070 30 34 86.
www.agriturist.it

Consorzio Agri-turismi di Sardegna
Via Duomo 17, Oristano.
Road map B4.
Tel 0783 41 16 60.

Terranostra
Via dell'Artigianato 13,
Cagliari. Road map C6.
Tel 070 211 02 96.
www.terranostra.
sardegna.it

Turismo Verde
Via Libeccio 31, Cagliari.
Road map C6.
Tel 070 37 37 33
www.turismoverde.it

FARM HOLIDAYS

L'Agnata
San Bachisio, Tempio
Pausania. Road map C2.
Tel 079 67 13 84.
www.agnata.it

Agriturismo Costiolu
Bitti (Nuoro). Road map
D3. Tel 0784 26 00 88 or
333 563 07 40.
www.agriturismo
costiolu.com

Agriturismo Li Scopi
Località Li Scopi (San
Teodoro). Road map D2.
Tel 0784 86 56 24.
www.agriturismo
liscopi.com

Azienda di Lucia Sotgiu
Via Amsicora 9, Nurachi
(Oristano). Road map B4.
Tel 0783 41 02 96.
www.terranostra.
sardegna.it

Fenu
Località Sa Tuerra, Teulada
(Cagliari). Road map C6.
Tel 070 92 83 013.

Il Cavallino
Padru (Nuoro). Road map
D2. Tel 0789 510 14.

Le Querce
Località Valli di Vatta, Porto
Cervo. Road map D1.
Tel 0789 992 48.
www.lequerce.com

Lu Striglioni
Murta Maris, Olbis
(Sassari). Road map D2.
Tel 0789 405 24 or
360 61 68 67.

Sa Perda Marcada
Sa Perda Marcada, Arbus
(Cagliari). Road map B5.
Tel 070 975 87 14.
www.saperdamarcada.it

Sos Rios
Sos Rios, Torpe (Nuoro).
Road map D4.
Tel 0784 82 60 72.
www.sosrios.it

Sardinia's Best: Hotels

The majority of the luxury hotels in Sardinia are to be found in the Gallura region and close to the beaches of the Costa Smeralda. However, there are increasing numbers of smaller quality hotels in other less famous and much less expensive areas of Sardinia. All the hotels on this map offer something special and are highly recommended for their particularly favourable position along the coast or in the mountains, for architecture that blends in with the landscape, and for excellent service. Book well in advance if you plan to stay in the high season and note that many hotels close for the winter.

Villa Las Tronas
This seaside villa at Alghero is now a comfortable hotel. All the rooms have views of the coast and the only "noise" is that of the sea (see p176).

THE
WESTERN
COAST

Le Dune
Tucked away among the Piscinas dunes, this hotel occupies two old mine buildings which have been restored with great attention to detail (see p174).

CAGLIARI
AND THE
SOUTH

Forte Village
At this seaside holiday village the hotels are surrounded by Mediterranean maquis. Facilities for relaxation are excellent, and include thalassotherapy pools (see p174).

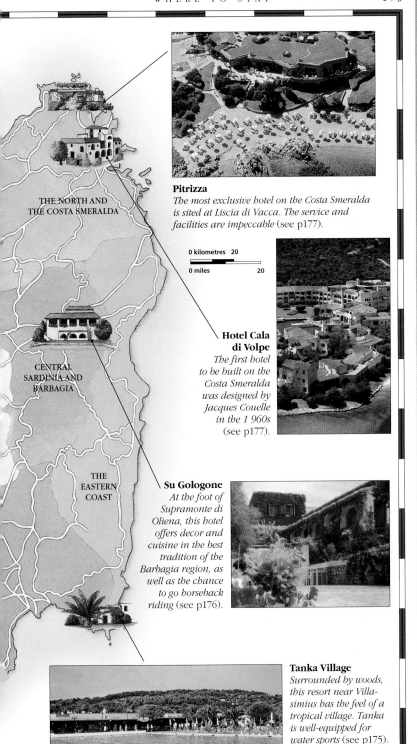

Pitrizza
The most exclusive hotel on the Costa Smeralda is sited at Liscia di Vacca. The service and facilities are impeccable (see p177).

THE NORTH AND
THE COSTA SMERALDA

0 kilometres 20

0 miles 20

**Hotel Cala
di Volpe**
*The first hotel
to be built on the
Costa Smeralda
was designed by
Jacques Couelle
in the 1960s
(see p177).*

CENTRAL
SARDINIA AND
BARBAGIA

THE
EASTERN
COAST

Su Gologone
*At the foot of
Supramonte di
Oliena, this hotel
offers decor and
cuisine in the best
tradition of the
Barbagia region, as
well as the chance
to go horseback
riding (see p176).*

Tanka Village
*Surrounded by woods,
this resort near Villa-
simius has the feel of a
tropical village. Tanka
is well-equipped for
water sports (see p175).*

Choosing a Hotel

Hotels have been selected across a wide price range for facilities, good value, and location. All rooms have private bath unless otherwise indicated. The hotels are listed by area; for map references, see back endpaper. Book in advance if you plan to stay in the high season, and note that many hotels close for the winter.

PRICE CATEGORIES
The following price ranges are for a double room per night, including breakfast, tax and service.

ⓢ Under €85
ⓢⓢ €85–€150
ⓢⓢⓢ €150–€250
ⓢⓢⓢⓢ €250–€350
ⓢⓢⓢⓢⓢ Over €350

CAGLIARI AND THE SOUTH

ARBUS Le Dune
€€€
Via Bau 1 - Fraz. Piscinas di Ingurtosu, 9031 **Tel** *070 97 71 30* **Fax** *070 97 72 30* **Rooms** *25*   **Road map B5**

Located in a carefully restored seafront mine building – an officially recognized national heritage monument – this hotel is extremely atmospheric, and a stay here is a memorable experience. There are sweeping panoramic views over the coast, the long stretch of sandy beach and the famous Piscinas dunes. **www.leduneingurtosu.it**

CAGLIARI Hotel 4 Mori
€
Via GM Angioj 27, 9124 **Tel** *070 66 85 35* **Fax** *070 66 60 87* **Rooms** *42*   **Road map C6**

In the heart of the city, this small friendly hotel was completely refurbished in 2004. Rooms are simple and clean, with whitewashed walls and wooden furniture. The hotel offers good value for its excellent position, near Via Roma and Largo Carlo Felice; excellent for sightseeing, shopping and eating. **www.hotel4mori.it**

CAGLIARI Hotel Aurora
€
Salita Santa Chiara 19, 9124 **Tel** *070 65 86 25* **Fax** *070 640 50 50* **Rooms** *13*   **Road map C6**

A small, centrally located hotel in a 19th-century building off the busy Piazza Yenne. All of the rooms have been redecorated with murals. Rooms at the front are noisier as the building opposite holds a morning market. One of the cheaper hotels, it is well positioned near the major attractions. **www.hotelcagliariaurora.it**

CAGLIARI T Hotel
€€€
Via dei Giudicati, 9131 **Tel** *070 474 00* **Fax** *070 47 40 16* **Rooms** *207*   **Road map C6**

Not far from the city centre this well-equipped, smart and modern hotel is undoubtedly one of Cagliari's best. A wide range of services are provided, including wi-fi Internet connection in the conference rooms, a wellness centre with beauty treatments, massages a gym and a sauna. There's also a bar and restaurant. **www.thotel.it**

DOMUS DE MARIA Chia Laguna
€€€€€
Loc. Chia, 9010 **Tel** *070 923 91* **Fax** *070 923 0144* **Rooms** *372*   **Road map C6**

This large elegant hotel is situated on one of the best beaches in the area and has plenty to offer guests. As well as the private beach there is a swimming pool and other fitness facilities, including tennis courts. Health and beauty treatments are also available. **www.lemeridien-chialaguna.com**

ISOLA DI SAN PIETRO Hotel Hieracon
€€
Corso Cavour 62, 9014 **Tel** *0781 85 40 28* **Fax** *0781 85 48 93* **Rooms** *23*   **Road map B6**

This well-preserved villa was built in the Art Nouveau style at the end of the 19th century and has a number of attractive period rooms. The rooms at the back are quieter. The apartments are in the pretty Mediterranean garden where breakfast can be served. The hotel is near the ferry terminus. Pets are welcome. **www.hotelhieracon.com**

ISOLA DI SAN PIETRO Hotel Paola e Primo Maggio
€€
Località Tacca Rossa, 9014 **Tel** *0781 85 00 98* **Fax** *0781 85 01 04* **Rooms** *20*   **Road map B6**

Surrounded by greenery and overlooking the sea, this is a quiet modern family run pensione. The restaurant has a shady panoramic terrace for outside dining, and prides itself on quality Carloforte cooking. The rooms are simple but furnished with a homely feel. The main area is cosy and rustic. **www.carloforte.net/hotelpaola/index.htm**

PORTOSCUSO La Ghingetta
€€
Via Cavour 26 – Sa Caletta, 9010 **Tel** *0781 50 81 43* **Fax** *0781 50 81 44* **Rooms** *8*   **Road map B6**

This small hotel is located in a charming position right on the beach, with fantastic views over the sea and to the island of San Pietro. The rooms are all decorated in different styles. The hotel restaurant, which serves some top quality seafood dishes, is particularly recommended (see p184). **laghinghetta@tiscali.it**

SANTA MARGHERITA DI PULA Forte Village
€€€€
Statale 195 - km 39+600, 9010 **Tel** *070 921 71* **Fax** *070 92 12 46* **Rooms** *765*   **Road map B6**

This glamorous resort, set in a luscious well-maintained park, is actually made up of seven hotels, each with its own style. There is plenty to do, with tennis courts, a gym, spa treatments and a private beach, as well as organized activities for children and adults. **www.fortevillage.com**

Key to Symbols *see back cover flap*

THE EASTERN COAST

BARÌ SARDO La Torre

Loc. Torre di Bari, 8042 **Tel** *078 22 80 08* **Fax** *078 27 01 00* **Rooms** *60*   **Road map D4**

This hotel is set in a lovely garden and has a fantastic seafront location, opposite a picturesque 16th-century tower. The comfortable bedrooms open onto a central piazza-patio. Windsurfing, mountain bikes and tennis courts are available, and guided tours, walks and horse-riding can also be arranged. **www.hotellatorresardegna.it**

OROSEI Biderrosa

Loc. Su Ponte sa Mela, 8028 **Tel** *078 49 11 77* **Fax** *078 491 9240* **Rooms** *14*   **Road map D3**

This pleasant hotel, built in a Mediterranean style, is set in a splendid garden near the Biderrosa natural park, with its beautiful rugged landscape and fabulous white sandy beach. The bedrooms are simply furnished, and service is courteous. Ideal for a calm and relaxing break away from it all. **www.hotelbiderrosa.it**

OROSEI Torre Moresca

Loc. Cala Ginepro, 8028 **Tel** *078 49 12 30* **Fax** *078 49 12 70* **Rooms** *210*   **Road map D3**

Located near the marvellous beach of Cala Ginepro, with its fine sands and dense pine forests, this is a really well organized beach resort about 14 km (8.5 miles) from Orosei. It's also an attractively designed complex, with courtyards and gardens. All sorts of activities are available for both children and adults. . **www.torremoresca.it**

TORTOLÌ Victoria

Via Monsignor Virgilio 72, 8041 **Tel** *078 262 3457* **Fax** *078 262 4116* **Rooms** *60*   **Road map D4**

This well-established seaside hotel offers hospitable and courteous service. The bedrooms are spacious and comfortable, and there is a fabulous terrace where breakfast is served – a lovely place to linger and gaze out over the coast. The hotel restaurant serves good traditional Sardinian food. **www.hotel-victoria.it**

VILLASIMIUS Stella Maris

Loc. Campulongu, 9049 **Tel** *070 79 71 00* **Fax** *070 79 73 67* **Rooms** *53*   **Road map D6**

Surrounded by forests of juniper and pine, just metres from the beach, this hotel was originally built as a Jesuit retreat. Calm and tranquility still characterize the place, which has been transformed into a comfortable hotel with attractive, Mediterranean-style rooms. The restaurant, overlooking the sea, serves local specialities. **www.stella-maris.com**

VILLASIMIUS Cala Caterina

Lago Maggiore 32 – Simius, 9049 **Tel** *070 79 74 09* **Fax** *070 79 74 73* **Rooms** *48*   **Road map D6**

In a beautiful location on Sardinia's southeast coast, in a quiet area of natural beauty, Cala Caterina brings relaxation to its guests. Service is excellent and the structure itself is well designed, incorporating local stone and vegetation in the grounds. There's a smart restaurant and a poolside bar. **www.mobygest.it**

VILLASIMIUS Tanka Village

Villasimius, 9049 **Tel** *070 7951* **Fax** *070 79 70 08* **Rooms** *903*   **Road map D6**

A fantastic resort near Villasimius, set in a lovely location surrounded by trees. The facilities and services are excellent, with plenty of water sports, as well as a golf course, swimming pool and tennis courts. The quality accommodation is in either independent chalets or traditional hotel rooms. **www.atahotels.it**

CENTRAL SARDINIA AND BARBAGIA

ARITZO Sa Muvara

Via Funtana Rubia, 8031 **Tel** *0784 62 93 36* **Fax** *0784 62 94 33* **Rooms** *80*   **Road map C4**

In the heart of the Gennargentu, this welcoming countryside hotel benefits from a wonderful environment and pure spa water. It makes an ideal base for exploring Mount Gennargentu and the surrounding area. Jeep excursions are organized and bicycles are available. The excellent restaurant serves local food. **www.samuvarahotel.com**

GAVOI Taloro

SS Fonni-Gavoi, 8020 **Tel** *0784 530 33* **Fax** *0784 537 40* **Rooms** *90*   **Road map C3**

There's plenty to do at this comfortable, well-run hotel on the banks of Lago di Gusana. Among other services are a health and beauty centre with a sauna, and sports facilities include tennis, swimming and 5-a-side football. The hotel restaurant serves numerous Sardinian specialities. **www.hoteltaloro.it**

NUORO Hotel Grillo

Via Mons. Melas, 8100 **Tel** *0784 386 78* **Fax** *0784 320 05* **Rooms** *45*   **Road map D3**

This modern, recently refurbished hotel is situated in a quiet location just a short walk from the *centro storico*. The bedrooms are spacious and elegantly furnished, some with Jacuzzis. There is wi-fi Internet access in all rooms. It has a restaurant which serves good regional cuisine and is popular with the locals. **www.grillohotel.it**

OLIENA Cooperativa Enis

Loc. Monte Maccione, 8025 **Tel** *0784 28 83 63* **Fax** *0784 28 84 73* **Rooms** *17*   **Road map D3**

Located in a wonderful location near Oliena and the Gennargentu mountains, this hotel makes a good base for exploring the area, and they can organize guided tours of the national park. The hotel has panoramic terraces with fantastic views over the countryside and a good restaurant serving tasty local dishes. **www.coopenis.it**

OLIENA Su Gologone

Località Su Gologone, 8025 **Tel** *0784 28 75 12* **Fax** *0784 28 76 68* **Rooms** *70*   **Road map D3**

A rambling villa in the mountainous Sopramonte, Su Gologone is delightfully peaceful, with warm Sardinian hospitality. The stone buildings are set in parkland and shaded by olive trees. The hotel has an excellent restaurant and also offers a good range of sports, activities and excursions. Half-board only. **www.sugologone.it**

THE WESTERN COAST

ALGHERO Hotel Angedras

Via Frank 2, 7041 **Tel** *079 973 50 34* **Fax** *079 973 50 34* **Rooms** *52*   **Road map B2**

This is a stylish hotel ten minutes from Alghero Old Town in a quiet residential street. The decor combines traditional Sardinian features with modern elegance. Breakfast is a selection of typical Sardinian pastries made by the family bakery. Service is warm and friendly. The hotel provides a free shuttle service. Private beach. **www.angedras.it**

ALGHERO Villa Las Tronas

Lungomare Valencia 1, 7041 **Tel** *079 98 18 18* **Fax** *079 98 10 44* **Rooms** *25*   **Road map B2**

A mustard-coloured 19th-century villa on a promontory overlooking Capo Caccia is the setting for this comfortable elegantly decorated hotel. Public rooms are full of gilt and fine furniture, while the bedrooms are simpler but pretty. The garden and terraces overlook the sea. **www.hotelvillalastronas.it**

ARBOREA Ala Birdi

Strada a Mare 24 – n° 27, 9092 **Tel** *0783 805 00* **Fax** *0783 80 10 86* **Rooms** *364*   **Road map B4**

The riding stables here are among Europe's largest, catering to all abilities from the complete beginner to the experienced rider. There's plenty for non-riders too, of course, including walking, cycling and water sports. The hotel and chalets, set in a lovely pine forest, are attractive. **www.alabirdi.it**

BOSA Hotel al Gabbiano

Viale Mediterraneo 5, 8013 **Tel** *0785 37 41 23* **Fax** *0785 37 41 09* **Rooms** *32*   **Road map B3**

Ideally positioned on Bosa Marina, this family-run hotel has scenic views over the bay from the private beach. The staff can organize bike trips and other excursions. The rooms are clean, bright and airy. The hotel also has a country house located within the interior. Half-board only in July and August. **www.bosa.it/gabbianohotel**

CUGLIERI La Baja

Via Scirocco 20 – S. Caterina di Pittinuri, 9073 **Tel** *0785 38 91 49* **Fax** *0785 38 90 03* **Rooms** *29*   **Road map B3**

Set in a fabulous location near the ruins of the ancient city of Cornus, overlooking the attractive bay and Spanish Tower landmark, La Baja has plenty to offer guests. There are comfortable rooms and great facilities, including golf, horse-riding and cycling. The hotel restaurant serves traditional Sardinian cuisine. **www.hotellabaja.it**

ORISTANO Hotel Mistral 2

Via XX Settembre 34, 9170 **Tel** *0783 21 03 89* **Fax** *0783 21 10 00* **Rooms** *132*   **Road map B4**

The rooms at this well-built modern hotel are light, airy and comfortable, there are also some non-smoking rooms available. The hotel is located near the historic centre of Oristano, but outside the pedestrianized zone. There's a pleasant open-air café, a good hotel restaurant and a swimming pool. **www.shg.it**

TRESNURAGHES Piccolo Hotel Alabe

Via Lungomare 48 – Porto Alabe, 9079 **Tel** *0785 35 90 56* **Fax** *0785 33 01 42* **Rooms** *20*   **Road map B3**

This family-run hotel, situated in a delightful location on the coast near Bosa, is quite small. The bedrooms are comfortable, and all have balconies with sea views. The service is courteous and friendly. The hotel restaurant serves good, typical Sardinian home cooking, including excellent fish dishes. **piccolohotelportoalabe@virgilio.it**

THE NORTH AND COSTA SMERALDA

LA MADDALENA Miralonga

Via Don Vico, 7024 **Tel** *0789 72 25 63* **Fax** *0789 72 24 04* **Rooms** *50*   **Road map D1**

Situated on the stunning island of La Maddalena, not far from the port itself, this modern hotel is a great place to stay for a relaxing seaside holiday. It is, in fact, practically on the sea. Facilities include a swimming pool on the panoramic terrace and diving excursions. **www.miralonga.it**

Key to Price Guide *see p174* **Key to Symbols** *see back cover flap*

PALAU Excelsior Vanna

🚶📋🅿 €€€

Via Capo d'Orso 100, 7020 **Tel** *0789 70 95 89* **Fax** *0789 70 95 89* **Rooms** *39*   **Road map D1**

This traditional hotel is located in an admirable position a few hundred metres from the sea, in the bustling port of Palau. Some of the rooms have splendid views over the water and the islands. The hotel also has its own garden and there is a play area for children. **www.hotelvanna.it**

PALAU Capo d'Orso

🏋️🏖️🚶📋🅿 €€€€€

Loc. Cala Capra, 7020 **Tel** *0789 70 20 00* **Fax** *0789 70 20 09* **Rooms** *92*   **Road map D1**

A fantastic hotel in a peaceful romantic setting with lovely grounds, fabulous views and delightful bays on either side. The décor is elegant and comfortable, and there are great facilities, including a nine-hole golf course and beauty treatments. The hotel's two restaurants serve excellent Sardinian cuisine0. **www.delphina.it**

PORTO CERVO Capriccioli

🏋️🏖️🚶📋🅿 €€€

Località Capriccioli, 7020 **Tel** *0789 960 04* **Fax** *0789 964 22* **Rooms** *45*   **Road map D1**

One of the best value hotels on the expensive Costa Smeralda. This family-run hotel is set in a Mediterranean garden. The rooms are whitewashed and furnished with traditional wooden furniture. The hotel is close to the beach and has an excellent restaurant. A variety of excursions and activities are available. **www.hotelcapriccioli.it**

PORTO CERVO Le Ginestre

🏋️🏖️🚶📺📋🅿 €€€

Loc. Porto Cervo, 7020 **Tel** *0789 920 30* **Fax** *0789 940 87* **Rooms** *80*   **Road map D1**

This lovely hotel is set in a beautiful typically Mediterranean, park. Accommodation is in a variety of types of room, but the standards are high in all. There's a private beach with organized water sports, as well as tennis courts. The hotel restaurant serves good food, including many local specialities. **www.leginestrehotel.com**

PORTO CERVO Cala di Volpe

🏊🏋️🏖️🚶📺📋🅿 €€€€€

Loc. Porto Cervo, 7020 **Tel** *0789 97 61 11* **Fax** *0789 97 66 17* **Rooms** *125*   **Road map D1**

A fantastically designed resort overlooking the sea, built to recall a traditional fishing village, but with plenty of luxury. Traditional colours and tiles are used in the décor and the fabulous views along the coast from the balconies off each guest room are unforgettable. Plenty of leisure activities. **www.luxurycollection.com/caladivolpe**

PORTO CERVO Pitrizza

🏋️🏖️🚶📺📋🅿 €€€€€

Loc. Porto Cervo, 7020 **Tel** *0789 93 01 11* **Fax** *0789 93 06 11* **Rooms** *55*   **Road map D1**

An exclusive hotel that oozes luxury. The rooms are splendidly decorated, and furnished in keeping with the island's heritage – colours and materials echo Sardinia's natural beauty. The excellent recreational facilities include a seawater swimming pool carved out of the rock, water sports and a golf course. **www.luxurycollection.com/hotelpitrizza**

PORTO ROTONDO Sporting

🏋️🏖️🚶📺📋🅿 €€€€€

Porto Rotondo, 7020 **Tel** *0789 340 05* **Fax** *0789 343 83* **Rooms** *27*   **Road map**

An oasis of comfort on the Costa Smeralda, this hotel is a large complex with its own beach and a plethora of activities. The architecture and garden are typically Mediterranean. Rooms are airy, comfortably furnished and have private flower-filled terraces which open onto the beach. There is a piano bar. **www.sportingportorotondo.it**

SAN TEODORO L'Esagono

🏋️🏖️🚶📋🅿 €€

Via Cala d'Ambra 141, 8020 **Tel** *0784 86 57 83* **Fax** *0784 86 60 40* **Rooms** *83*   **Road map D2**

Set in luscious gardens, facing the Cala d'Ambra beach and just a short way from the centre of the village, this is an ideal place for a relaxing holiday. The bedrooms are very attractive and comfortable. L'Esagono started out as a restaurant – and is still a great place to eat. **www.hotelesagono.com**

SAN TEODORO Due Lune

🏋️🏖️🚶📺📋🅿 €€€

Loc. Puntaldia, 8020 **Tel** *0784 86 40 75* **Fax** *0784 86 40 17* **Rooms** *66*   **Road map D2**

In a fantastic position overlooking the coast, with its own private beach and a splendid nine-hole golf course, this hotel has attractive, fresh and airy rooms. There are facilities for diving, sailing and windsurfing, as well as four tennis courts and a restaurant serving traditional local food. **www.duelune.com**

SANTA TERESA DI GALLURA Grand Hotel Corallaro

🏋️🏖️🚶📺📋🅿 €€

Loc. Rena Bianca, 7028 **Tel** *0789 75 54 75* **Fax** *0789 75 54 31* **Rooms** *85*   **Road map C1**

This traditional hotel, set in pleasant grounds, offers simply furnished rooms and well-prepared local food – a good place to stay for a seaside holiday. There are fantastic views over the coast towards Corsica, and the lovely sandy beach is just metres away. Facilities include an indoor swimming pool. **www.hotelcorallaro.it**

SANTA TERESA DI GALLURA Shardana

🏋️🏖️🚶📋🅿 €€€

Loc. Santa Reparata, 7028 **Tel** *0789 75 40 31* **Fax** *0789 75 41 29* **Rooms** *75*   **Road map C1**

The hotel, set among junipers and myrtles, is on the coast just a few kilometres out of Santa Teresa itself, on the way to the attractive Capo Testa headland. Accommodation is in well-built chalets with simple but pleasantly furnished rooms. Watersports are available and there are fantastic activities for children. **www.hotelshardana.com**

SASSARI Hotel Leonardo da Vinci

🚶📋🅿 €€

Via Roma 79, 7100 **Tel** *079 28 07 44* **Fax** *079 285 22 33* **Rooms** *116*   **Road map B2**

A large, modern, comfortable hotel just a few minutes' walk from Piazza Italia and the city centre. The rooms and furnishings are functional, but there is a sense of space and tranquillity. The main hall and bar are paved in coloured marble and furnished with banks of sofas. **www.leonardodavincihotel.it**

WHERE TO EAT

The relatively recent arrival of tourism in Sardinia means that it is an excellent place for appreciating regional variations in cuisine. Fish and seafood fill restaurant menus along the coast, while meat and stuffed pasta are commonly found in the interior. In fact, restaurants that do not serve typical regional dishes are a rarity. The rhythm for mealtimes is Mediterranean, with lunch being served from

Lucia Pennisi and home-made, fresh pasta, Sant'Antioco

1–3pm and the evening meal from 9–10:30pm. In many cases restaurants stay open until midnight, especially in summer. Almost all restaurants and trattorias close one day a week and close for a month for annual holidays, so check business hours if you have chosen a particular destination. All the restaurants listed on pages 184–7 have been chosen as among the best in their category.

The Locanda Rosella at Giba, in the Cagliari region

TYPES OF RESTAURANTS

In terms of price, cuisine and atmosphere, there is not much difference between a restaurant (ristorante) and a trattoria in Sardinia. Even a fairly expensive restaurant may still be decorated in a functional, country style, with simple furniture. The pizzerias are rarely luxurious, but have the advantage of offering decent eating at lower prices. If you can, choose pizzerias with wood-burning ovens; the quality is better. In the summer, refreshment stalls on the beaches sell sandwiches and fish and pasta dishes for those spending the day at the seaside. In general, the bars here do not offer snacks and sandwiches for a quick meal.

PRICES AND PAYING

A three-course meal will cost about €15–€30. In top restaurants the bill may add up to €35–€45 euros but

only rarely will it go above €50. In pizzerias you can have a two-course meal with a glass of beer or half-litre of wine for €15–20. The bill always includes a cover charge (coperto or pane e coperto), which varies from €1–€3, and service. Although it isn't customary among the locals to leave a tip in Sardinian restaurants, in the more exclusive resorts waiters have become accustomed to receiving tips (generally 10–15 per cent of the bill) from foreign tourists.

Many restaurants accept major credit cards (such as VISA, MasterCard, American Express and Diners) but, just in case, be prepared to pay in cash, especially when you go to bars, cafés or smaller, family-run establishments.

FIXED-PRICE MENUS

Some restaurants offer menus at fixed prices (menù a prezzo fisso or menù turistico).

Agriturismi (see p170) prepare a fixed menu of Sardinian specialities daily, giving you a chance to try regional dishes such as porceddu (suckling pig), which you would have to order in advance in restaurants. Upmarket restaurants may offer a special menu called a menù degustazione or menù gastronomico, for a fixed price. This usually gives you the chance to taste five or six house specialities.

CLOSING DAYS

All restaurants close for one day each week, except during the high season (July and August). The closing days for each establishment recommended in this guide are clearly shown in the listings on pp184–7. Most places also close for about one month for annual holidays,

Dal Corsaro, one of Cagliari's top restaurants (see p184)

usually in the winter, except for the restaurants in Cagliari, which are closed in August.

VEGETARIAN FOOD

Sardinia is not ideal for strict vegetarians. People who eat fish, but not meat, will not have problems along the coast. In the interior the choice may be limited to pasta and soup dishes with fresh bread and cheeses. (However, do not forget that some soup dishes may be prepared with meat stock.) If you don't see anything suitable on the menu, explain your situation to the waiter. The chef will usually cook you something special.

Aperitif time in an Alghero bar

Pane Frattau, a dish of stock-softened bread, cheese and tomato sauce

THE MENU

Restaurants do not always provide a written menu. Where this happens, the waiter will give you a list of the day's dishes at your table and help you to choose. You may wish to begin with an *antipasto,* or starter, such as sliced sausage, cured hams or vegetables in oil, artichoke hearts or olives perhaps. Coastal restaurants offer seafood appetizers (clams, baby squid, cuttlefish, sea anemones and assorted molluscs). This is followed by the first course *(primo),* which may consist of soup, pasta, ravioli or, occasionally, a rice dish. The second course *(secondo)* will be meat or fish, and may include the famous *porceddu* (suckling pig). Some

first courses, such as *pane frattau (carasau* bread in broth) or *fregula* pasta with clams, make substantial meals. The meal ends with cheese, fruit or dessert such as ice cream, with coffee and perhaps a Sardinian liqueur *(see p183).*

RESERVATIONS

Restaurants are often crowded, particularly in the evening and during the summer. Consequently it is advisable to book ahead even in the cheaper establishments, or else arrive fairly early to avoid a long wait.

WINE AND DRINKS

Most restaurants, even those in the medium-price range, will stock a good selection of regional wines and liqueurs *(see pp182–3).* Some may offer non-Sardinian wines. Almost all restaurants also provide a house wine.

CHILDREN

Children are welcome in restaurants, especially family-run ones, where staff are more inclined to prepare half portions or even special dishes for them.

SMOKING

Smoking in public establishments in Italy is now banned. Some places may have terraces or outside tables where smoking is permitted.

WHEELCHAIR ACCESS

Only a few restaurants in Sardinia are equipped with ramps and adapted toilet facilities for the disabled. However, few restaurants have steps, and access is not normally a problem. It is a good idea to call the restaurant beforehand to ensure an easily accessible table and assistance when you arrive.

FOOD FESTIVALS

The best way to get a taste of the real Sardinia is at one of the frequent *sagre* or festivals. These pleasant occasions are usually dedicated to one particular dish or product, such as wine, cheese or fish. One of the most interesting is the picturesque tuna festival held around the end of May at Carloforte on the Island of San Pietro, where you can try tuna cooked in a multitude of ways. Fish in general is the theme in September at Cagliari's Sagra del Pesce and also in August when Oristano hosts the Festa del Mare. Another popular festival, dedicated to chestnuts and hazelnuts, is held in Aritzo in October, while the following month, the Sagre delle Olive at Gonnosfanadiga, near Cagliari, features all sorts of other produce as well as olives. The various religious and folk festivals held throughout the year all have a gastronomic element, often including spit-roast *porceddu* - suckling pig.

The Flavours of Sardinia

There is a huge contrast between the extravagant lifestyle of Costa Smeralda and the hard lives of Sardinia's farmers and shepherds that inspired the *cucina povera* – a "poor cooking" style of food. But even the most fashionable restaurants serve versions of these simple tasty dishes, the most famous of which is *porceddu*, traditional spit-roasted suckling pig. Remote from the mainland, rugged and dry, the island has a distinctive cuisine, taking its flavours from the herbs that grow on the hillsides. Other popular ingredients include honey, wild-boar ham and salami, goat's and ewe's cheeses and seafood.

Sardinian herbs

Market vendor offering a wide range of local cheeses

INLAND INFLUENCES

Centuries of seaborne invasion required Sardinians to make the most of available inland ingredients. Vines and olive trees grow everywhere so families made their own wine and oil. Wild herbs flavoured anything that could go into the pot. Rabbit, hare, game birds and even thrushes were easily caught, and lamb or mutton was usually available. Offal is still used, and local specialities include pigs' trotters, cooked in a piquant sauce, and lambs' feet, which are braised in tomato sauce while their intestines are spit-roasted *(cordula)*. *Porceddu* (suckling pig) is spit-roasted over a fire of myrtle and juniper wood and basted until the skin is crisp and the herb-scented meat is tender. Sausages and salami are also made from pork. The meat of the young goats that climb the mountains is cooked with herbs and wine; *capretto al finocchietto* is kid cooked with fennel. Lamb and kid were also roasted by hunters in pits dug in the ground – a technique now reserved for celebrations. Wheat was introduced by the Romans, and bread-making is a local art. Among the many types is the crisp, circular *pane carasau*,

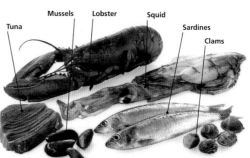

Tuna **Mussels** **Lobster** **Squid** **Sardines** **Clams**

Some of the superb seafood caught in the clear waters around Sardinia

SARDINIAN DISHES AND SPECIALITIES

Many local dishes are unique to the island. Sardinian pastas include little ball-shaped *fregula*; similar to couscous, it is often simmered in lamb stock and flavoured with saffron and Pecorino to make *succu*. It is also served with clams, or in broth as a soup. Ravioli-like *culungiones* may be filled with cheese and fresh mint and served with a tomato sauce, while semolina *gnocchetti* (dumplings)

Fresh green figs

are delicious served with a hearty meat sauce such as *sugo di cinghiale* (wild boar). *Suppa cuata* is layers of bread, grated cheese, nutmeg and parsley, baked in lamb stock. Pork, beans and vegetables go into *favata*, a hearty winter stew. *Stufato di capretto* is a more extravagant dish – a rich casserole made with kid (young goat), wine, artichokes and saffron. Sometimes eggs are added to make a kind of fricassée.

Pesce Spada alla Sardegna *is a swordfish steak with a sauce of tomatoes, wine, mint, saffron and chilli.*

Tresses of vine-ripened tomatoes hanging on a local produce stall

bass, bream, swordfish and tuna are grilled with herbs or fried in a semolina-flour batter. Risottos, pasta dishes and fish soups make use of the plentiful squid, cuttlefish, anchovies and shellfish. Octopus, prawns, mussels, clams, scallops and squid are boiled and dressed in oil and vinegar as *antipasti*. *Burrida* is fish marinated in vinegar with walnuts and parsley, and *bottarga* is the dried and salted roe of grey mullet or tuna, which may be served sliced as an *antipasto* or grated over pasta.

that shepherds would take to work with them. When moistened and topped with a sauce, Pecorino cheese and egg, it is called *pane frattau*. Pecorino is Sardinia's most renowned cheese: soft when young, it hardens with age and is then used grated. *Pecorino pepato* contains peppercorns. Other cheeses include *fiore Sardo* and *dolce Sardo*. Soft ricotta is used in savoury and sweet dishes.

COSMOPOLITAN COASTS

The Romans, Arabs, Genoese and Spanish who colonized the island brought with them their culinary influences. Saffron, an Eastern import, still adds colour and perfume to numerous savoury and sweet recipes. The west coast has Catalan-influenced dishes that stem from the era of Spanish

rule. *Panadas* are savoury pies filled with meat or cheese and vegetables; the most popular type is stuffed with eel *(panada di anguillas)*. Lobster *alla Catalana*, stewed with wine, peppers and tomatoes, is a typical dish from Alghero. Mullet, sea

Newly harvested olives ready to be taken to the mill for pressing

SARDINIAN SWEETS

Soft almond nougat is a speciality of Tonara. Many Sardinian biscuits and sweets were originally made for religious festivals:

Aranciata or Aranzada Preserved orange peel with honey and nuts.

Caschettes Rose-shaped nut- and honey-filled pastries, given to brides at weddings.

Gianchittos Toasted almond and lemon peel meringues.

Papassinos Walnut, raisin and almond biscuits.

Sebadas Ricotta and citrus peel fritters, covered in honey.

Sos guelfos Balls of almond or hazelnut paste.

Sospiri di Ozieri Iced almond paste and citrus sweets, wrapped in bright paper.

Malloreddus *are gnocchi-like dumplings served with a fresh tomato sauce and minced sausage meat.*

Agnello alla zafferano, *saffron- and garlic-scented lamb stew, is shown here served with* fregula *pasta.*

Pardulas *(or* casadinas*) are fresh cheese pastries that are flavoured with cinnamon, saffron and lemon.*

What to Drink in Sardinia

Grapevines first came to Sardinia from the eastern Mediterranean, where the Phoenicians had long cultivated vineyards. The warm climate tends to yield very ripe grapes, which are then turned into strong, deeply coloured wines. Lighter, fruity *novellos* are also worth trying. Good-quality Sardinian wines are widely available in shops, but it also pays to go directly to the suppliers. All types are made, from red *(rosso)*, white *(bianco)* and rosé *(rosato)* to rich dessert wines. Many qualify for the status of *denominazione di origine controllata* (DOC), with guaranteed provenance and quality standards. Sardinian wines are almost always made from a single grape variety. Perhaps the best-known is Vernaccia di Oristano, the first to gain DOC status in Sardinia.

Old winemaking equipment

WHITE WINES

The white wines of Sardinia go well with fish and seafood dishes, and some are sturdy enough to go with meat dishes such as pork. Nuragus is a widely planted white grape, producing rather neutral, soft and fruity wines. Vermentino is also widely grown and the wines have more complex flavours. Both Vermentino di Sardegna and Vermentino di Gallura, made mostly around Sassari and Nuoro province, tend to be fairly strong. There is also a sparkling version. DOC Vermentino from Cala Viola and Usini is very good. The Campidano area produces the fruity, dry white Semidano.

Vernaccia

Slightly sparkling Sinis

Grape harvesting

RECOMMENDED WHITES

- **Cantina Sociale della Riforma Agraria, Alghero**
  Vermentino di Sardegna Aragosta
- **Cantina Sociale Gallura**
  Vermentino
- **Tenuta Sella & Mosca, Alghero**
  Terre Bianche

RED WINES

The best-known red wine is Cannonau, which is usually full-bodied and strong, although some lighter versions are made. Most Cannonau is produced in the province of Nuoro in eastern Sardinia. It goes well with roast meat and game. Another wine to drink with game and mature cheese is Monica di Sardegna, a dry red with intense perfume that should be drunk young. Less common but equally good DOC reds are the light, dry Mandrolisai, Campidano di Terralba and Carignano del Sulcis. Other reds, such as Tanca Farrà di Alghero and Terre Brune del Sulcis, blend Sardinian and imported grape varieties. The most expensive Sardinian red wine is Turriga.

Cannonau grapes

Nieddera rosé and Cannonau

RECOMMENDED REDS

- **Azienda Giuseppe Cabras, Nuoro**
  Cannonau
- **Tenuta Sella & Mosca, Alghero**
  Anghelu Ruju
- **Attilio Contini, Cabras**
  Nieddera

DESSERT WINES

Sardinia produces a number of sweet dessert wines, both white and red. Besides mature white Vernaccia and sweet red Cannonau, there is Moscato di Sardegna, made from Muscat grapes and bottled at three years old. It is sweet but has good acidity, and an alcoholic content of 15°. Tempio Pausania Muscat tends to be lightly fizzy, while the Cagliari version is strong and sweet. The red Girò di Cagliari and amber-coloured Nasco are also strong and sweet. Two dessert wines made from semi-dried grapes come from the Alghero area: Torbato and the port-like Anghelu Ruju, both produced with Cannonau grapes. The Bosa and Cagliari Malvasia wines are similar to Vernaccia.

Cantina Sociale della Vernaccia at Oristano

Sparkling Vernaccia

Malvasia di Bosa

Vernaccia grapes

Moscato grapes

Malvasia grapes

Harvesting black grapes from Cannonau vines

RECOMMENDED DESSERT WINES

- *Centro Enologico Sardo, Villacidro*
  Malvasia
- *Centro Enologico Sardo, Villacidro*
  Moscato Dolce (Muscat)
- *Fratelli Serra, Zeddiani*
  Vernaccia
- *Meloni Vini, Selargius*
  Malvasia di Cagliari
- *Cantina Sociale Dolianova*
  Moscato di Cagliari

DIGESTIVI

The best-known spirit in Sardinia is *abbardiente* (named from the Spanish *aguardiente)*, a *grappa* or eau-de-vie. Among the best are made from the strong-tasting Cannonau and the more delicate Malvasia. Grappa here is also called *fil'e ferru* (iron wire), from the wire used to mark hiding places for illegally produced grappa. Grappa flavoured with wild fennel, juniper and thistle is a relatively new style. The most famous liqueur, however, is Mirto, both red and white, made with wild myrtle leaves and berries. The Sardinians' favourite is Zedda Piras.

Cork-covered bottles with characteristic decorative motifs

Choosing a Restaurant

The restaurants in this guide have been selected across a wide range of price categories for their good value, exceptional food and/or interesting location. This chart lists the restaurants by region. The entries are listed in alphabetical order within each price category. For map references, see inside back cover.

PRICE CATEGORIES
The following price ranges are for a three-course meal for one, including a half-bottle of house wine, cover charge, tax and service.
Ⓢ Under €25
ⓈⓈ €25–€35
ⓈⓈⓈ €35–€45
ⓈⓈⓈⓈ €45–€55
ⓈⓈⓈⓈⓈ Over €55

CAGLIARI AND THE SOUTH

CAGLIARI Antica Hostaria   €€
Via Cavour 60, 9124 **Tel** *070 66 58 70*   **Road map C6**

A comfortable atmospheric restaurant in an old building on the backstreets of the Marina district. The cuisine is good, based on traditional and local produce. Seasonal specialities include risotto with radicchio, spaghetti with clams and dried mullet roe, game and fish. They also have a good wine list.

CAGLIARI Saint Remy   €€
Via San Salvatore da Horta 7, 9125 **Tel** *070 65 73 77*   **Road map C6**

This unusual restaurant is part of an attractive former monastery, dating from the 17th century. The menu includes a wide range of Sardinian specialities, in particular several traditional dishes from Cagliari. There is a great choice of fish as well as some delicious pasta dishes, including the cous cous-like *fregula*, served with clams.

CAGLIARI Dal Corsaro   €€€€
Viale Regina Margherita 28, 9124 **Tel** *070 66 43 18*   **Road map C6**

An elegant restaurant with a pleasant atmosphere and a refined service, in which to enjoy regional dishes such as fish ravioli, original creations (white trevally with aubergine (eggplant) and basil, or fillet steak *all'Angelu Ruju*), and some Cagliari classics. Vegetarian dishes are also available. There is a good wine list.

CALASETTA Da Pasqualino   €€
Via Regina Margherita 85, 9011 **Tel** *0781 884 73*   **Road map B6**

Delicious fish, particularly tuna-based specialities, are served in this simple and relaxed family trattoria in the old quarter of the town. The menu includes fish soups, *bottarga* (tuna roe), *musciame* (sun-dried tuna), spaghetti with fresh tuna, a local version of cous cous and lobster. The wines are all local.

CARLOFORTE Al Tonno di Corsa   €€
Via G Marconi 47, 9014 **Tel** *0781 85 51 06*   **Road map B6**

On a hill behind the seafront in the old town, this restaurant offers local cuisine with some Tunisian influences. The menu features seafood antipasti, cous cous, *musciame* (sun-dried tuna), fresh pasta with basil and marjoram or seafood sauce and a variety of tuna dishes, including tuna stomach with potatoes. The décor is rustic and charming.

CARLOFORTE Da Nicolo   €€€€
Corso Cavour 32, 9014 **Tel** *0781 85 40 48*   **Road map B6**

The food served here is tantalizingly tasty. It is firmly rooted in the local cuisine of Carloforte, which is, in fact, a surprising mixture of North African, Ligurian and Sardinian influences. The main house speciality is fresh tuna – try it with caramelized saffron. Another delicious dish is *cashcà* – a kind of cous cous cooked with vegetables.

NUXIS Letizia   €€
Via San Pietro 12, 9010 **Tel** *0781 95 70 21*   **Road map C6**

Letizia is an environmentally friendly centre for tourists in the middle of the Sulcis park. Herbs and vegetables are grown with care and you can find out how you can grow and use them. The restaurant serves some exceptionally tasty dishes – either traditionally Sardinian or more innovative in style – made with freshly picked produce.

PORTOSCUSO La Ghinghetta   €€€€€
Via Cavour 26, 9010 **Tel** *0781 50 81 43*   **Road map B6**

Small and elegant, this restaurant is set in a charming fishing village facing the island of San Pietro. The almost exclusively fish-based menu adds a twist to local specialities. Fish and prawn tartare with quails' eggs and caviar, smoked fish, lobster terrine and ice cream with caramelized fruit all feature on the menu. It is advisable to book ahead.

TEULADA Ristorante Sebera   €€
Via San Francesco 10, 9019 **Tel** *070 927 0876*   **Road map C6**

The décor at this welcoming hotel restaurant is attractively rustic with checked tablecloths, and the standard of service is excellent. The menu covers a good range of typical Sardinian specialities, including plenty of fish dishes. *Spaghetti ai frutti di mare* is one of the house favourites and the local *fregola* is also delicious.

Key to Symbols *see back cover flap*

THE EASTERN COAST

ARBATAX Il Faro
€€
Piazzale Porto Frailis, 8041 **Tel** *0782 66 74 99*
Road map D4

A table on the summer terrace, overlooking the sea at Arbatax, is a fantastic place to eat, and the interior of the restaurant is very pleasant too. The food served is principally based on traditional and simply prepared Sardinian recipes, with a good range of fresh fish. Pizzas are also available.

BAUNEI Golgo
€
Loc. San Pietro, 8040 **Tel** *0782 61 06 75*
Road map D4

This rustic restaurant is located in an attractive traditional stone building amid lovely countryside, near the mountain village of Baunei. You'll find authentic local food, prepared according to tradition. Sit outside to enjoy the views, and the tasty home cooking. A good place to try the *porceddu* (suckling pig) or some Pecorino sheep's cheeses.

DORGALI Ispinigoli
€€
Loc. Ispinigoli, 8022 **Tel** *078 49 52 68*
Road map D3

Inland, near the beautiful Ispinigoli caves, this restaurant is part of a hotel. The menu features a lot of local dishes based on the area's meat products and delicious cheeses, as well as some fresh fish brought in from the coast. There is a good choice of food for vegetarians, too, and an excellent wine list.

OROSEI Su Barchile
€€€€€
Via Mannu 5, 8028 **Tel** *078 49 88 79*
Road map D3

This welcoming restaurant is located in the old town centre of Orosei. There is a good range of deliciously fresh locally caught fish, mostly prepared according to local recipes. There is also an interesting choice of other Sardinian dishes, but specialities such as roast suckling pig should be ordered in advance. There are plenty of vegetarian options.

TORTOLÌ Da Lenin
€€
Via San Gemiliano 19, 8041 **Tel** *078 62 44 22*
Road map D4

Memorable fish dishes are served at this informal restaurant. The menu, which changes according to the season and depends on what fresh ingredients are available, is mainly based on seafood. The home-made pasta dishes are exceptional – one to try is fish-filled ravioli served with *bottarga* – the local speciality dried mullet roe.

VILLASIMIUS Moro
€€
Via Cagliari, 9049 **Tel** *070 79 81 80*
Road map D6

This friendly, informal place is ideal for either a relaxing evening or for entertaining the kids. The garden tables are especially attractive on a warm summer's evening. The menu includes a good range of typical Sardinian specialities, both meat- and fish-based – much of the meat is cooked over an open fire. Delicious home-made pasta is also served.

VILLASIMIUS Da Barbara
€€€
SP Villasimius – Fraz. Sinnai-Solanos, 9049 **Tel** *070750630*
Road map D6

This family run restaurant, not far out of Villasimius itself, is worth seeking out for the excellent standard of the fish dishes served. It is the kind of place frequented by local residents, who come here to enjoy traditional and tasty local flavours cooked as they should be. The service is courteous and the atmosphere is warm and welcoming.

CENTRAL SARDINIA AND BARBAGIA

NUORO Canne al Vento
€€
Via G Biasi 123, 8100 **Tel** *0784 20 17 62*
Road map D3

This restaurant offers classic Barbagia dishes, excellent cheeses, roast meats – suckling pig, boar and lamb – octopus salad and *seadas* (fried pastries filled with melted Pecorino cheese and coated in honey). The restaurant is named after the novel by the Nobel Prize-winning novelist Grazia Deledda, who was born in Nuoro.

NUORO Da Giovanni Si Mangia
€€
Via IV Novembre 9, 8100 **Tel** *078 43 05 62*
Road map D3

This simple, traditional trattoria is located right in the centre of Nuoro. The food served is all typical of the Barbagia area, with a mixture of fish- and meat-based dishes. Wild boar and goat are among the local specialities served, as well as lobster, baked fish and mixed seafood salads.

OLIENA CK
€
Corso M L King 2–4, 8025 **Tel** *0784 28 80 24*
Road map D3

This family-run restaurant (pronounced "chee kappa") in a pale pink villa in the historic town centre offers local cuisine and uses a wood oven. Highlights of the menu include home-made pasta (including *busa*, traditionally made using wire) with walnut sauce, roast meats, a fine selection of cheeses and a good wine list.

OLIENA Su Gologone   €€€€€

Località Su Gologone, 8025 **Tel** *0784 28 75 12*   **Road map D3**

Surrounded by greenery, Su Gologone is only 12 km (7 miles) from Nuoro. It is known for its meat dishes (roast suckling pig, lamb and goat), *pane frattau* (Sardinian flatbread baked with stock, cheese, tomatoes and egg), ravioli, *malloredus* (Sardinian pasta often in a tomato sauce with sausage) and *seadas* (fried pastries).

THE WESTERN COAST

ALGHERO La Cuina   €

Via Cavour 110, 7041 **Tel** *079 97 69 38*   **Road map B2**

A cosy trattoria on the outskirts of Alghero old town. Locally caught fish is the speciality: mixed seafood antipasti, *zuppa di pesce* (fish soup), squid ink risotto and fried fish. Finish off with a home-made Sardinian dessert. The décor is classic, with vaulted ceilings and exposed brickwork. This restaurant offers excellent service and value.

ALGHERO Il Pavone   €€

Piazza Sulis 3–4, 7041 **Tel** *079 97 95 84*   **Road map B2**

A smart restaurant on the edge of the old town, overlooking the lively Piazza Sulis serving seasonal Mediterranean and innovative Sardinian cuisine: fresh figs with anchovies and chilli, squid ink pasta with smoked ricotta and lemon sorbet with spicy chocolate. Fish dishes are the speciality, and the service is good.

ALGHERO Al Tuguri   €€€

Via Maiorca 113/115, 7041 **Tel** *079 97 67 72*   **Road map B2**

Located in the old part of central Alghero, this small restaurant is set in an atmospheric 15th century building, with an open fire in one of the dining rooms. The menu features a good range of traditional Sardinian dishes, sometimes with inspired variations, depending on the time of year and the freshest seasonal ingredients available.

ALGHERO/FERTILIA Sa Mandra   €€

Strada Aeroporto Civile 21, 7041 **Tel** *079 99 91 50*   **Road map B2**

This classic Sardinian *agriturismo* has a rustic but the food is fit for a king. The fixed menu of traditional pastoral fare includes a selection of pecorino cheeses, hams and salamis, a variety of home-made pastas, roast suckling pig and lamb with fresh vegetables, followed by home-baked Sardinian sweets. The value is amazing.

BOSA Mannu da Giancarlo e Rita   €€

Viale Alghero 28, 8013 **Tel** *0785 37 53 06*   **Road map B3**

A smart, modern restaurant in a family-run hotel, offering extremely good local fish specialities. Bosa is famous for fresh lobster, which they serve here in a variety of sauces and styles. They also have meat dishes such as, roast suckling pig and gnocchi with lamb. The restaurant prides itself on the freshness of the produce they use.

CABRAS Sa Funtà   €€€€

Via Giuseppe Garibaldi 25, 9072 **Tel** *0783 29 06 85*   **Road map B4**

Sa Funtà is a rather refined restaurant, located in the lakeside village of Cabras. Traditional dishes are served but they are prepared with an added touch of creativity. Much care is taken over the choice of ingredients: the olive oil and vegetables are produced using organic techniques and the fish served is mainly from the local freshwater lake.

ORISTANO Il Faro   €€

Via Bellini 25, 9170 **Tel** *0783 700 02*   **Road map B4**

One of Sardinia's best restaurants, Il Faro is well-known for its traditional cuisine. They serve regional dishes based on what is fresh at the market that day, particularly fish and seafood. Typical dishes include octopus with vegetables, seafood soup, pasta with aubergine (eggplant), mushrooms and truffles and lobster. There are delicious home-made desserts.

ORISTANO Da Giovanni   €€€€

Via Cristoforo Colombo 8 – Torre Grande, 9170 **Tel** *078 32 20 51*   **Road map B4**

Opened by acclaimed local chef Giovanni Sebis in the early 1960s, this restaurant near the tree-lined seafront has an excellent reputation. The locally caught fish is selected with care, and cooked mostly according to traditional recipes. The delicious lobster ravioli are certainly worth trying as is the *spaghetti con bottarga* – the speciality mullet roe.

PORTO TORRES Li Lioni   €€€

SS 131 – Loc. Li Lioni, 7046 **Tel** *079 50 22 86*   **Road map B2**

A lovely welcoming restaurant, set in its own garden, a few kilometres from Porto Torres. Great care is taken over the quality of the food and the preparation methods. The meats - porcetto, lamb and so on - are all cooked in an olive-wood burning fireplace and the pasta and desserts are home-made. The wine served is produced locally.

STINTINO Silvestrino   €€€

Via Sassari 12/14, 7040 **Tel** *079 52 30 07*   **Road map B2**

This centrally located restaurant and hotel, here since 1948, has gained a good reputation, particularly for the excellent seafood dishes served. The local lobster is one dish worth trying – it comes with a delicious sauce. The décor inside the restaurant is pleasant enough, but in summer the terrace tables are a more attractive place to dine.

Key to Price Guide *see p184* **Key to Symbols** *see back cover flap*

THE NORTH AND COSTA SMERALDA

ARZACHENA Grazia Deledda

Strada per Baja Sardinia, 7021 **Tel** *0789 989 90*   **Road map D1**

The décor at this hotel restaurant recalls the life and times of Grazia Deledda, Sardinia's famous author who won the Nobel prize for literature in 1926. The location is lovely, overlooking the stunning coastline. The standard of the food served is excellent – there are many traditional Sardinian specialities including lots of delicious local fish.

LA MADDALENA Mangana

Via Mazzini 2, 7024 **Tel** *0789 73 84 77*   **Road map D1**

This picturesque restaurant, with a great veranda for al fresco dining, overlooks the pretty port of La Maddalena. The atmosphere is intimate and warm and there's often live piano music. The menu features numerous Sardinian specialities, with the fresh, locally caught fish being a particular strong point. Tasty pizzas are also available.

LA MADDALENA La Grotta

Via Principe di Napoli 2, 7024 **Tel** *0789 73 84 77*   **Road map D1**

This attractively rustic restaurant, located at the centre of La Maddalena, has been a local favourite since the late 1950s. The same family, originally from the Naples area, has been in charge since then, adapting well to the increase in tourism over the years. The *zuppa di pesce* (fish soup) is one speciality to try.

OLBIA Gallura

Corso Umberto 145, 7026 **Tel** *0789 246 48*   **Road map D2**

One of the finest seafood restaurants in Sardinia. The cuisine is creative and the ingredients are organic. Swordfish with saffron is a speciality. Fish can be grilled, poached or roasted in the wood-burning oven. There are also meat dishes, goat and rabbit and pasta with wild boar. The desserts are equally as delicious.

PALAU Da Franco

Via Capo d'Orso 1, 7020 **Tel** *0789 70 95 58*   **Road map D1**

An attractive wood-panelled interior with a fabulous terrace overlooking the port, quality tableware and courteous service at this exclusive restaurant – a favourite among the jet-set. The menu features seafood and other Sardinian specialities, including delightful cheeses. The standard is fantastic – exquisite flavours and perfectly presented dishes.

PORTO CERVO Gianni Pedrinelli

Località Piccolo Pevero, 7020 **Tel** *0789 924 36*   **Road map D1**

The regional menu in this delightful restaurant offers a wealth of fish dishes, such as lobster pasta and salt fish, but the house speciality is *porcettu allo spiedo* (spit-roast suckling pig). The restaurant combines style and tradition in a large airy whitewashed room with arched doorway, wooden beamed ceilings and tiled floors.

PORTO ROTONDO Da Giovannino

Piazza Quadrata 1, 7026 **Tel** *0789 352 80*   **Road map D1**

A sophisticated restaurant decorated to the finest detail and with a lovely garden. It is popular with Italian politicians and media types, who dine on expensive but delicious Mediterranean specialities, such as scampi sushi with lemon juice, swordfish with tomatoes and capers and grilled squid. Superb wine list.

SAN TEODORO Lea Cana

Loc. Monti Pitrosu, 8020 **Tel** *0784 83 50 91*   **Road map D2**

This friendly family-run restaurant serves fragrant pizzas as well as plenty of genuine Sardinian dishes. The rustic, typically Sardinian décor is attractive, and there is a large garden area with granite tables. The house specialities include *culungiones* (a traditional filled pasta dish), tasty fish soup and delicious *seadas*. Local wines.

SANTA TERESA DI GALLURA Canne al Vento

Via Nazionale 23, 7028 **Tel** *0789 75 42 19*   **Road map C1**

This friendly restaurant in Santa Teresa di Gallura, at the northernmost point of Sardinia, serves some delicious traditional dishes. Fish is the main speciality, cooked in a variety of ways. One to try is the excellent *zuppa di pesce* (fish soup); portions are large and hearty. The wine list features a well-picked selection of Sardinian wines.

SASSARI Il Cenacolo

Via Ozieri 2, 7100 **Tel** *079 23 62 51*   **Road map B2**

The traditional menu here offers the very best of sea and land regional specialities according to the season: there are mushrooms in autumn, seafood in summer and vegetables all year round. An elegant restaurant with a pleasant atmosphere in the centre of the city.

SASSARI Liberty

Piazza N Sauro 3 (corso Vittorio Emanuele), 7100 **Tel** *079 23 63 61*   **Road map B2**

Elegant and refined, this restaurant excels on all fronts, with a menu that is fish-based. Start with the *antipasto Liberty*, a delicious array of fish and seafood, and follow with *gnocchetti camustia* (smoked ricotta and calamari dumplings), spaghetti with lobster or oven-baked fish with potatoes and artichokes. Excellent wine list.

SHOPS AND MARKETS

Sardinia produces a great variety of handicrafts that are hard to find in other regions of Italy. Among these are hand-woven rugs, linen napkins, *pibbiones* (embroidered fabrics) and baskets. Traditional materials and techniques are used for all these products, and while some are still made in the traditional style, others have been adapted to more modern tastes. Crafted goods are often made to a very

Local olives

high standard of design and workmanship, and include coral and filigree pins and brooches, pottery and crockery, and items made from cork and wrought iron.

In the larger towns and tourist resorts, traditional souvenirs are sold, such as ashtrays in the shape of nuraghi, costumed dolls and seashell pictures. Specialities such as pecorino cheese, salted mullet roe, sweets and wine are also worth trying.

OPENING HOURS

Shops in Sardinia generally open at 9am, close at 1pm for lunch and reopen 4:30–8pm (5–8:30pm or later in summer). Large supermarkets and larger clothes stores are open throughout the day. In the cities most shops close for a few weeks in August, while on the coast they tend to open on a seasonal basis (June to September).

A potter at the wheel

HOW TO PAY

The majority of the larger shops and department stores accept credit cards, but it is advisable to check in advance. The smaller shops and artisan's workshops will generally prefer payment in cash. You must get a receipt *(scontrino)* when you pay; it is required by law and it may be asked to produce it as you leave the shop. It will also be needed should you want to change purchased articles later on.

DEPARTMENT STORES

The main department store in Cagliari is **La Rinascente** in Via Roma. Other large stores are **Upim** and **Standa**, which you will also find in other Sardinian towns and cities. Recently, large shopping centres have grown up on the outskirts of towns, with a wide selection of goods on offer, from shoe shops and clothing stores to supermarkets and fast food restaurants.

HANDICRAFTS

Local handicrafts are on sale all over Sardinia. In the villages, women display their wares, such as baskets, rugs or ceramics, outside their homes.

Shops that belong to the *Istituto Sardo Organizzazione Lavoro Artigianale* (**ISOLA**), Sardinian Institute of Handicrafts, offer quality products from the local craftsmen's cooperatives, including rugs, tablecloths, leather, jewellery, baskets, pottery, carved wood

Local handicrafts for sale in a certified ISOLA shop

and wrought-iron objects. All ISOLA products carry a seal of quality guaranteeing their origin and authenticity.

You can find good bargains at the *Fiera del Tappeto* (Carpet Fair), held at Mogoro in late July–August. Handicrafts can also be purchased at holiday farms. Other useful addresses can be found in the Esit publication *Sardegna – Un Mare di Tradizioni*.

A fish stall in Cagliari's covered market, San Benedetto

REGIONAL SPECIALITIES

Gastronomic specialities in Sardinia are sold in the food section of supermarkets as well as in delicatessens and specialist shops or directly from the producers.

The **Mercato Coperto di San Benedetto** in Cagliari is the largest covered market in Italy. It offers an excellent choice of regional delicacies. *Bottarga* (mullet roe) can be bought at **Vaghi**, on Via Bayle, which also sells sea urchin pâté. Salted *bottarga* can be bought from the manufacturer

San Francesco's feast day celebrated at Lula with barbecued *porceddu*

A dish of typical Sardinian honey

at **Fratelli Manca** in Cabras. Smoked fish is on sale at **Sarda Affumicati** in Buggerru.

Cakes and sweets are also a Sardinian speciality and a fine selection is on offer in several shops, including **Sorelle Piccioni** in Quartu Sant'Elena, **Colomba Codias** in Olbia and **Acciari** at Porto Torres. A visit

to a winery (*cantina*) to taste the wines before buying can prove both interesting and good value. It is sometimes possible to taste wines in a wine shop (*enoteca*).

Other useful addresses of shops and workshops are listed in the publication by Esit, *Sardegna – Un Mare di Delizie.*

DIRECTORY

HANDICRAFTS

Alghero
Centro Forme
Via Lamarmora 64/66.
Tel 079 97 53 52.

Cagliari
ISOLA
Via Bacaredda 184.
Tel 070 40 47 91.
www.regione.
sardegna.it/isola

Olbia
Sardartis srl
SS125, km 313.
Tel 0789 669 33.

Cerasarda
Road for Palau, km 2,800.
Tel 0789 500 32.
www.cerasarda.it

Oristano
Cooperativa Sutrobasciu
Via Gramsci 1.
Tel 0783 99 05 81.
www.sutrobasciu.com

Porto Cervo
ISOLA
Sottopiazza.
Tel 070 40 47 91.

Sant'Antioco
Cooperativa Sant'Antioco Martire
Lungo Mare Vespucci 30.
Tel 0781 820 85.

Sassari
ISOLA
Viale Mancini.
Tel 070 40 47 91.

REGIONAL SPECIALITIES

Alghero
Sella & Mosca
I Piani. *Tel* 079 99 77 00.
www.sellaemosca.com

Buggerru
Sarda Affumicati
Portixeddu.
Tel 0781 549 14.
www.sardaffumicati.com

Cabras
Fratelli Manca
Via Cima 5.
Tel 0783 29 08 48.
www.orodicabras.com

Cagliari
Mercato San Benedetto
Via Cocco Ortu.
Tel 070 28 37 52.

Olbia
Colomba Codias
Via Australia 12.
Tel 0789 682 26.

Ozieri
Pasticceria Pietro Pinna
Via Pastorino 35.
Tel 079 78 74 51.

Porto Torres
Acciaro
Corso Vittorio Emanuele 36.
Tel 079 51 46 05.

Quartu Sant'Elena
Sorelle Piccioni
Via Marconi 312.
Tel 070 81 01 12.

Sassari
Fratelli Rau
Via Gorizia 7.
Tel 079 29 22 64.

Tonara
Salvatore Pruneddu
Via Porru 7.
Tel 0784 638 05.

WINE

Cabras
Azienda Attilio Contini
Via Genova 48.
Tel 0783 29 08 06.
www.vinicontini.it

Cagliari
Antica Enoteca Cagliaritana
Scalette Santa Chiara.
Tel 070 65 56 11.
www.enoteca-cagliaritana.it

Jerzu
Jerzu Antichi Poderi
Via Umberto I 1.
Tel 0782 700 28.
www.jerzuantichipoderi.it

Olbia
Cantina della vigne di Piero Mancini
Tel 0789 50 717.
www.pieromancini.it

Oristano
Cantina Sociale della Vernaccia
Loc. Rimedio.
Tel 0783 331 55.
www.vinovernaccia.com

Quartu Sant'Elena
Cantina Sociale
Via Nazionale, Maracalagonis.
Tel 070 78 98 65.
www.cantinadiquartu.it

Sant'Antioco
Cantina Sociale
Via Rinascita 46.
Tel 0781 830 55.

Sennori
Tenute Dettori
Tel 079 51 47 11.
www.tenutedettori.it

Serdiana
Cantina Argiolas
Via Roma 56/58.
Tel 070 74 06 00.

What to Buy in Sardinia

Sardinia offers a great variety of traditional island products and local handicrafts, ranging from hand-woven rugs, bedspreads and pillowcases to baskets woven in asphodel, reed or raffia. Some of the finest baskets are made in Flussio and Castelsardo. Other household articles, such as kitchenware and tableware, are made of cork or ceramics, materials which are also used to make large plates, statues and bas-reliefs. Filigree jewellery production is widespread and worn by the women for festivals and weddings; the best is made in Alghero and Bosa.

Filigree pendant

Gold buttons

Pin and earrings

JEWELLERY

Traditional Sardinian jewellery, such as earrings, brooches and buttons, often worn with local dress, is made of filigree and coral. Goldsmiths also make bracelets and necklaces in modern designs, including elegant coral spirals.

Cork ice bucket

At Calangianus, *in the Gallura region of the Costa Smeralda, cork is used to make numerous household articles such as boxes, umbrella stands, bowls and ice buckets.*

Circular amphora

Flower vase

Vases and jugs made to a modern design

POTTERY

Sardinian pottery is hand-thrown and glazed with natural colours. The most common articles are vases, plates and jugs and the designs are simple and fluid. Some potters have modified traditional designs to suit modern tastes.

Basket-weaving *is an ancient craft that is still widely practised. Baskets are made of straw, raffia, dwarf palm, asphodel, corn sheaves or wicker in delicate, natural colours.*

Rug made in Nule

Tapestry from Mogoro

A *pibbiones* rug

RUGS AND TAPESTRIES

Among the typical hand-woven articles are woollen rugs, linen bedspreads and napkins, and tapestries. The rugs are made from coloured wool with lively geometric or floral designs. The *pibbiones* rugs consist of an embroidered raised pattern knitted with small needles on neutral coloured fabric.

Wood carving *is an ancient Sardinian tradition. The most common articles produced are chests, kitchen implements, chopping boards and ceremonial masks.*

Lace-making *is a rare craft that requires great skill. At Oliena you can find delicate shawls made of black silk embroidered with bright colours. At Bosa you can still see women making filet lace.*

Carved mask

Lacework from Dorgali

GASTRONOMIC DELICACIES

Typical Sardinian products include cakes and cheeses which vary from region to region. Other specialities include jam, wine and liqueurs, such as myrtle (*mirto*) and lemon (*limoncino*), salted mullet roe and vegetables in oil.

Typical Sardinian cakes

Salted mullet roe

Myrtle liqueur

Typical Sardinian delicacies

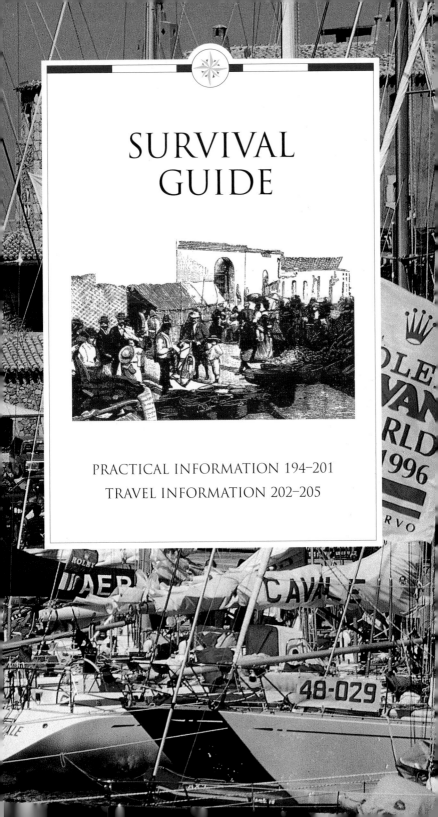

SURVIVAL
GUIDE

PRACTICAL INFORMATION

Beaches and clean blue sea are the principal attractions for visitors to Sardinia, and the coastline, especially in the northeast, gets very crowded from early July to late August. Visiting the island out of season can have its advantages, apart from avoiding the bustling crowds. The weather can be very hot in midsummer and visits to the towns and countryside, rich in history, ancient culture, old traditions and spellbinding scenery, are all the more easily appreciated in spring, early summer and autumn.

Tourist information sign

Tourism is a relatively new phenomenon in Sardinia, and the familiar problems of funding and staffing for monuments and museums occur here as on the mainland. Do not be surprised to see signs such as *chiuso per restauro* (closed for restoration). Provision of information for travellers is far from perfect but is improving; there are now more tourist offices, opening at regular hours, able to provide maps and guides to help you plan your time. Attempts to speak Italian, however halting, are always appreciated.

Cooling off in midsummer

WHEN TO VISIT

In July and August practically the whole of Italy goes on holiday and everywhere is overcrowded, in particular the ferries to and from Olbia and Cagliari, and the seaside hotels and resorts. Prices are much higher and you need to plan your visit ahead to make sure of accommodation. The most crowded areas are the Costa Smeralda, the beaches near the Golfo di Cagliari and the area around Stintino.

The best months to visit the beautiful interior are May, June and September. Spring is particularly delightful, when flowers are in bloom.

In winter the cold can be quite intense, especially at higher altitudes.

TOURIST INFORMATION

Tourist information facilities in Sardinia are currently undergoing a substantial change. The local tourist offices (Azienda Autonoma di Soggiorno e Turismo) have been abolished, along with the provincial tourist offices (Entre Provinciale Per il Turismo), so tourism is now the responsibility of the comune (local town council) and the local Pro Loco (Town

Hall). Some Sardinian towns have already set up new tourism offices – mainly those in well-established tourist areas – while others are in the process of doing so.

In the meantime, local papers – L-Unione Sarda, La Nuova Sardegna and Il Sardegna are useful sources of information, providing complete day-by-day listings of activities and events.

There are also useful websites aimed at tourists in Sardinia. Two of the best are www.sardinia.net and www.sardiniapoint.it They list holiday accommodation, events and festivals.

IMMIGRATION AND CUSTOMS

European Union (EU) residents and visitors from the United States, Canada, New Zealand, Australia, Japan, need no visa for up to three months but must have one for a longer stay. Non-European Union citizens must carry a valid passport with them, while for EU citizens an ID with photo will suffice. It is however, adviseable to check the requirements before travelling. Non-EU citizens can bring in either 400 cigarettes or 100 cigars or 500 grams of tobacco, 1 litre of spirits, 2 litres of wine and 50 grams of perfume. Valuable goods may be imported only for strictly personal use.

Snowy scene in the interior, not unusual in midwinter

◁ The yachting centre of Porto Cervo

SHOPS, BANKS AND POST OFFICES

This guide provides the opening hours for the island's museums and archaeological sites. Shops are open from 8 or 9am to 1pm and from 3:30 or 4pm (in winter) or 5pm (in summer) to 7 or 8pm from Monday to Saturday, with one early closing day during the week. Banks are open from Monday to Friday from 8:30am to 1:30pm and 2:30pm to 3:30pm. Small post offices are open from 8am to 1:15pm, while larger offices open until 6:45pm (1:15pm on Saturday). The Italian national telephone company, Telecom Italia, runs both coin-operated and card

An elegant shop offering Sardinian handicrafts

(scheda telefonica) public phones in all towns. For English-language information on post office services, visit www.poste.it

MUSEUMS AND MONUMENTS

Normally museums and archaeological zones are open every day except Monday. However, in winter, some sites close in the afternoon and, in summer, opening hours are extended.

Museum entrance fees vary and, in line with EU rules, there are discounts or free entry for children, young people under 18, senior citizens and group bookings.

Churches in the interior are usually closed in the middle of the day and may only be open for mass. If a church is closed, the parish priest *(parroco)* or sexton may open it for you as a special favour for a short visit. A small contribution to church funds will always be welcome in return for assistance.

FESTIVALS

Sardinia's festivals have a very long history and are colourful and unusual affairs. The busiest times of year for seeing traditional festivals are

Traditional rituals, still part of the community year in Sardinia

Carnival, Easter and 15 August. Town halls provide information on feast days and festivals, and dates are also given in the information for each town in this guide. For an overview of the main festivals and events in Sardinia, see pages 26–9.

DISABLED TRAVELLERS

Unfortunately, special facilities for the disabled are rare, even in the larger towns, and touring can be quite a frustrating experience for wheelchair users.

For further information on advice and assistance for the disabled, contact the offices of the Sardinian provinces.

DIRECTORY

SARDINIAN PROVINCES

Provincia di Cagliari
www.provincia.cagliari.it

Provincia del Medio Campidano
www.provincia.mediocampidano.it

Provincia di Carbonia-Iglesias
www.provincia.carboniaiglesias.it

Provincia di Oristano
www.provincia.or.it

Provincia di Nuoro
www.provincia.nuori.it

Provincia di Ogliastra
www.provincia.ogliastra.it

Provincia di Olbia Tempio
www.provincia.olbiatempio.it

Provincia di Sassari
www.provincia.sassari.it

EMBASSIES AND CONSULATES

Australia
Roma. **Tel** 06 852 721.

Canada
Roma. **Tel** 06 85 444 2911.

United Kingdom
Cagliari. **Tel** 070 82 86 28.
Roma. **Tel** 06 42 20 00 01.

United States
Roma. **Tel** 06 46 741.

ITALIAN TOURIST OFFICES ABROAD

1 Princes Street,
London W1R 8AY,
UNITED KINGDOM.
Tel 020 740 812 54.
www.enit.it
www.italiantouristboard.co.uk

175 Bloor Street E.,
Suite 907, South Tower,
Toronto, Ontario
M4W 3R8, CANADA.
Tel 416 925 4882.
www.italiantourism.com

630 Fifth Ave,
Suite 1565,
New York, NY 10111,
UNITED STATES.
Tel 212 245 5618.
www.italiantourism.com

COUNTRY CODES

To call Italy from these countries, dial the code and then the number.

Australia
Tel 00 1139.

Canada
Tel 011 39.

United States
Tel 011 39.

United Kingdom
Tel 00 39.

Personal Security and Health

On the whole, Sardinia is a safe place for visitors and only a few precautions are needed for a pleasant stay. There is some petty crime, so take extra care of money and belongings in the busy passenger terminals of the ports and in cities. Do not leave valuables in your car if the parking place is unsupervised. On the whole, rural areas are generally safer than cities. During the summer, forest fires are a very serious problem, so be sure to follow the instructions of the local police or firemen should an emergency arise. If you fall ill, the nearest pharmacy *(farmacia)* is a good first stop.

CREDIT CARDS AND LOST PROPERTY

It is never a good idea to carry a lot of cash with you. The major credit cards (Visa, MasterCard, American Express and Diners Club) are accepted by the majority of shops, restaurants and hotels on the island. It is reasonably easy to find automatic cash dispensers *(bancomat)* in all the large cities, but interest will be charged on currency exchange withdrawals, so you may prefer to carry travellers' cheques as well.

Generally speaking, it is safe to park where you like, as car theft is not common, especially in small towns. However, if anything is stolen, go immediately to the local police or carabinieri to report the theft; you will need the report for the insurance claim.

FIRE HAZARDS

Unfortunately, forest fires are a real problem in Sardinia, especially in the summer. Except for rare cases

Fire, a constant danger

of accidental fire that may be caused by a thrown-away cigarette, most fires on the island are started deliberately. In some instances forest and brush are destroyed to make way for more grazing land but, more often than not, the motive is to clear space for new buildings. In an attempt to halt the practice, a law has been passed prohibiting con-struction in areas destroyed by fire, but even this has not stopped arsonists. In the dry heat of summer, fire spreads rapidly in the undergrowth of

the maquis, and the main enemy of the firemen is the wind, which is capable of carrying the fire a long way in a very short time. Fire-fighting is carried out by the local fire brigades as well as the state forest rangers, volunteers and specially equipped fire-fighting planes positioned in key areas of the island.

MEDICAL TREATMENT

Should you need medical assistance during your stay, Sardinia has a network of hospitals and casualty departments *(pronto soccorso)*, as well as pharmacies which can dispense advice as well as medicines. European Union nationals are entitled to Italian medical care, but you need to carry an EHIC card.

In all the tourist resorts there is a *Guardia Medica* (emergency treatment centre) equipped to give medical attention to summer visitors. These seasonal surgeries are often closed in the winter and, in an emergency in low season, you will have to go to one of the main hospitals.

Pharmacies in Sardinia are open from Monday to Friday, 9am–1pm and 4–7pm and Saturday morning. Lists of the night and holiday opening rotas for the local area are carried on the chemist's door.

FIRE PREVENTION RULES

1. Always take care to extinguish cigarettes before discarding them.
2. Never light a fire except in areas where this is explicitly permitted.
3. If you see a fire, you must report it to the local firemen.
4. Do not stop or park your car to watch a fire; you may block the roads and interfere with fire-fighting operations.
5. Pay attention to the wind direction: it is highly dangerous to be down-wind of a fire, as it may spread quite rapidly and catch you unawares.

Policemen on horseback at the Poetto beach near Cagliari

COUNTRYSIDE CODES

During your stay you are likely to spend a good deal of time exploring outdoors, so be prepared for any problems that may occur.

In the summer, whether you are on the beach or in the interior, be wary of too much sun, as it may cause serious burns and sunstroke. If it is windy, you may not be aware you are burning.

If a storm breaks and you need to take shelter, do not head for isolated trees or rocky peaks, which may attract lightning.

Although you cannot simply camp wherever you like, you can make private arrangements with landowners to pitch your tent away from official camping sites. Make sure you take away all your rubbish and do not light fires.

Bear in mind that grazing in the open countryside is still quite common in Sardinia: pigs, sheep, cows and horses may well decide to see whether campers have anything good to eat in their tents. In hilly areas sheepdogs

Livestock often graze on fields near campsites.

should be avoided, since they are trained to chase away any potential intruders.

While walking or trekking in the countryside you may come across gates or fences barring your way. It is always a good idea, if possible, to ask whether you can go through. Having done so, remember to close the gate so that animals are unable to escape. If you plan a lengthy hike, make sure you carry enough water with you, as villages may be few and far between. Lastly, despite the wildness, there are no poisonous snakes.

CURRENCY

Thirteen European countries have replaced their traditional national currencies with the euro. Austria, Belgium, Finland, France, Germany, Greece, Ireland, Italy, Luxembourg, Netherlands, Portugal, Spain and more recently Slovenia chose to join the new currency.

The euro was introduced on 1 January 1999, but only for banking purposes. Notes and coins came into circulation on 1 January 2002. All euro notes and coins can be used anywhere inside the participating member states.

Euro bank notes have seven denominations. The €5 note (grey in colour) is the smallest, followed by the €10 note (pink), €20 note (blue), €50 note (orange), €100 note (green), €200 note (yellow) and €500 note (purple). The euro has eight coin denominations: €1 and €2; 50 cents, 20 cents, 10 cents, 5 cents, 2 cents and 1 cent. The €2 and €1 coins are silver and gold in colour. The 50-, 20- and 10-cent coins are gold. The 5-, 2- and 1-cent coins are bronze.

Visitors will find automatic exchange machines at the airports. However, it is always a good idea to have some euros at hand for any immediate expenses.

Euro notes

USING BANKS

Bank opening hours are usually 8:30am–1:30pm and 3–4:30pm from Monday to Friday. All banks close at weekends and on public holidays. Credit cards, once regarded with suspicion in Sardinia, are now accepted without question by hotels, restaurants and shops, especially those in the tourist areas. All the major credit cards are accepted, the most popular cards being Visa and MasterCard. You will not have difficulty in finding an automatic cash dispenser *(bancomat)* in all the larger towns and in some of the smaller villages.

Water Sports

Despite the impressive beauty of its interior, Sardinia's fame is more strongly associated with the sea. The development of the tourist industry means that the island now offers a good range of facilities for water sports, in particular sailing, windsurfing and scuba diving. There are diving centres and sailing schools in almost all the coastal resorts, and many of the holiday villages are well-equipped for water sports. Canoeing is a different matter, since the lack of navigable rivers limits your choice in the interior, and sea canoeing is only practised in a few places along the coast.

Diving in the crystal-clear waters of Sardinia

Sailing along the coast

strong and variable winds. A good source of useful information for a sailing holiday is volume 1A of *Portolano del Mediterraneo* (Mediterranean Pilot's Book), which is published by the Istituto Idrografico della Marina Militare. Another useful publication is the pamphlet *I Porti Turistici della Sardegna* (Sardinian Yacht Harbours), available from all tourist information offices. You need permission from the harbour master to moor in most of Sardinia's harbours.

SCUBA DIVING

The coastline offers plenty of opportunities for experienced divers. Among the most famous spots for diving are the coasts of Asinara and Gallura, Capo Caccia, Carloforte, the Golfo di Orosei and the area around the island of Tavolara. Many diving centres – often based at sports shops – organize diving trips. You can also buy or rent diving equipment and get advice on diving sites.

SAILING

With its marvellous sea and coastline, Sardinia is regarded as a paradise for boating of all kinds, whether your preferred style is a billion-dollar luxury yacht on the Costa Smeralda or a simple dinghy for hire from one of the more affordable centres. The conditions vary considerably and even experienced sailors find the Sardinian coast a challenge because of the

WINDSURFING

Windsurfing equipment is available for hire at almost all the tourist beaches. Some of the sailing centres also offer boards for hire and can organize lessons.

Windsurfing in the open sea

DIRECTORY

WINDSURFING BEACHES

The following beaches are the best on the island for windsurfing (see pp18–19)

Bosa Marina
Poetto – Cagliari
Calagrande – Isola di
  Sant'Antioco
Saline – Isola di Sant'Antioco
Monti d'a Rena – La Maddalena
Porto Massimo – La Maddalena
Porto Taverna – Porto San Paolo
  Lotzorai
Marinella – Olbia
Porto Istana – Olbia
Torre Grande – Oristano
Porto Pollo – Palau
Capo Testa – Santa Teresa di
  Gallura
La Cinta – San Teodoro
Putzu Idu – San Vero Milis

The Centro Velico Caprera sailing school

The safety rules for sailing also apply to this sport: the winds can be very strong and fickle (especially the mistral), so do not go too far out.

CANOEING

Although there are very few navigable rivers for canoeing in the interior – and the variable weather makes practising the sport even more difficult – you can canoe in the lakes or along certain stretches of the coast.

OTHER SPORTS

There are numerous coves along the Sardinian coasts where you can explore the rocks and the water and observe the varied marine life. Snorkelling is perhaps best left to the experienced: strong winds and currents can easily create difficult and dangerous conditions.

Subaqua fishing with a harpoon and aqualung is not permitted but freshwater fishing is possible in the lakes and reservoirs. You will need a permit to fish in the rivers.

In some holiday villages water-based tours are offered to guests, and some also provide dinghies in which to explore the coastline.

Canoeing in the fabulous Cala Sisine cove

DIRECTORY

SAILING AND WINDSURFING CENTRES

Carloforte Yacht Club
Tel 0781 85 64 57.
www.carloforte
yachtclub.org

Centro Velico Caprera – La Maddalena
Porto Palma.
Tel 0789 73 85 29.
www.centrovelico
caprera.it

Circolo Nautico Arbatax
Tel 0782 66 75 66.

Circolo Nautico Olbia
Via Genova 69.
Tel 0789 261 87.

Circolo Nautico Oristano
Tel 0783 21 01 72.

Club Nautico La Maddalena
Via G Cesare 20.
Tel 0789 72 79 85.

Windsurfing Club Cagliari
Marina Piccola.
Tel 070 37 26 84 or

328 611 68 98. **www.**
windsurfingclubcagliari.it

Windsurfing Vela Club Portoscuso
Portoscuso.
Tel 0781 50 95 38.

Yacht Club Alghero
Tel 079 95 20 74.
www.yachtclubalghero.it

Yacht Club Cagliari
Marina Piccola.
Tel 070 37 03 50.
www.yachtclub-cagliari.com

Yacht Club Costa Smeralda – Porto Cervo
Porto Cervo.
Tel 0789 90 22 00.
www.yccs.it

Yacht Club Porto Rotondo
Tel 0789 340 10.
www.ycpr.it

DIVING CENTRES

Air Sub Service – Villasimius
Tel 070 79 20 33
or 070 50 68 63 (winter).
www.airsub.com

Anthias
Palau. Tel 0789 86 311
or 339 891 79 67.
www.anthiasdiving.com

Aqua Diving Center Puntaldia
Puntaldia, San Teodoro.
Tel 0784 86 43 90
or 348 511 23 33.

Area Mare Diving
Cannigione.
Tel 338 822 11 35.
www.areamare.com

Centro Sub Caribù
c/o Hotel Capo Caccia.
Tel 079 94 66 66.
www.hotel
capocaccia.it

Centro Sub Iuledda Compagnia dell'Avventura
Cannigione, Arzachena.
Tel 0789 862 53
or 347 461 62 92.
www.isuledda.it

Centro Sub Tavolara
Porto San Paolo.
Tel 0789 403 60.
www.centrosub
tavolara.com

Isla Diving
Carloforte.
Tel 0781 85 56 34 or
335 46 25 02
www.isladiving.it

L'Argonauta Diving Center
Cala Gonone.
Tel 0784 930 46 or

347 530 40 97.
www.argonauta.it

Nautica – Portisco
Tel 0789 335 12.

Orso Diving Club – Poltu Quato
Porto Cervo
Tel 0789 990 01.
www.orsodiving.com

Oyster Sub Diving Center
Palau.
Tel 0789 70 20 70.
www.oystersub.com

Tanka Village Diving Center – Villasimius
Tel 070 79 54 64 or
338 674 14 72. **www.**
subcentertanka.com

CANOEING

Associazione Italiana Kayak da Mare – Cagliari
Tel 070 66 04 89.

Canoa Club Oristano
Tel 0783 21 03 35.

Federazione Italiana Canoa
Cagliari. **Tel** 070 65 27 48.
www.federcanoa.it

Outdoor Sports

Neglected for years because attention was focused on tourist development along the coast, the interior landscape of Sardinia offers plenty of opportunity to practise outdoor sports. The countryside can be explored on foot or on horseback – riding centres have made great advances in recent years and are in great demand. Facilities for hiking and rock climbing are good and increasing numbers of mountain climbing routes are in the process of being marked out.

The Su Rei riding centre in Sulcis

HORSE RIDING

Sardinia is ideally suited for trekking and horse riding. Horses have long been an integral part of the island's culture, as the animal has been part of local life since Phoenician times: many of the religious feast days and festivities include breakneck rides and horse races.

The many isolated minor roads, mule tracks and paths, far away from traffic and noise, particularly in the interior, are ideal for pleasant rides, and many are not too difficult for beginners.

There are nearly 100 Sardinian equestrian clubs and centres, large and small, offering facilities for this sport. Most are equipped to organize lessons and rides for beginners as well as extended treks for experienced riders.

Most of the stables and clubs are located near Cagliari, Nuoro and Oristano, but there has been an increase in the number of holiday farms *(see p170)* offering horse riding and riding excursions for their guests, whatever their ability.

Supramonte, Giara di Gesturi and the Valle della Luna are three of the most interesting and popular destinations for those who love long treks in the Sardinian countryside.

ROCK CLIMBING

In the 1960s the Italian mountaineer Alessandro Gogna published *Mezzogiorno di Pietra* (Midday Stone), which opened up the possibilities for rock climbing in Sardinia. Since those days enthusiasm for the sport has grown considerably, and the island's most challenging

Cliffs at the seaside with facilities for rock climbing

rocks and cliffs are tackled by climbers from all over Italy and Europe. Among the most popular climbing areas are Supramonte (Surtana, l'Aguglia), the cliffs at Iglesiente (Domusnovas), where hand- and foot-holds have recently been placed, and the Isili area in Nuoro province.

Essential reading for rock climbers who decide to come here is *Pietra di Luna* (Moon Stone) by Maurizio Oviglia, the most up-to-date guide to rock climbing in Sardinia.

Additional information can be obtained at the **Sezione di Cagliari del Club Alpino Italiano**. Programmes are organized by a number of companies, including **Barbagia Insolita** and **Keya**. Climbing lessons are available from **Nuovi Equilibri**.

WALKING AND TREKKING

Wild mountains, hills dotted with prehistoric ruins, forests and maquis vegetation make up most of the terrain in the interior of Sardinia. The countryside is rugged but unspoilt and ideal for walking, hiking and more strenuous treks. However, facilities are few and far between, clearly signposted footpaths are rare and there are very few refuges or stopping places. It is always advisable to carry an up-to-date map and to take plenty of water when walking.

The most rewarding and popular areas are Supramonte, the Gennargentu massif and the Sulcis area (which offers an unusual blend of hiking and industrial archaeology). Some stretches of the steep coastline are more suited to those with climbing experience.

In the Supramonte area experienced mountaineers can even tackle the wild and precipitous Su Gorroppu gorges. The trek takes a couple of days and special rock climbers' equipment is needed in order to make it down the vertical walls of the falls. This particular excursion is, therefore, not suitable for beginners.

THE SELVAGGIO BLU ROUTE

Its very name – Wild Blue – is the best possible description of this difficult route along the Golfo di Orosei, starting from Santa Maria Navarrese and ending at Cala Luna. The Selvaggio Blu was conceived a few years ago by Mario Verin and Peppino Cicalò. The course requires excellent

physical condition and preparation (since part of it consists of stretches of rock climbing, some of the descents are achieved by abseiling and you have to walk with a heavy load because of the distance between water supply sources) but the rewards are some of the most spectacular views of the Sardinian coast. The town of Baunei publishes a guide to Selvaggio Blu; for information, or if you are interested in buying the book, call 0782 61 08 23.

A stretch of the Selvaggio Blu trail

Whether walking or climbing, or a combination of both, make sure you have the best map possible to hand (a good map is published by IGM). You should also carefully calculate the time the tour will take and how much food and water will be needed, as it is possible to walk for kilometres without stumbling across a village.

SPELEOLOGY

The mountains of Sardinia are riddled with dozens of fascinating caves to be explored, some of which have tourist facilities. The temperature inside is likely to be relatively high, more or less the yearly average of the surrounding area. Bear in mind that some of the difficult caves, such as the Golgo abyss (at Su Sterru), the Grotta Verde at Capo Caccia or the Su Palu cave near Orosei, are only open to experienced speleologists.

GOLF COURSES

Sardinia has some famous golf courses, including the one at the **Pevero Golf Club** in Porto Cervo, designed by the architect Robert Trent Jones. This 18-hole golf course is internationally known for its tournaments.

OTHER SPORTS

The island's sports activites are not confined to the mountains and caves in its interior. More traditional sports such as tennis, football, swimming and five-a-side football can be pursued in the many sports grounds and courts throughout the island.

The golf course at Pevero

DIRECTORY

HORSE RIDING

Associazione Ippica Montalbo
Tel 0784 85 41 16.
www.posadacavallo.it

Centro Sportivo Le Dune
Loc. Porto Pollo (Palau).
Tel 0789 704 153.

Idee Natura in Sardegna
Capoterra, Cagliari.
Tel 070 711 212.
www.ideenatura insardegna.it

Cooperative Goloritze
Ogliastra.
Tel 368 702 89 80.
www.coopgoloritze.com

WALKING TOURS

Cooperativa Goloritze
Tel 368 702 89 80.
www.coopgoloritze.com

Barbagia Insolita
Oliena. *Tel 0784 28 60 05.*
www.barbagiainsolita.it

Club Alpino Italiano
Cagliari. *Tel 070 66 78 77.*
www.caica.sardegna.it

Compagnia dell'Avventura
Cannigione.
Tel 0789 862 53.

Cooperativa Ghivine
Dorgali. *Tel 0784 967 21.*

Cooperativa Turistica Enis
Oliena. *Tel 0784 28 83 63.*

Keya
Orosei.
Tel 348 6530 682/683.
www.keya-sardegna.it

Nuovi Equilibri
Tel 338 132 61 56.
www.nuoviequilibri.com

Scoprisardegna
Porto Torres.
Tel 328 456 46 82.
www.scoprisardegna.com

Terranova Escursioni
Olbia. *Tel 328 739 4526.*
www.terranovaescursioni.it

Terre Protette
Roma. *Tel 06 9784 1775/6.*

Zente
Dorgali.
Tel 349 666 2264.
www.zente.it

SPELEOLOGY

Federazione Speleologica Sarda
Via De Magistris, Cagliari.
Tel 070 27 23 31.
www.sardegnaspeleo.it

Società Speleologica Italiana
Via Zamboni 61, Bologna.
Tel 051 25 00 49.
www.speleo.it

GOLF COURSES

Villaggio Arbatax Golf Club
Tel 0782 66 835.

Is Molas Golf Club
Pula. *Tel 070 924 10 13.*

Pevero Golf Club
Porto Cervo.
Tel 0789 95 80 20/00.
www.golfclubpevero.com

TRAVEL INFORMATION

Sardinia is served by Europe's major air–lines, including British Airways, the Sardinian Meridiana and the Italian carrier, Alitalia.

A Meridiana airlines plane

Low-cost flights are available from Ryanair and easyJet. In addition, many charter flights operate in summer, often with low fares or as part of a package deal. During summer there are also more direct flights available. If no direct flights or suitable connections are available, Alitalia and Meridiana provide regular domestic flights from Italy's

mainland cities throughout the year. The island is also served by an excellent network of ferries from ports on the Italian mainland. Slower ferries offer a long crossing, with berths for overnight trips, whereas the faster and more expensive ferry lines can almost halve the travelling time. During the peak summer season of July and August it is not easy to find places on passenger and, in particular, car ferries, so make sure to book your place well in advance.

ARRIVING BY AIR

The main airports in Sardinia are Cagliari's **Elmas** airport, Alghero's **Fertilia** airport and the **Olbia-Costa Smeralda** airport. These are not far from their respective city centres and offer taxi services as well as public transport into town. In Alghero, for example, a bus runs according to the flight timetable, linking the airport to the city centre (call 079 95 04 58 for details). In the summer there is also a coach service from Olbia airport to the towns on the Costa Smeralda.
  Alitalia and the Sardinian airline **Meridiana** serve Cagliari and Olbia from a

number of Italian cities, providing links to major European capitals. Meridiana also flies daily from Gatwick to Cagliari via Florence. **British Airways** flies from London Heathrow to Cagliari. Low-cost airline **Ryanair** serves Alghero direct from London Stansted, East Midlands and Liverpool airports, while **easyJet** serves Olbia from London Gatwick and Cagliari from London Luton.
  Long-haul passengers will almost inevitably have to change in an Italian mainland or other European city. If you are travelling from the United States, American, United Airlines and Delta offer direct

A Sardinia Ferries car ferry

flights to Rome or Milan where you can get a connection to one of the island's airports. Canadian Airlines flies from Canada and Qantas flies from Australia. Alitalia also has a regular service between these countries and Rome.

Olbia's airport serving the east and the Costa Smeralda

A Tirrenia line car ferry

TICKETS AND FARES

If you are based in the UK, Ryanair and easyJet usually provide the cheapest flights. However, it is also worth scouring the small ads of newspapers for cut-price charters and discounted scheduled flights. Fares vary greatly during the year, but the most expensive periods are summer, Christmas and Easter holidays. Meridiana offers low-season economy flights.

For intercontinental flights the most economical option is to take a budget flight to London, Berlin or Barcelona and get a Ryanair or easyJet flight from there to the island.

FERRY SERVICES

Sardinia is easily reached by ferry from Italy's mainland ports which are accessible by train. The crossing can be long (16 hours from Naples to Cagliari, 7 hours between Civitavecchia and Olbia), although the more expensive ferry lines offer a faster service. For overnight crossings, passengers can book a cabin. Ferry services leave from Civitavecchia, Fiumicino, Naples, Genoa, Livorno, Palermo and Trapani. They dock at Sardinia's tourist ports of Arbatax, Cagliari, Olbia, Golfo Aranci, Palau and Porto Torres. **Sardinia Ferries'** fast service connects Livorno and Civitavecchia with Golfo Aranci in just over four hours. **Tirrenia** offers a similar service from La Spezia and Civitavecchia to Olbia (a four-to five-hour trip). There are also ferries from Bonifacio in Corsica, bound for Santa Teresa di Gallura and between Palau and Porto Vecchio in Corsica during the high season. **Moby** sails from mainland Italy to the Sardinian port of Olbia and between Bonifacio (Corsica) and Santa Teresa di Gallura.

PACKAGE HOLIDAYS

Most travel agencies, both in Italy and abroad, offer holidays to Sardinia. The sea and coast are the greatest attractions, but there are also options for holidays in the interior. Many holiday villages provide a wide range of entertainment and sports facilities, including diving and windsurfing, sailing lessons and horseback riding.

A Moby ferry

DIRECTORY

AIRLINES

Alitalia
Domestic flights
Tel 848 86 56 41.
International flights
Tel 848 86 56 42.
Elmas airport, Cagliari
Tel 070 24 00 79.
Fertilia airport, Alghero
Tel 079 935 03 3/7.
www.alitalia.it

British Airways
Tel 0870 850 9850 (UK).
Tel 199 71 22 66 (Italy).
www.ba.com

easyJet
Tel 0905 821 0905 (UK).
Tel 899 678 990 (Italy).

www.easyjet.com

Meridiana
Information/reservations
Tel 199 111 333.
Elmas Airport, Cagliari
Tel 070 24 01 69 or
070 65 13 81.
Costa Smeralda Airport, Olbia
Tel 078 956 34 44.
Rome
Tel 06 47 80 42 22 or
06 65 95 38 80.
Milan
Tel 02 74 85 22 00 or
02 58 49 73 33.
www.meridiana.it
UK
15 Charles II Street, London.
Tel 020 7839 2222.

Ryanair
Tel 0870 333 12 53 (UK).
Tel 199 114 114 (Italy).
www.ryanair.com

FERRY COMPANIES

Grandi Navi Veloci
Information/reservations
Tel 899 199 069.
Olbia *Tel 0789 20 01 26.*
Porto Torres
Tel 079 51 60 34.
Genova *Tel 010 20 94 51.*
www.gnv.it

Moby
Milan *Tel 02 86 52 31.*
Olbia *Tel 078 92 79 27.*
Cagliari *Tel 070 65 53 59.*
Rome *Tel 06 42 01 14 55.*

www.moby.it

Corsica Sardinia Ferries
Information/reservations
Tel 199 400 500.
www.corsicaferries.com

Tirrenia
Information/reservations
Tel 199 123 199 or
081 317 29 99.
Cagliari *Tel 070 65 46 64.*
Olbia *Tel 0789 20 71 09.*
Porto Torres
Tel 079 514 10 7/8.
www.tirrenia.it

TRAIN COMPANIES

Ferrovie dello Stato
Tel 848 88 80 88.
www.trenitalia.it

Getting Around Sardinia

Many of Sardinia's roads are characterized by an interminable number of curves and tight bends: annoying if you are in a hurry, but pleasant if you're on holiday and can take time to enjoy the scenery. With the exception of a few major roads, such as the SS131 which connects the four corners of the island, the roads wind their way over hills and across plains so that, even though the traffic outside the towns is light, always calculate plenty of time when planning a tour. The empty roads, on the other hand, are perfect for cyclists.

cyclists, moped riders and passengers must wear helmets.

PARKING

In winter, parking at the beach is normally free. In summer, car park attendants charge by the hour, half a day, or a full day. The Costa Smeralda has the highest charges. Cagliari's Poetto beach always has free parking.

TRAVELLING BY CAR

Given the inefficient public transport system, and the spectacular natural scenery, travelling by car is the best way to become acquainted with the island.

It is important, however, to be aware of the issues that may occur. Minor roads will often be blocked by flocks of sheep, adding to your travel time. Road signs are not always clear and may be missing just when you need them most. Should this occur, the best thing to do is to ask someone on the way – Sardinians will happily help. Another potential problem is petrol, as there are not many filling stations in the interior. Lastly, you will often find yourself forced to take difficult dirt roads, particularly when looking for an out-of-the-way church or archaeological site.

Always carry a good, up-to-date road map. One of the best is published by the Touring Club Italiano, to a scale of 1:200,000. Keep your vehicle and identity documents (including driving licence) with you in the car at all times, since the police often do spot checks.

A flock of sheep blocking a country road

RENTING A CAR

Most international car rental companies are represented in Sardinia, with offices in the main port towns (Olbia, Cagliari, Porto Torres) and in the airports of Cagliari Elmas, Olbia-Costa Smeralda and Alghero Fertilia. Hertz offers discounts for those who fly with Meridiana and Ryanair.

A number of holiday companies offer fly-drive deals.

RULES OF THE ROAD

The speed limits are 50 km/h (30 mph) in town and 90 km/h (55 mph) on major roads. Seat belts are required, and motor

BOAT HIRE

In many ports it is possible to charter yachts, from one day to one week. The prices may include a crew or simply the use of the boat. Hiring a boat enables you to see the island away from the busy resorts. For information, make enquiries with the harbour authorities or boat owners.

BICYCLING AND MOUNTAIN BIKING

The quiet roads along the coast or the stunning countryside in the interior are ideal for long trips by bicycle. If you prefer more arduous exercise, the steeper mountain roads are suitable for mountain bikes. Tourist offices will have suggestions for local bicycle routes and several associations exist with information about off-road tours by mountain bike. Cyclists should wear high-visibility clothing.

TRAIN TRAVEL

Sardinia has an efficient – if slow – railway service. There are several daily departures from Cagliari to Sassari, Porto

Car rental, a convenient and comfortable way to see the island

A bicycle tour among the olive groves near Sassari

della **Sardegna** (Sardinian Railway) organizes train rides from Cagliari to Mandas and Seui on the Trenino Verde *(see pp92–3)*. "Vintage" wagons from 1913 are pulled by steam locomotives from the 1930s.

TRAVELLING BY COACH

The Azienda Regionale Sarda Trasporti (ARST) coach company network covers most towns, cities and resorts in Sardinia. In order to meet the needs of the ever-growing number of visitors, ARST has issued a special tourist pass (biglietto turistico), available to non-residents only, between 1 June and 30 September. The pass allows you to travel on all ARST coaches, and can be purchased for a period of 7, 14, 21 or 28 days.

Other bus companies operate within specific towns or provinces. Tickets are sold in newspaper kiosks and at tobacconists, as well as bus stations. For more information, contact the local tourist office.

Torres and Olbia, and the journey takes around 4 hours. However, a new high-speed train line is being built. When it is complete, the journey will take just over two hours.

Local trains between Cagliari and Iglesias and Oristano depart regularly, as do trains between Alghero and Sassari. The journeys are surprisingly cheap: 13 euros one-way between Cagliari and Olbia.

A train ride in true late-19th- century style, such as on the Cagliari–Sòrgono route *(see p109)*, is an enjoyable and relaxing way to see the island's stunning scenery, which has fascinated travellers for many centuries. In spring, the **Ferrovie**

The narrow-gauge train known as the Trenino Verde

DIRECTORY

RENTING A CAR

Avis
Tel 199 100 133.

Europcar
Tel 800 014 410.

Hertz
Tel 199 11 22 11.

Maggiore
Tel 848 86 70 67.

MOUNTAIN BIKING

Bike Club Sardegna
Cagliari.
Tel 328 976 68 45.
www.bikesardegna.it.

Dolcevita Bike Tours
Pula. *Tel* 070 920 98 85.
www.dolcevitabiketours.com

Federazione Ciclista Italiana
Tel 070 66 32 43. **www**.federciclismo.it/sardegna

Mountain Bike Club Taxus Baccata
Gonnasfanadiga.
Tel 070 979 98 64.

Mountain Bike Porto Conte Escursioni
Alghero.
www.mtbportoconte.it

Skedaddle Sardinia
Porto Columbu.
Tel 070 925 31 75.
www.skedaddle.co.uk

Team Spakkaruote Sud West Sardinia
Carbonia. **www**.spakkaruote.it

TRAIN TRAVEL

Ferrovie della Sardegna
Via Cugia 1, Cagliari.
Tel 070 34 23 41.
www.ferroviesardegna.it

Trenitalia
Tel 892 021, 199 30 30 60 *(disabled users)*.
www.trenitalia.it

ARST INFORMA-TION OFFICES

Tel 800 86 50 42.
www.arst.sardegna.it

Cagliari
Tel 070 409 83 24.

Gùspini
Tel 070 97 02 36.

Lanusei
Tel 078 24 02 92.

Nuoro
Tel 078 429 50 38.

Olbia
Tel 078 955 30 00.

Oristano
Tel 078 37 17 76.

Sassari
Tel 079 263 92 00.

General Index

Phrase Book

In an Emergency

Help!	Aiuto!	eye-**yoo**-toh
Stop!	Fermate!	fair-**mah**-teh
Call a doctor.	Chiama un medico	kee-**ah**-mah oon **meh**-dee-koh
Call an ambulance.	Chiama un' ambulanza	kee-**ah**-mah oon am-boo-**lan**-tsa
Call the police.	Chiama la polizia	kee-**ah**-mah lah pol-ee-**tsee**-ah
Call the fire brigade.	Chiama i pompieri	kee-**ah**-mah ee pom-pee-**air**-ee
Where is the telephone?	Dov'è il telefono?	dov-**eh** eel teh-**leh**-foh-noh?
The nearest hospital?	L'ospedale più vicino?	loss-peh-**dah**-leh pee-**oo** vee-**chee**-noh?

Communication Essentials

Yes/No	Si/No	see/noh
Please	Per favore	pair fah-**vor**-eh
Thank you	Grazie	**grah**-tsee-eh
Excuse me	Mi scusi	mee **skoo**-zee
Hello	Buon giorno	bwon **jor**-noh
Goodbye	Arrivederci	ah-ree-veh-**dair**-chee
Good evening	Buona sera	**bwon**-ah **sair**-ah
morning	la mattina	lah mah-**tee**-nah
afternoon	il pomeriggio	eel poh-meh-**ree**-joh
evening	la sera	lah **sair**-ah
yesterday	ieri	ee-**air**-ee
today	oggi	**oh**-jee
tomorrow	domani	doh-**mah**-nee
here	qui	kwee
there	la	lah
What?	Quale?	**kwah**-leh?
When?	Quando?	**kwan**-doh?
Why?	Perchè?	pair-**keh**?
Where?	Dove?	**doh**-veh?

Useful Phrases

How are you?	Come sta?	**koh**-meh stah?
Very well, thank you.	Molto bene, grazie.	**moll**-toh **beh**-neh **grah**-tsee-eh
Pleased to meet you.	Piacere di conoscerla.	pee-ah-**chair**-eh dee coh-**noh**-shair-lah
See you later.	A più tardi.	ah **pee-oo** tar-dee
That's fine.	Va bene.	va **beh**-neh
Where is/are...?	Dov'è/Dove sono...?	dov-**eh**/dov-eh **soh** noh?
How long does it take to get to...?	Quanto tempo ci vuole per andare a...?	**kwan**-toh **tem**-poh chee voo-**oh**-leh pair an-**dar**-eh ah...?
How do I get to...?	Come faccio per arrivare a...?	koh-meh **fah**-choh pair arri-**var**-eh ah...?
Do you speak English?	Parla inglese?	**par**-lah een-**gleh**-zeh?
I don't understand.	Non capisco.	non ka-**pee**-skoh
Could you speak more slowly, please?	Può parlare più lentamente, per favore?	pwoh par-lah-reh pee-oo len-ta-**men**-teh pair fah-**vor**-eh?
I'm sorry.	Mi dispiace.	mee dee-spee-**ah**-cheh

Useful Words

big	grande	**gran**-deh
small	piccolo	**pee**-koh-loh
hot	caldo	**kal**-doh
cold	freddo	**fred**-doh
good	buono	**bwoh**-noh
bad	cattivo	kat-**tee**-voh
enough	basta	**bas**-tah
well	bene	**beh**-neh
open	aperto	ah-**pair**-toh
closed	chiuso	kee-**oo**-zoh
left	a sinistra	ah see-**nee**-strah
right	a destra	ah **dess**-trah
straight on	sempre dritto	**sem**-preh **dree**-toh
near	vicino	vee-**chee**-noh
far	lontano	lon-**tah**-noh
up	su	soo
down	giù	joo
early	presto	**press**-toh
late	tardi	**tar**-dee
entrance	entrata	en-**trah**-tah
exit	uscita	oo-**shee**-ta
toilet	il gabinetto	eel gah-bee-**net**-toh
free, unoccupied	libero	**lee**-bair-oh
free, no charge	gratuito	grah-**too**-ee-toh

Making a Telephone Call

I'd like to place a long-distance call.	Vorrei fare una interurbana.	vor-**ray** far-eh oona in-tair-oor-**bah**-nah
I'd like to make a reverse-charge call.	Vorrei fare una telefonata a carico del destinatario.	vor-**ray** far-eh oona teh-leh-fon-**ah**-tah ah **kar**-ee-koh dell dess-tee-nah-**tar**-ree-oh
I'll try again later.	Ritelefono più tardi.	ree-teh-**leh**-foh-noh pee-oo **tar**-dee
Can I leave a message?	Posso lasciare un messaggio?	**poss**-oh lash-**ah**-reh oon mess-**sah**-joh?
Hold on.	Un attimo, per favore	oon **ah**-tee-moh, pair fah-**vor**-eh
Could you speak up a little please?	Può parlare più forte, per favore?	pwoh par-**lah**-reh pee-oo for-teh, pair fah-**vor**-eh?
local call	telefonata locale	te-leh-fon-**ah**-tah loh-cah-leh

Shopping

How much does this cost?	Quant'è, per favore?	kwan-**teh** pair fah-**vor**-eh?
I would like...	Vorrei...	vor-**ray**
Do you have...?	Avete...?	ah-**veh**-teh...?
I'm just looking.	Sto soltanto guardando.	stoh sol-tan-toh gwar-dan-doh
Do you take credit cards?	Accettate carte di credito?	ah-chet-**tah**-teh **kar**-teh dee **creh**-dee-toh?
What time do you open/close?	A che ora apre/ chiude?	ah keh **or**-ah **ah**-preh/kee-oo-deh?
this one	questo	**kweh**-stoh
that one	quello	**kwell**-oh
expensive	caro	**kar**-oh
cheap	a buon prezzo	ah bwon **pret**-soh
size, clothes	la taglia	lah **tah**-lee-ah
size, shoes	il numero	eel **noo**-mair-oh
white	bianco	bee-**ang**-koh
black	nero	**neh**-roh
red	rosso	**ross**-oh
yellow	giallo	**jal**-loh
green	verde	**vair**-deh
blue	blu	bloo

Types of Shop

antique dealer	l'antiquario	lan-tee-**kwah**-ree-oh
bakery	il forno /il panificio	eel forn-oh /eel pan-ee-**fee**-choh
bank	la banca	lah **bang**-kah
bookshop	la libreria	lah lee-breh-**ree**-ah
butcher	la macelleria	lah mah-chell-eh-**ree**-ah
cake shop	la pasticceria	lah pas-tee-chair-**ee**-ah
chemist	la farmacia	lah far-mah-**chee**-ah
delicatessen	la salumeria	lah sah-loo-meh-**ree**-ah
department store	il grande magazzino	eel **gran**-deh mag-gad-**zee**-noh
fishmonger	il pescivendolo	eel pesh-ee-ven-doh-loh
florist	il fioraio	eel fee-or-**eye**-oh
greengrocer	il fruttivendolo	eel froo-tee-**ven**-doh-loh
grocery	alimentari	ah-lee-men-**tah**-ree
hairdresser	il parrucchiere	eel par-oo-kee-**air**-eh
ice cream parlour	la gelateria	lah jel-ah-tair-**ree**-ah
market	il mercato	eel mair-**kah**-toh
newsstand	l'edicola	leh-**dee**-koh-lah
post office	l'ufficio postale	loo-**fee**-choh pos-**tah**-leh
shoe shop	il negozio di scarpe	eel neh-**goh**-tsioh dee **skar**-peh
supermarket	il supermercato	eel su-pair-mair-**kah**-toh
tobacconist	il tabaccaio	eel tah-bak-**eye**-oh
travel agency	l'agenzia di viaggi	lah-jen-**tsee**-ah dee vee-**ad**-jee

Sightseeing

art gallery	la pinacoteca	lah peena-koh-**teh**-kah
bus stop	la fermata dell'autobus	lah fair-**mah**-tah dell **ow**-toh-booss
church	la chiesa	lah kee-**eh**-zah
	la basilica	lah bah-**seel**-i-kah
closed for holidays	chiuso per le ferie	kee-**oo**-zoh pair leh **fair**-ee-eh
garden	il giardino	eel jar-**dee**-no
library	la biblioteca	lah beeb-lee-oh-**teh**-kah
museum	il museo	eel moo-**zeh**-oh
railway station	la stazione	lah stah-tsee-**oh**-neh
tourist information	l'ufficio di turismo	loo-**fee**-choh dee too-**ree**-smoh

Numbers

1	uno	oo-noh
2	due	doo-eh
3	tre	treh
4	quattro	kwat-roh
5	cinque	ching-kweh
6	sei	say-ee
7	sette	set-teh
8	otto	ot-toh
9	nove	noh-veh
10	dieci	dee-eh-chee
11	undici	oon-dee-chee
12	dodici	doh-dee-chee
13	tredici	tray-dee-chee
14	quattordici	kwat-tor-dee-chee
15	quindici	kwin-dee-chee
16	sedici	say-dee-chee
17	diciassette	dee-chah-set-teh
18	diciotto	dee-chot-toh
19	diciannove	dee-chah-noh-veh
20	venti	ven-tee
30	trenta	tren-tah
40	quaranta	kwah-ran-tah
50	cinquanta	ching-kwan-tah
60	sessanta	sess-an-tah
70	settanta	set-tan-tah
80	ottanta	ot-tan-tah
90	nòvanta	noh-van-tah
100	cento	chen-toh
1,000	mille	mee-leh
2,000	duemila	doo-eh mee-lah
5,000	cinquemila	ching-kweh mee-lah
1,000,000	un milione	oon meel-yoh-neh

Time, Days, Months, Seasons

one minute	un minuto	oon mee-noo-toh
one hour	un'ora	oon or-ah
half an hour	mezz'ora	medz-or-ah
a day	un giorno	oon jor-noh
a week	una settimana	oona set-tee-mah-nah
Monday	lunedì	loo-neh-dee
Tuesday	martedì	mar-teh-dee
Wednesday	mercoledì	mair-koh-leh-dee
Thursday	giovedì	joh-veh-dee
Friday	venerdì	ven-air-dee
Saturday	sabato	sah-bah-toh
Sunday	domenica	doh-meh-nee-kah
January	gennaio	jen-nah-yo
February	febbraio	feb-bra-yo
March	marzo	mar-tzo
April	aprile	a-pree-leh
May	maggio	mah-jo
June	giugno	joo-nyo
July	luglio	loo-lyo
August	agosto	ag-os-toh
September	settembre	set-tem-bre
October	ottobre	ot-toh-bre
November	novembre	no-vem-bre
December	dicembre	dee-chem-bre
Spring	primavera	pree-mah-veh-ra
Summer	estate	es-tah-te
Autumn	autunno	ow-toon-noh
Winter	inverno	een-vair-no
Christmas	Natale	nah-tah-le
Christmas Eve	la Vigilia di Natale	vee-jee-lya dee nah-tah-le
Good Friday	Venerdì Santo	ven-air-dee san-toh
Easter	Pasqua	pas-kwa
New Year	Capodanno	kah-poh-dan-noh
New Year's Eve	San Silvestro	san seel-ves-tro
Whitsun	Pentecoste	pente-kos-te

Travelling

adult	l'adulto	ad-ool-toh
airport	l'aeroporto	a-air-oh-por-toh
baggage claim	il ritiro bagagli	ree-tee-roh bah-gal-yee
boarding card	la carta d'imbarco	kar-tah deem-bar-koh
boat	la barca	bar-kah
booking office	la biglietteria	beel-yet-teh-ree-ah
bus	l'autobus	ow-toh-booss
bus stop	la fermata dell'autobus	fer-mah-tah del-ow-toh-booss
check-in desk	l'accettazione	achet-ah-tzyoh-neh
luggage	i bagagli	bah-gal-yee
child (male)	il bambino	bam-bee-noh
child (female)	la bambina	bam-bee-nah
coach (bus)	la corriera	kor-ee-air-ah
connection	la coincidenza	ko-een-chee-den-tza

Couchette	la cuccetta	koo-chet-tah
customs	la dogana	doh-gah-nah
delay	ritardo	ree-tar-doh
domestic	nazionale	natz-yoh-nah-leh
exit gate	l'uscita	oo-shee-tah
fare	la tariffa	tah-reef-fah
ferry	il traghetto	trah-get-toh
first class	prima classe	pree-mah klas-seh
flight	il volo	voh-loh
left luggage	il deposito bagagli	deh-poh-zee-toh bah-gal-yee
lost property	l'ufficio oggetti smarriti	oof-fee-cho ojet-tee zmar-ree-tee
luggage trolley	il carrello	kar-rel-loh
non-smoking	non fumatori	noh-n foo-mah-toh-ree
passport	il passaporto	pas-sah-por-toh
platform	il binario	bee-nah-ree-o
railway	la ferrovia	fer-roh-vee-a
reservation	la prenotazione	pre-noh-tatz-yoh-neh
return ticket	andata e ritorno	an-dah-tah ay ree-tor-no
seat	il posto	poss-toh
second class	seconda classe	sek-on-da klas-seh
single ticket	solo andata	soh-loh an-dah-tah
smoking	fumatori	foo-mah-toh-ree
station	la stazione	statz-yoh-neh
supplement	il supplemento	soop-leh-men-toh
taxi	il taxi	tak-si
ticket	il biglietto	beel-yet-to
timetable	l'orario	oh-rah-ry-oh
train	il treno	treh-noh
underground	la metropolitana	met-roh-poh-lee-tah-nah

Motoring

Fill her up	il pieno	eel pyeh-noh
Do you do repairs?	Effettua riparazioni?	ef-fet-tua ree-paratz-yoh-nee?
I'd like to hire a car	Vorrei noleggiare una macchina	vor-ray noh-ledg-ah-re oona mah-keena
automatic	con il cambio automatico	kon eel kam-bee-oh ow-toh-mah-tee-koh
boot	il portabagagli	porta-bah-gal-yee
car	l'automobile, la macchina	ow-toh-moh-bee-leh, mah-kee-nah
car ferry	il traghetto	trah-geh-to
diesel oil	gasolio	gaz-oh-lyo
garage (repairs)	il meccanico	mek-ah-neeko
four-star petrol	benzina super	ben-dzee-na soo-per
licence	la patente	pah-ten-teh
motorbike	la motocicletta	moh-toh-chee-kleh-ta
motorway	l'autostrada	ow-toh-strah-da
petrol	la benzina	ben-dzeena
petrol station	la stazione di servizio	statz-yoh-neh dee sair-veetz-yo
ring road	raccordo anulare	rak-or-do an-oo-lah-re
road	la strada	strah-da
traffic lights	il semaforo	sem-ah-foh-roh
unleaded petrol	benzina senza piombo	ben-dzeena sen-dza peeom-boh

Signs You May See On the Road

accendere i fari	ach-en-deh-reh ee fah-ree	headlights on
caduta massi	kah-doo-tah mah-see	falling rocks
divieto di accesso	dee-vyeh-toh dee ach-eh-so	no entry
divieto di sosta	dee-vyeh-toh dee sos-tah	no stopping
dogana	dog-ah-nah	customs
escluso residenti	es-kloo-so reh-zi-den-ti	residents only
ghiaccio	gyah-cho	ice
lavori in corso	lah-voh-ree een kor-so	roadworks
nebbia	neb-bya	fog
parcheggio a pagamento	par-kej-yo a pah-gah-men-toh	paying car park
parcheggio custodito	par-kej-yo koo-sto-dee-toh	car park with attendant
pedaggio	peh-daj-yo	toll
pericolo	peh-ree-koh-loh	danger
rallentare	rah-lehn-tah-reh	reduce speed
senso unico	sen-tzo oo-nee-ko	one way
uscita camion	oo-shee-tah kah-myon	works exit
zona pedonale	dzoh-na peh-doh-nah-leh	pedestrian area

Staying in a Hotel

English	Italian	Pronunciation
Do you have any vacant rooms?	Avete camere libere?	ah-**veh**-teh kah-mair-eh **lee**-bair-eh?
double room	una camera doppia	oona kah-mair-ah **doh**-pee-ah
with double bed	con letto matrimoniale	kon **let**-toh mah-tree-moh-nee-**ah**-leh
twin room	una camera con due letti	oona kah-mair-ah kon **doo**-eh **let**-tee
single room	una camera singola	oona kah-mair-ah **sing**-goh-lah
room with a bath, shower	una camera con bagno, con doccia	oona kah-mair-ah kon **ban**-yoh, kon **dot**-chah
I have a reservation.	Ho fatto una prenotazione.	oh **fat**-toh oona preh-noh-tah-tsee-**oh**-neh
balcony	balcone	bal-**coh**-neh
breakfast	prima colazione	**pree**-ma coh-lah-**tzyoh**-neh
key	la chiave	lah kee-**ah**-veh
porter	il facchino	eel fah-**kee**-noh
room service	servizio in camera	ser-**vitz**-yoh een **cah**-meh-rah

Eating Out

English	Italian	Pronunciation
Have you got a table for…?	Avete una tavola per…?	ah-**veh**-teh oona **tah**-voh-lah pair…?
I'd like to reserve a table.	Vorrei riservare una tavola.	vor-**ray** ree-sair-**vah**-reh oona **tah**-voh-lah
the bill, please.	il conto, per favore.	**kon**-toh pair fah-**vor**-eh
I am a vegetarian.	Sono vegetariano/a.	**soh**-noh **veh**-jeh-tar-ee-**ah**-noh/nah
beer	la birra	**bee**-rah
bread	il pane	**pah**-neh
bottle	la bottiglia	bot-**teel**-yah
breakfast	la prima colazione	pree-mah koh-lah-tsee-**oh**-neh
butter	il burro	**boor**-roh
carafe	la caraffa	kah-rah-**fah**
child's portion	una porzione per bambini	portz-**yoh**-neh pair bam-**bee**-nee
coffee	il caffè	kaf-**feh**
cover charge	il coperto	koh-**pair**-toh
cup	la tazza	**tat**-zah
dessert	il dessert	des-**ser**
dinner	la cena	**cheh**-nah
dish of the day	il piatto del giorno	pee-**ah**-toh dell **jor**-no
first course	il primo	**pree**-moh
fixed price menu	il menù a prezzo fisso	meh-**noo** ah **pret**-soh fee-soh
fork	la forchetta	for-**ket**-tah
glass	il bicchiere	bee-kee-**air**-eh
half-litre	da mezzo litro	da **met**-zoh **lee**-troh
knife	il coltello	kol-**tel**-loh
litre	un litro	**lee**-troh
lunch	il pranzo	**pran**-tsoh
main course	il secondo	seh-**kon**-doh
medium (meat)	al punto	al **poon**-toh
menu	il menù	meh-**noo**
milk	il latte	**lat**-teh
pepper	il pepe	**peh**-peh
plate	il piatto	p-**yat**-toh
rare (meat)	al sangue	al **sang**-gweh
receipt (in bars)	lo scontrino	skon-**tree**-noh
(in restaurants)	la ricevuta	ree-cheh-**voo**-tah
restaurant	il ristorante	rees-toh-**ran**-teh
salad	l'insalata	een-sah-**lah**-tah
salt	il sale	**sah**-leh
sandwich	il panino	pan-**ee**-noh
serviette	il tovagliolo	toh-val-**yoh**-loh
snack	lo spuntino	spoon-**tee**-noh
soup	la minestra	mee-**nes**-trah
spoon	il cucchiaio	koo-kee-**eye**-oh
starter	l'antipasto	an-tee-**pas**-toh
sugar	lo zucchero	dzoo-keh-roh
tea	il tè	teh
teaspoon	il cucchiaino	kook-yah-**ee**-noh
tip	la mancia	**man**-cha
vegetables	il contorno	eel kon-**tor**-noh
waitress	la cameriera	kah-mair-ee-**air**-ah
waiter	il cameriere	kah-mair-ee-**air**-eh
water	l'acqua	**ak**-wah
fizzy/still	gassata/naturale	gah-**zah**-tah/ nah-too-**rah**-leh
well done (meat)	ben cotto	ben **kot**-toh
wine	il vino	**vee**-noh
wine list	la lista dei vini	**lee**-stah day **vee**-nee

Menu Decoder

Italian	Pronunciation	English
abbacchio	ab-**ak**-yoh	spring lamb
acciughe	ach-**oo**-geh	anchovies
aceto	ach-**eh**-toh	vinegar
acqua minerale	**ah**-kwah mee-nair-**ah**-leh gah-**zah**-tah/ nah-too-**rah**-leh	mineral water
gassata/naturale		fizzy/still
aglio	**al**-ee-oh	garlic
agnello	ah-**niell**-oh	lamb
al forno	al **for**-noh	baked
alla griglia	ah-lah **greel**-yah	grilled
albicocche	al-bee-**kok**-eh	apricots
ananas	an-an-ass	pineapple
anatra	**an**-at-rah	duck
anguria	an-**goo**-rya	water melon
antipasti	ahn-ti-**pas**-ti	starters
aperitivo	apeh-ree-**tee**-voh	aperitif
aragosta	ara-**goss**-tah	lobster
arancia	ah-**ran**-cha	orange
aringa	ah-**reen**-gah	herring
arrosto	ar-**ross**-toh	roast
asparagi	as-**pah**-rah-ji	asparagus
baccalà	bak-al-**la**	dried cod
basilico	bas-**ee**-lee-ko	basil
besciamella	besh-ah-**mel**-ah	white sauce
birra	**beer**-rah	beer
bistecca	bees-**tek**-ka	steak
bottarga	bot-**ahr**-gah	salted mullet roe
branzino	bran-**zee**-no	sea bass
brasato	bra-**sah**-toh	braised beef
bresaola	breh-**sah**-oh-lah	slices of cold, wind-dried beef with oil and lemon
brioche	bri-**osh**	type of croissant
brodo	**broh**-doh	clear broth
budino	boo-**dee**-noh	pudding
burro	**boor**-oh	butter
caffè	kah-**feh**	espresso coffee
caffè corretto	kah-**feh** koh-**reh**-toh	espresso coffee with a dash of liqueur
caffè lungo	kah-**feh loon**-goh	weak espresso coffee
caffè macchiato	kah-**feh** mak-**yah**-toh	espresso coffee with a dash of milk
caffè ristretto	kah-**feh** ree-**streh**-toh	strong espresso coffee
caffelatte	kah-**feh-lah**-teh	half coffee, half milk
calamari	kah-lah-**mah**-ree	squid
calzone	kal-**zoh**-neh	folded pizza filled with tomato and mozzarella
camomilla	kah-moh-**mee**-lah	camomile tea
cannella	kan-**el**-ah	cinnamon
cannelloni	kan-eh-**loh**-nee	stuffed pasta tubes
cappuccino	kap-oo-**chee**-noh	coffee with foaming milk
carciofi	kar-**choh**-fee	artichokes
carne	**kar**-neh	meat
carote	kar-**roh**-teh	carrots
castagne	kas-**tan**-yeh	chestnuts
cavolfiore	kavol-**fyoh**-reh	cauliflower
cavolo	**kah**-voh-loh	cabbage
cefalo	**che**-fah-loh	grey mullet
cernia	**cher**-nya	grouper (fish)
ciambella	cham-**bella**	ring-shaped cake
cicoria	chih-**kor**-ya	chicory
ciliege	chil-**yej**-eh	cherries
cioccolata	choc-oh-**lah**-tah	chocolate
cipolle	chip-oh-leh	onions
coniglio	kon-**ee**-lyo	rabbit
contorni	kon-**tor**-nee	vegetables
coperto	kop-**er**-toh	cover charge
coppa	**koh**-pah	cured pork, sliced finely and eaten cold
cordula	**kor**-doo-lah	Sardinian spit-roasted plaited lamb entrails
cotoletta	kot-oh-**let**-ta	pork or lamb chop
cozze	**kot**-zeh	mussels
crema	**kreh**-mah	custard dessert
crespella	**kres**-pel-lah	savoury pancake
crostata di frutta	kros-**tah**-tah dee **froo**-tah	fruit tart
datteri	**dat**-eh-ree	dates
digestivo	dee-jes-**tee**-voh	digestive liqueur
dolci	**dol**-chi	desserts, cakes
espresso	es-**pres**-soh	strong black coffee
fagiano	fah-**jah**-noh	pheasant
fagioli	fah-joh-lee	beans
fagiolini	fah-joh-**lee**-nee	long, green beans
fegato	**feh**-gah-toh	liver
fettuccine	feh-too-**chee**-neh	ribbon-shaped pasta
fichi	**fee**-kee	figs

filetto	fee-**leh**-toh	fillet (of beef)
finocchio	fee-**noh**-kyo	fennel
formaggio	for-**maj**-yo	cheese
fragole	**frah**-goh-leh	strawberries
frappé	frap-**eh**	whisked fruit or milk drink with ice
fregula	**freh**-goo-lah	small, granular pasta
frittata	free-**tah**-tah	type of omelette
fritto	**free**-toh	deep fried
fritto misto	**free**-toh mees-toh	seafood in batter
frittura di pesce	free-**too**-rah dee **pesh**-eh	variety of fried fish
frutta	**froo**-tah	fruit
frutta secca	**froo**-tah sek-kah	dried fruit
frutti di mare	**froo**-tee dee **mah**-reh	seafood
funghi	**foon**-g-ee	mushrooms
gamberetti	gam-beh-**reh**-tee	shrimps
gamberi	**gam**-beh-ree	prawns
gamberoni	gam-beh-**roh**-nee	king prawns
gelato	gel-**ah**-toh	ice cream
gnocchi	**nyok**-ee	small flour and potato dumplings
gorgonzola	gor-gon-**zoh**-lah	strong, soft blue cheese
granchio	**gran**-kyo	crab
granita	gra-**nee**-tah	drink with crushed ice
grissini	gree-**see**-nee	thin, crisp breadsticks
insalata	een-sah-**lah**-tah	salad
involtini	een-vol-**tee**-nee	meat rolls stuffed with ham and herbs
lamponi	lam-**poh**-nee	raspberries
latte	**lah**-teh	milk
lattuga	lah-**too**-gah	lettuce
leggero	leh-**jeh**-roh	light
legumi	leh-**goo**-mee	pulses
lenticchie	len-**teek**-yeh	lentils
lesso	**less**-oh	boiled
lepre	**leh**-preh	hare
limone	lee-**moh**-neh	lemon
lingua	**leen**-gwa	tongue
macedonia di frutta	mach-eh-**doh**-nya dee **froo**-tah	fruit salad
maiale	mah-**yah**-leh	pork
mandarino	man-dah-**ree**-noh	mandarin
mandorla	**man**-dor-lah	almond
manzo	**man**-dzo	beef
mascarpone	mah-skar-**poh**-neh	soft, sweet cheese
mela	**meh**-lah	apple
melanzane	meh-lan-**zah**-neh	aubergines
melone	meh-**loh**-neh	melon
menta	**men**-tah	mint
merluzzo	mer-**loo**-tzoh	cod
minestrone	mee-nes-**troh**-neh	thick vegetable soup
mirtilli	meer-**tee**-lee	bilberries
more	**mor**-eh	blackberries
nasello	nah-**seh**-loh	hake
nocciole	noch-**oh**-leh	hazelnuts
noce moscata	**noh**-che mos-**kah**-tah	nutmeg
noci	**noh**-chi	walnuts
olio	**oh**-lyo	oil
orata	oh-**rah**-tah	gilthead bream
origano	oh-**ree**-gah-noh	oregano
ossobuco	os-oh-**boo**-ko	stewed shin of veal
ostriche	**os**-tree-keh	oysters
pane	**pah**-neh	bread
carasau	cah-rah-**sahw**	crisp, circular bread
panino	pah-**nee**-noh	filled roll
panna	pah-**nah**	cream
parmigiana di melanzane	par-mee-**jah**-nah dee meh-lan-**zah**-neh	aubergine, tomato, mozarella and parmesan bake
parmigiano	par-mee-**jah**-noh	parmesan cheese
pasticcio	pas-**tich**-oh	pasta and meat bake
patate	pah-**tah**-teh	potatoes
pecorino	peh-coh-**ree**-noh	strong, hard ewe's milk cheese
penne	peh-**neh**	pasta quills
pepe	**peh**-peh	pepper (spice)
peperoncino	peh-peh-**ron**-chee-noh	cayenne pepper
peperoni	peh-peh-**roh**-nee	peppers
pera	**peh**-rah	pear
pesca	**pes**-kah	peach
pesce	**pesh**-eh	fish
piselli	pee-**seh**-lee	peas
polenta	poh-**len**-tah	boiled cornmeal with meat or vegetables
pollo	**poh**-loh	chicken
polpette	pol-**peh**-teh	meatballs
polpettone	pol-**peh**-toh-neh	meatloaf
pomodori	poh-moh-**doh**-ree	tomatoes
pompelmo	pom-**pel**-moh	grapefruit
porceddu	por-**ched**-doo	roast suckling pig
porri	**poh**-ree	leeks
prezzemolo	pretz-**eh**-moh-loh	parsley
primi piatti	pree-mee **pyah**-tee	first courses
prosciutto	pro-**shoo**-toh	ham
cotto/crudo	**kot**-toh/**kroo**-doh	cooked/cured
prugne	**proo**-nyeh	plums
radicchio	rah-**deek**-yo	red chicory
ragù	rah-**goo**	mince and tomato sauce
ravanelli	rah-vah-**neh**-lee	radishes
ravioli	rah-vee-**oh**-lee	square-shaped egg pasta filled with meat
razza	**rah**-tzah	skate
ricotta	ree-**kot**-tah	white, soft cheese
ripieno	ree-**pyeh**-noh	stuffed
riso	**ree**-soh	rice
risotto	ree-**soh**-toh	rice cooked in stock
rognone	ron-**yoh**-neh	kidney
rosato	roh-**sah**-toh	rosé wine
rosolato	roh-soh-**lah**-toh	fried
rosmarino	ros-mah-**ree**-noh	rosemary
salame	sah-**lah**-meh	salami
sale	**sah**-leh	salt
salsa	**sal**-sah	sauce
salsiccia	sal-**see**-cha	sausage
salvia	**sal**-vya	sage
scaloppine	skah-loh-**pee**-neh	veal escalopes
seadas	say-**ah**-dahs	sweet cheese and lemon fritters
secco	**seh**-koh	dry
secondi piatti	seh-**kon**-dee **pyat**-ee	main courses
sedano	**seh**-dah-noh	celery
selvaggina	sel-vah-**jee**-nah	game
semifreddo	**seh**-mee-**freh**-doh	ice cream and sponge dessert
senape	**seh**-nah-peh	mustard
seppie	**sep**-pee-eh	cuttlefish
servizio compreso	ser-**vitz**-yo com-**preh**-soh	service charge included
servizio escluso	ser-**vitz**-yo es-**cloo**-so	service charge not included
sogliola	**sol**-yoh-lah	sole
sorbetto	sor-**bet**-toh	sorbet
speck	sp-**ek**	cured, smoked ham
spezzatino	spetz-ah-**tee**-noh	stew
spiedini	spyeh-**dee**-nee	meat or fish on a spit
spinaci	spee-**nah**-chee	spinach
spremuta	spreh-**moo**-tah	freshly squeezed juice
spumante	spoo-**man**-teh	sparkling wine
stufato	stoo-**fah**-toh	casserole
tacchino	tak-**ee**-noh	turkey
tagliatelle	tah-lyah-**teh**-leh	flat strips of egg pasta
tartine	tar-**tee**-neh	small sandwiches
tartufo	tar-**too**-foh	ice cream covered in cocoa
tè	**teh**	tea
tiramisù	tee-rah-mee-**soo**	dessert of coffee-soaked sponge, Marsala and mascarpone
tisana	tee-**zah**-nah	herbal tea
tonno	toh-**noh**	tuna
torta	**tor**-tah	tart, cake
torta salata	**tor**-tah sah-**lah**-tah	savoury flan
tortellini	tor-teh-**lee**-nee	stuffed pasta shapes
triglia	**tree**-lya	red mullet
trippa	**tree**-pah	tripe
trota	**troh**-tah	trout
uova	oo-**wo**-va	eggs
uova sode	oo-**wo**-va **soh**-deh	hard-boiled eggs
uva	**oo**-va	grapes
verdura	ver-**doo**-rah	vegetables
vino	**vee**-noh	wine
vino bianco	**vee**-noh **byan**-ko	white wine
vino da dessert	**vee**-noh dah deh-**ser**	dessert wine
vino da pasto	**vee**-noh dah **pas**-toh	table wine
vino da tavola	**vee**-noh dah **tah**-voh-lah	table wine
vino rosso	**vee**-noh **ros**-soh	red wine
vitello	vee-**tel**-loh	veal
vongole	**von**-goh-leh	clams
zafferano	zah-feh-**rah**-noh	saffron
zucca	**dzoo**-kah	pumpkin
zucchero	**dzoo**-kair-oh	sugar
zucchine	dzoo-**kee**-neh	courgettes
zuppa	dzoo-**pah**	soup
zuppa inglese	dzoo-**pah** een-**gleh**-seh	trifle

Acknowledgments

Dorling Kindersley would like to thank the following organizations and people whose contributions have made the preparation of this book possible:

Special Assistance

Agriturismo di Lucia Sotgiu, Agriturismo Sa Perda Marcada, Hertz, Claire Littlejohn, Hotel Mediterraneo, Greca Mattan, Meridiana, Anna Chiara Montefusco, Filomena Rosato, Anna Sacripanti, Terranostra Sardegna.

Design and Editorial

ADDITIONAL PICTURE RESEARCH Ellen Root
REVISIONS EDITOR Anna Freiberger
REVISIONS DESIGNER Conrad Van Dyk
Beverley Ager, Gillian Allen, Uma Bhattacharya, Emma Bird, Samantha Borland, Antonugo Cerletti, Michelle Clark, Michelle Crane, Cooling Brown, Felicity Crowe, Vivien Crump, Fay Franklin, Vinod Harish, Mohammad Hassan, Elinor Hodgson, Annette Jacobs, Jasneet Kaur, Vincent Kurien, Sarah Lane, Georgina Matthews, Gillian Price, Lee Redmond, Azeem Siddiqui, Ellie Smith, Tiziana Tuveri, Sylvia Tombesi-Walton, Helen Townsend, Ingrid Vienings.

Additional Photography Ian O'Leary

Picture Credits

Key: t=top; tl=top left; tlc=top left centre; tc= top centre; trc=top right centre; tr=top right; cla=centre left above; ca=centre above; cra=centre right above; cl=centre left; c=centre; cr=centre right; clb=cent re left below; crb=centre right below; cb=centre below; bl=bottom left; br=bottom right; b=bottom; bc=bottom centre; bcl=bottom centre left; bcr=bottom centre right.

All the photographs were taken by the photographic agency Overseas S.r.l., except for the following:

Alamy Images, London: Arco Images 11clb; Claudio H. Artman 10c; Authors Image/Mickael David 180cl; bildagentur-online.com/th-foto 11tl; CuboImages srl/Marco Casiraghi 146tr, 179cl, 197tr; Robert Harding Picture Library Ltd/J Lightfoot 11br; Andrew Woodley 170bl; Alfio Elio Quattrocchi, Cagliari: 22tr, 39t, 42cl, 53t, 62b, 70tr, 106tr, 109cr, 145t, 149t, 165b, 190bl, 191br.

Corbis: Owen Franken 181c; Michelle Garrett 181tl; Cristina Gambaro, Milan: 25b, 70cl, 70c, 91c, 108t, 109cl, 140b.

European Commission, 197b

Fabio Braibanti, Milan: 139, 147tr, 179c, 188cl, 191bl, 191tr, 191crb; Fabio De Angelis, Milan: 32tr, 32cra, 143bl, 190c, 191cr; Fabrizio Ardito, Rome: 24tr, 24br, 25cr, 32cr, 33bl, 33br, 37t, 59b, 82b, 83b, 85b, 85c, 96b, 99c, 99cr, 102b, 103cl, 104t, 104bl, 105t, 106tl, 106cr, 106b, 108c, 111tl, 111cr, 116tr, 116cl, 119cl, 120t, 121t, 124l, 124c, 124b, 125t, 150t, 150b, 151tr, 151cr, 151br, 151cl, 152tl, 153tl, 155cr, 156tl, 156tr, 156c, 156b, 157tl, 157tr, 157c, 157b, 158tr, 158c, 158b, 159tl, 159tr, 159b, 164cr, 165t, 165c; Antonio Mannu, Sassari: 26tr, 28tc, 32bl, 41br, 43cr, 48tr, 52cl, 72tl, 95b, 102bcl, 103tl, 113b, 117tl, 117cra, 117bcr, 118cl, 118bl, 119cl, 121tl, 126tr, 126cr, 126bl, 127cr, 128tl, 129cr, 129b, 134cl, 134br, 135tl, 136t, 136bl, 154bm, 154bl, 157cr, 157br, 160tl, 160cl, 160br, 162tr, 162bl, 163tc, 163b, 189tr; Foto Carfagna + Associati, Rome: 133br; Francine Reculez, Milan: 180, 181, 191bc.

Grazia Neri: Remo Casilli 45cra.

Hemispheres Images: Jean du Boisberranger 50.

Il Dagherrotipo: Marco Melodia 10cla; Ilisso Edizioni, Nuoro: 159cra, 159crb; Image Bank, Milan: 51bc, 127, 130t, 138.

Marka, Milan: Lorenzo Sechi 10tc; Moby Lines Ferry, Italy: 203cr.

Raccolta Delle Stampe Achille Bertarelli, Milan: 30b, 36, 37c, 37bl, 38c, 38b.

Starwood Hotels & Resorts Worldwide Inc.: 173cr.

Tirrenia Di Navagazione S.P.A, Italy: 203tl.

Jacket
Front – 4Corners Images: Ripani Massimo main image; Alamy Images: Michael Grant clb. Back – 4Corners Images: Fantuz Olimpio clb; Spila Riccardo tl; DK Images: John Heseltine cla; Hemispheres Images: Ingolf Pompe bl. Spine – 4Corners Images: Ripani Massimo t; Alamy Images: Paul Carstairs b.

All other images @ Dorling Kindersley. For further information see: www.dkimages.com

---

SPECIAL EDITIONS OF DK TRAVEL GUIDES

DK Travel Guides can be purchased in bulk quantities at discounted prices for use in promotions or as premiums. We are also able to offer special editions and personalized jackets, corporate imprints, and excerpts from all of our books, tailored specifically to meet your own needs.

To find out more, please contact:
(in the United States) **SpecialSales@dk.com**
(in the UK) **Sarah.Burgess@dk.com**
(in Canada) DK Special Sales at **general@tourmaline.ca**
(in Australia) **business.development@pearson.com.au**

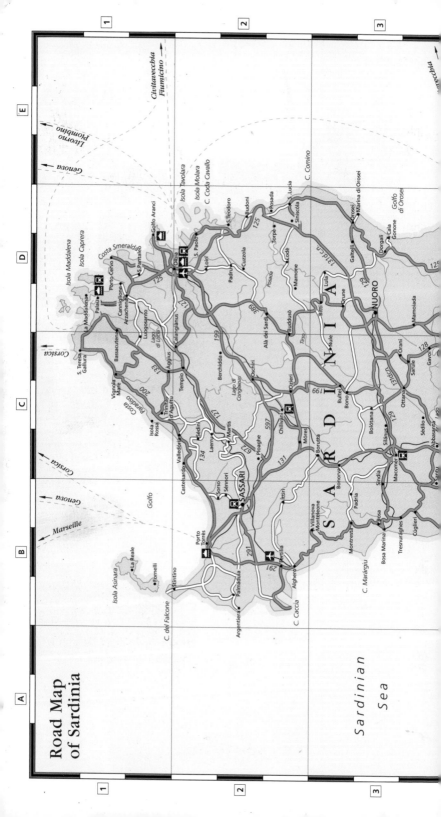

Road Map
of Sardinia